A CHART shewing the several Places of Action between the ENGLISH and SPANISH Fleets, with the Places where several of the SPANISH Ships were destroyed in their return to SPAIN, North about the BRITISH ISLANDS.

Armada

Peter Padfield

Armada

A celebration of the four hundredth anniversary
of the defeat of the Spanish Armada
1588–1988

London
Victor Gollancz Ltd
1988

First published in Great Britain 1988
by Victor Gollancz Ltd
14 Henrietta Street, London WC2E 8QJ

British Library Cataloguing in Publication Data
Padfield, Peter
Armada.
1. Armada 1588
I. Title
942.05′5   DA360

ISBN 0–575–03729–6

Designed by Alan Bartram
Typeset by Nene Phototypesetters Ltd,
Northampton
Printed in Italy by Imago Publishing Ltd

JACKET
Launch of the English fireships
off Calais.
Netherlandish school, *c.*1590.

ENDPAPERS
An Armada track chart engraved and
published by John Pine, 1690–1756. It
is derived from an original published
in 1590 and shows the course of the
English and Spanish fleets. The
elaborate allegorical border represents
Protestant England's defeat of
Catholic Spain.

HALF–TITLE
Visscher's engraving of the
merchantman *Griffin*, commissioned
as an armed auxiliary for the English
fleet.

FRONTISPIECE
The Armada in the Strait of Dover.
Flemish school, *c.*1610.
    The view shows a combination of
various incidents. To the right,
England is defended by the fleet, and,
on shore, by an army with Queen
Elizabeth's standard. To the left are
Armada vessels flying Spanish and
Catholic flags. Armada beacons
appear in the distance.
    The Stuart arms and initials IR at the
top suggest this rare miniature of an
historical event may have been done
for James I.

TITLE–PAGE
One of a set of silver medallions
produced by the Dutch in 1588–89 to
celebrate deliverance from the enemy.

ILLUSTRATION ACKNOWLEDGEMENTS
The author and publishers wish to
thank the following for kind
permission to reproduce the
illustrations which appear on the
pages listed:
Bibliothèque Nationale, Paris 30
Climatic Research Unit, University of
East Anglia 50, 160, 185
Department of the Environment,
London 84, 88
The Marquess of Salisbury, Hatfield
House 14, 24, 25, 36, 39, 52, 54, 55,
61, 76, 96, 101, 133, 134, 168, 193
The Marquess of Tavistock, and the
Trustees of the Bedford Estates,
Woburn Abbey 21, 167
National Maritime Museum, London
jacket, endpapers, 1, 2, 3, 8, 10, 11, 17,
29, 37, 40, 45, 59, 60, 72, 73, 78, 79,
99, 105, 109, 110, 112, 113, 120, 121,
126, 129, 136, 146, 147, 151, 155, 157,
159, 161, 172, 173, 174, 175
National Portrait Gallery, London 33,
64
The National Trust Photographic
Library 33
Northern Ireland Tourist Board 183
Rotunda Museum, Woolwich 92, 93
Collections Ulster Museum 177, 180,
181, 184
The Trustees, Victoria and Albert
Museum, London 83

Contents

Acknowledgements

My wife, Jane, did much of the research for this book, which would not have been the same without her work and talent for serendipity. Both of us benefited from the generous lending facilities of the University of East Anglia library, whose staff we should like to thank and, as always, the Woodbridge Library and inter-lending service.

Lionel Willis has made an imaginative contribution with his splendid cut-away paintings of contemporary warships incorporating the latest research, and with maps and battle diagrams; I should like to thank him and John Taylor, who gathered the illustrations – including some unusual ones never published before – for the pictorial interest of the book.

I should also like to thank David Lyon, formerly Curator of naval ordnance at the National Maritime Museum, Greenwich, and Dr Margaret Rule of the *Mary Rose* Trust, Portsmouth for their help with queries; Krystina Behnke of Berlin for her help with the late Frank Lynder's researches into the Armada wreck off Norway, and from Norway, Mr Bjørn Ringstad of Fylkehuset, Molde, and Mr Bjørn Jonson Dale of Oslo for their researches into the oral tradition of the wreck – or wrecks?

I am grateful to Professor Hubert Lamb and Dr K. S. Douglas of the Climatic Research Unit, University of East Anglia, for permission to reproduce weather maps from their studies, *Weather Observations and a tentative Meteorological analysis of the Period May to July, 1588* and *A Meteorological Study of July to October, 1588*, both published at the University of East Anglia, and I am grateful to the Editor of the *Mariner's Mirror*, the Journal of the Society for Nautical Research, for permission to quote from 'Gorgas' Seafight' by Tom Glasgow Jr, as indeed to the authors of the numerous articles in *Mariner's Mirror* who have contributed hugely to this book.

1

The Prudent King

King Philip II of Spain (1527–98, reigned 1556–98).

Philip II of Spain did not reach conclusions lightly; his decision to invade England was no exception. Exactly when he made it is open to doubt; it is even questionable whether the 'Armada' he sent north in 1588 was intended to mount a serious invasion, or whether he expected the threat of its presence would be sufficient to overawe the English Queen, Elizabeth I, and bring her to terms. Certainly he hoped this. Probably he did not expect it.

Again it is not clear whether his despatch of the Armada sprang from positive strategic ideas or was a desperate act to preserve face, or to preserve his credit in the financial market-place. His more able advisors had been stressing the strategic importance of England for years, but the matter had never got beyond discussion. His Netherlands dominions were in revolt and he was determined to reassert his authority there; afterwards it would be time to consider England; that was his attitude as late as August 1585. That autumn he learned that Elizabeth had concluded a treaty with the Dutch rebels, agreeing to send them troops and money to stiffen their resistance; he also learned that Francis Drake had sailed into Vigo Bay with a sizeable squadron and pillaged and threatened the port of Vigo itself. He was used to English and French mischiefs overseas; to be insulted on his own coast was a different matter. He asked his most experienced Admiral, the Marquis of Santa Cruz, and his most successful military commander, the Duke of Parma, to propose detailed plans for the invasion of England. The Pope had already urged such a course to bring the Protestant English back to the True Faith, and in January 1586, Philip wrote to him to ask for a contribution towards the huge expenses. The Pope replied that Philip's real concerns were with grand strategy and revenge, not religion.

In March news arrived that Drake, having crossed the Atlantic to the Caribbean, had taken, sacked and extorted ransom from Santo Domingo, former capital of the island of Hispaniola, and Cartagena, capital of the mainland, thus 'Spanish Main' viceroyalty of New Granada. Both were designated as strongpoints in the defensive system of the area, but were scarcely fortified, and had fallen easily.

Already the vital sea route to the Netherlands had been cut by rebel control of the islands commanding the mouths of the Scheldt and the other river highways, and an English force under the Earl of Leicester had landed to aid the rebels; now it seemed as if England were seriously threatening the equally vital collection points for the treasure fleets from Spain's American possessions. Philip was made aware of the alarm of the merchant and financial community and their growing conviction that England was the key to the safety of both the Netherlands and the Indies. From this point on, Philip's instructions suggest that his priorities had changed: England was to be called to order first; after that it would be time to deal with the Dutch rebels. It is still possible to wonder how much this was a result of mercantile unease, how much a 'forward' naval

Sir Francis Drake crowned in Nova
Albion, 1579. Engraving in J L
Gottfried's edition of Theodor de
Brys *Americae*.

During his famous voyage around
the world in the *Golden Hind* (1577–
80), Drake found anchorage near
modern San Francisco, where he was
welcomed and crowned by Indians.
He took formal possession of the area
on behalf of Queen Elizabeth and
named it Nova Albion.

strategy, how much simple concern for *reputacion*, which has always been as
important as either in imperial calculations; it is difficult to fault the Pope's
judgement that it had little to do with religion.

There is a sense, however, in which it had everything to do with religion. If
one accepts that Philip's chief concerns were to preserve the vast inheritance left
him by his father, and defend the faith, it follows that strategic and financial
measures were merely means to these great ends. It seems he did think in this
way; he was a man of his time. In that sense the old assertion that his was a war of
religion can be accepted. It is a picture which transforms itself according to the
angle from which it is viewed. From here politics and finance and grand strategy
fill the frame; shift and they have merged into a Cross.

Philip's character has been a puzzle to historians. He seldom spoke or wrote of
himself; he has come down as the monarch of the golden age of Spain, in Fernand
Braudel's imagery, 'silently reading at his desk, annotating reports in his hasty
handwriting, far from other men, distant and pensive'[1] – a private enigma.

He was the son of the Emperor Charles V, grandson on his mother's side of Ferdinand of Aragon and Isabella of Castile – the joint monarchs who had united Spain and repossessed the southern regions of the peninsula for Christendom – on his father's side of the Habsburg Emperor Maximilian I, whose possessions included both the Austro-Hungarian empire and the provinces of the Dukes of Burgundy, Franche-Comté, Luxemburg and the Netherlands. His father, Charles V, had come into this vast inheritance, which included in the Mediterranean the Balearics, Sardinia, Sicily, the kingdom of Naples occupying the southern half of Italy and Milan in north Italy, in the Atlantic the Canary Islands, the Caribbean islands of Cuba and Hispaniola, and the ever-expanding 'New World' in central America, above the isthmus the viceroyalty of New Spain (Mexico), below it New Granada (Venezuela/Colombia), and Peru.

In defending this unwieldy empire against the Ottoman Turks on the eastern and Mediterranean flanks, France on the western flank, and latterly trying vainly to quell heresy and revolt among German principalities in the north and centre, Charles overspent all the income he could squeeze from his dominions several times over. He met the deficit by borrowing on his Castilian Crown with its possessions in the New World. The loans were taken out with international bankers and secured on future treasure shipments or taxes at rates of interest which grew with the scale of his indebtedness; towards the end in the 1550s he was paying practically 50%, and to some Genoese bankers over 75% interest. He also sold annuities paying five to seven per cent interest called *juros* which were assigned to specific Castilian taxes or dues; servicing these swallowed up more and more of the revenue not already set against his loans. The Castilian Crown was thus put in pawn while ordinary and extraordinary taxation was forced up to levels which helped to depress industry and crush the common people.

Philip grew to maturity very close to these financial problems and their evil consequences, for Charles spent his time travelling and campaigning, and from the age of 16 Philip represented him in Castile. At the age of 17, he wrote to tell his father of a deficit of over three million ducats 'and we do not know from where or how to meet it, since income from the Indies is committed for several years.'[2] At the age of 18 he told him that 'the common people . . . are reduced to such utter misery that many of them walk naked.'[3]

By 1556, when Philip was 28, Charles had lost hope and his bankers' confidence; he abdicated, leaving his Austrian possessions to his brother, Ferdinand, the rest of his empire to Philip. Splendid as it appeared, the centrepiece Castile was technically bankrupt; the following year Philip had to suspend payments from the Castilian treasury and he converted all outstanding loans into *juros* at five per cent interest. It is not surprising he became known as the 'prudent King' who hated war.

Yet prudence in the form of diligence and long reflection before decisions was a mark of his character. His portraits suggest a pensive man of great seriousness. His policies suggest his guiding aim was to follow his father's precept to allow God to use him 'as His instrument' to preserve his inheritance in the True Faith. For this he used the Inquisition. Early in his reign its activities were extended to repress all forms of dissent; all books were censored, all manuscripts censored before they could be printed, the import of foreign books in Spanish translation was banned, free-speaking academics were imprisoned. So great was the fear of contamination from outside that Philip ordered home all Spaniards studying at foreign universities; the only exceptions were orthodox universities in Rome, Bologna, Naples and Coimbra; for the rest of his reign these remained the only institutions which Spanish students were allowed to attend abroad.

King Philip II of Spain.
Seventeenth-century Spanish school.

Queen Elizabeth I
(1533–1603, reigned 1558–1603).
John Bettes the Younger, fl. 1578–99.

It is interesting that this drastic action followed a letter from his father the previous year expressing his anxieties over the spread of heresy and suggesting a radical solution such as he had introduced in Flanders and Hungary: rather than allowing pardons with a light penance for those who recanted, thus allowing them, 'particularly if they are educated persons', to continue their heretical activities, 'an order was issued declaring that all people of whatever state and condition who came under certain specified categories were to be *ipso facto* burned and their goods confiscated. Necessity obliged me to act in this way.'[4]

Charles' hatred of heresy was far from being purely religious; it was as much political, born out of his battles with Lutherism in Germany; heresy had become synonymous in his mind with rebellion. It is likely that Philip thought in the same way. In the Spanish peninsula rebellion was feared chiefly from Moorish subjects who might be agents of the Turks, and the influential ranks of the former Jews, known as '*Conversos*' after their forbears had accepted Christian baptism. Once again one is confronted with a picture that transforms itself with the angle of view: the Inquisition was at one and the same time an expression of religious fundamentalism and an instrument of state terror to preserve internal security.

That Philip continued to heed his father's advice even after the abdication is in keeping with all that is known or suspected of his character. Charles was everything Philip was not; a reckless warrior prince, at home on the battlefield or in Court, whose great campaigns were inspired by a sense of mission, and whose personal warmth and enthusiasm inspired others – not least his son and heir. Philip was a cold man, at least that was the impression he gave ambassadors and foreign monarchs; with his close family, especially his daughters, he was warm and affectionate. He liked flowers and gardens, woods and birds and animals more than Courts – not that too great a sensitivity should be read into this since he also liked hunting and watching netted deer being torn to pieces by dogs. But where Charles had flair, Philip seems to have lacked obvious talent; where Charles led from the saddle and was a personal monarch to his subjects throughout the empire, Philip pondered at his desk and was seldom seen by any of his people. One of the clues to his character may be that he measured himself against his father and found himself wanting. One of his few personal comments suggests something of the sort; writing to his chief advisor in 1569, he said he felt like abdicating:

I know very well that I should be in some other station in life, one not as exalted as the one God has given me, which for me alone is terrible. And many criticize me for this. Please God that in heaven we shall be better treated.[5]

This might simply have been a symptom of the deep depression he fell into at this time after the death of his son, Don Carlos, soon after the death of a wife he loved, Elizabeth de Valois. It may have been a cry of exhaustion, for in his imperial role he set himself a superhuman task: he attempted to read every despatch and master every fact and opinion concerning policy in every part of his empire. As he expressed it himself 'Being a King . . . is none other than a form of slavery which carries a Crown'.[6]

He took advice from councils or *ad hoc* committees which dealt with different areas, generally through a document called a *consulta*, which abstracted the main points of discussion and the council's recommendations, leaving a wide margin for his comments. It is these comments which have exercised historians trying to peer into his mind; they touch every conceivable subject from widows' pensions to the prime issues of the day and give the impression that he made little difference between them. He has been called Chief Clerk of the Spanish Empire. No great visions have been discerned, only constant, pragmatic reaction to events. In the words of Fernand Braudel:

> He saw his task as an unending series of small details. Every one of his annotations is a small, precise point, whether an order, a remark, correction of a spelling mistake or geographical error. Never do we find general notions or grand strategies under his pen.'[7]

Other clues to his character and outlook are to be found in the Palace of San Lorenzo de Escorial, which he built on the side of a bare mountain outside Madrid. It was conceived as a monastery and mausoleum for his family, and himself, as much as a royal residence, above all perhaps as a personal retreat. His suite of rooms was next to the Chapel at the centre of the complex of buildings arranged around courtyards to form a pattern to commemorate the martyrdom of Saint Lorenzo, burned over a gridiron. From his bedchamber he could look through a window to the high altar, and hear Masses said for the souls of his parents, whose remains he had interred beneath. The paintings he chose to decorate his apartments were especially revealing, but of what? They were Hieronymus Bosch's *The Garden of Earthly Delights*, *The Haywain*, *The Seven Deadly Sins*.[8] Their extraordinary earthiness, the symbolism of eternal punishment awaiting earthly vice must have spoken to the same morbid humours which had caused him to build his palace as a refuge from the world and a tomb.

His personal life had given him frequent cause to reflect on mortality. His mother, whom he had loved and greatly respected, had died when he was 12; he had led the funeral cortege from Toledo to Granada during which time the heat had caused the body to decompose to such an extent it was unrecognisable when the coffin was opened. At the age of 16 he married the Portuguese Infanta, Maria; two years later she died after childbirth; the son she bore him, Don Carlos, grew into a subnormal youth with a cruel disposition who was judged unfit to rule; he died at the age of 23 after Philip had been forced to put him under guard. Meanwhile, Philip had married Mary, Queen of England, an unhappy childless affair undertaken out of duty to his father, who as one of his last acts as Emperor had sought to bind England into the Spanish-Netherlands orbit against France. After Mary died, Philip made a proposal to her successor, Elizabeth; she strung him along in her way, then turned him down, on which he married the 13-year-old Elizabeth de Valois; she did not join him in the marriage bed until she was 17, then bore two daughters and at the age of 21 died in childbirth. He had loved her. His final marriage was to Ana of Austria; she bore five children but four died young, leaving one son, Philip, as her heir. Ana herself died soon afterwards in 1580.

It is not surprising if Philip, when he raised his tired eyes from the papers that came in unceasingly from every quarter of his earthly world, rested his gaze on the world to come.

And if he conceived no grand designs, although this was undoubtedly based on fundamentals in his personality, he must have seen it as proper humility before God's grand design. Thus he instructed his son, who became Philip III, that a good prince had first to be a good Christian: 'If you are forced to take a stand as champion or defender of our sacred religion, even should you lose all your Kingdoms, God will receive you in glory, which is truly the only goal worth striving for.'[9]

This suggests that he saw himself, not only as a prisoner to his papers, but a prisoner to circumstances outside his control. Of course he was right. The events which he struggled to deal with were shaped by conquistadores and prospectors

Escorial Palace under construction.

in America, financiers in Germany, Italy and Flanders, merchant syndicates in France, England and the Netherlands, governors and traders in the Portuguese Indies as the system known as mercantilism, or more loosely capitalism, burst the bounds of the Mediterranean Sea and shifted the economic centre of gravity to the Atlantic Ocean. The process had begun before Charles' reign, even before Vasco de Gama rounded the Cape of Good Hope and sailed into the Indian Ocean; it reached fruition during Philip's reign.

The mechanism was trade, the motive power was the drive for profit, the fuel was finance, the moving parts were a few thousand men seeking to improve their lot; the dynamism of the system was irresistible. Neither Philip nor his great imperial rival at the other end of the Mediterranean, Suleiman the Magnificent, nor the naval campaigns they waged year after year with fleets of galleys in the Middle Sea could affect the changing pattern. The last great trial of strength at Lepanto after Suleiman's death was won decisively by Philip's half-brother, Don John of Austria, in command of the Christian fleet; that had no effect. It was an anachronism. The Portuguese were in command of the Indian Ocean and the trade which had flowed liberally from the spice islands and India through Egypt and the eastern Mediterranean to Europe was being diverted via the Cape into the Atlantic, or leaking through Portugal's eastern ally, Persia. Suleiman's successors turned towards Persia; Philip was able to turn towards the Atlantic.

Spain and Portugal claimed the Atlantic monopoly; they had agreed their spheres of influence either side of a line drawn 370 leagues west of the Cape Verde Islands: to the west of the line Spain had her central American possessions and beyond them the Pacific; to the east of the line Portugal had the bulge of the

Brazilian coast, stations on the west and east coasts of Africa and India, and the east Indies islands. The spice trade from the Indies and the gold and silver from the New World were at the heart of the Atlantic system but planters and ranchers had followed the original conquistadores creating the conditions for a circular web of trade, supplying them with European manufactures and plantation slaves from Africa, taking their sugar, tobacco, hides and other produce back to Europe.

The region which benefited most from this ever-growing cycle was the Netherlands; this was partly because of the accident of belonging to the Spanish crown, chiefly because of its geographical situation on the one hand at the mouth of a great river system from southern Europe and the German mining regions around Augsberg and Nurnberg, on the other hand between the Atlantic and the Baltic which supplied the masts, timbers, pitch, tar, turpentine, flax needed in ever-increasing quantities for the ships maintaining the Atlantic system. Thus Antwerp, which was made northern entrepot for Portuguese and Spanish spices and colonial produce, became centre of the most prosperous and industrially advanced region of Europe, virtually the workshop and armaments centre of the Spanish and Portuguese empires. Spanish treasure was drawn in in payment, augmenting the upward spiral, and Antwerp became financial capital of the Spanish empire.

All northern Europe naturally, but particularly the Atlantic coastal fringe, was affected by this movement of wealth. The first to attempt to break into the system at source around the Azores where the homeward fleets collected and on the Spanish 'Main' itself were French privateer squadrons with merchant or royal backing sailing from the Biscay and Channel ports. As early as 1523 the Angos of Dieppe cut out several ships carrying Cortez' loot from the palace of Montezuma; a decade later they repeated their success with a treasure fleet in the Indies. By the time Philip came to the throne French squadrons were sacking and pillaging throughout the Spanish islands and off the Florida channel, creating a reign of terror which Drake was scarcely to equal.

The English at this time were in the Spanish orbit, their merchants and seafarers trading more or less legitimately in the peninsula and Atlantic islands, although prohibited from the West Indies, America or the slaving coast of Africa. 'Legitimately' is not a word that corresponds to the realities of 16th-century seafaring: traders were smugglers or pirates as opportunity offered. The more rigidly Spain and Portugal tried to enforce the monopolies they claimed, the more the outsiders used force and corruption to break in. The French were more notorious in the Caribbean; the English, with the advantage of splendid, deep-water harbours along the flank of the Channel route to the Netherlands, specialised in smuggling and piracy; these 'illegal' means of profitable exchange became institutionalised within the legal organs of trade and within society up to the Court and the Queen.

Far more serious for Spain than the petty plundering of the French or English were the changes being wrought in the Netherlands themselves by Atlantic wealth; for this increased the power and ambition of the burghers of the sea ports and industrial centres, increasing the natural tensions between them and the feudal nobles and Church leaders. Since men thought in religious terms, this tension found expression in religious argument. Philip, believing with his father – and no doubt correctly – that heresy and rebellion were synonymous, attempted to increase the Church's power by creating 14 new Bishoprics in the Netherlands, each with its staff of Inquisitors. This provoked uproar and helped to focus the dissent into an independence movement, for the Inquisition was labelled 'Spanish', and it was not difficult to create a horror propaganda around it and incite the mob to Calvinist rage. Much the same social tensions in the maritime west of France produced a similar dissenting movement, the Huguenots; and France broke in civil war. Philip, warned by this and perceiving the different Protestant revolts as an international conspiracy, saw his duty plain: he sent an army north under the Duke of Alva to crush the revolt. Alva used the cruellest methods of repression but only succeeded in consolidating a fiercer spirit among the Protestant rebels, led by William of Orange. Meanwhile rebel sailors, known as 'Sea Beggars' – Beggars was a term of abuse used against the rebels which they had adopted – used English and French ports as bases, and joined Huguenot privateers in plundering Spanish trade. In the winter of 1568–9 they succeeded in cutting off the Netherlands from Spain by sea.

Philip recalled Alva and tried a policy of conciliation. Things had gone too far by then. Meanwhile the costs of the campaigns and the disruption at the industrial-commercial heart of his empire reduced his finances to the sorry state they had been in earlier; in 1575 he again stopped payments from the Castilian Treasury. The following year the Army in the Netherlands, unpaid, mutinied and sacked and pillaged Antwerp.

By this time England had moved into the anti-Spanish camp. This was partly because she had little to fear from France, split in civil war, chiefly because she was a very poor country and Elizabeth, her courtiers and merchants needed the quick profits promised by plundering Spanish trade and treasure. Drake was only the most notorious and successful of a steady stream of English sea rovers drawn to the alluring triangle between the Spanish Indies and the isthmus over which the silver shipments from Peru were carried.

Two things came to Philip's rescue – both outside his control: first and most important was a dramatic increase in the quantity of silver coming from the New World mines; by 1580 his 'Royal Fifth' of the value of the annual shipments amounted to two million ducats (rather over half a million pounds sterling) equal to the total value of the annual shipments at the beginning of his reign.[10] Although this still failed to bridge the gap between tax income and mounting military and naval expenditure necessary to defend his frontiers on land, in the Mediterranean, the Atlantic, pay the Army of the Netherlands and attend to England, it bestowed on his Crown a dazzling lustre in the eyes of the world, and renewed his bankers' confidence. This renewed confidence allowed him to pursue imperial policies with greater freedom than before.

The second stroke of fortune concerned Portugal. In 1578 the young King, Dom Sebastian, was killed leading a crusade into Morocco. His successor was an old man, Cardinal Henry of Portugal, who had taken the vows of celibacy and had no direct heirs. Philip had a claim to the throne through the female line and he began pressing it on influential groups within the country, not a difficult task since the Protestant assault on the trade routes was affecting Portugal as much as Spain, and forcing both powers towards an alliance to protect their oceanic monopolies. The increasing treasure from the New World was another powerful argument, for Portugal was desperately short of specie needed to lubricate her Indian Ocean and eastern trade. So it was that when Cardinal Henry died in January 1580, most of the nobles and the financial and commercial community of Lisbon came out in favour of Philip. The exceptions were the *Conversos* who feared the rigorous extension of the Inquisition that was bound to follow him into Portugal. These and sections of the lower clergy supported the claim of the illegitimate Dom Antonio who began the struggle for the succession by seizing Lisbon and the Crown treasury. Philip was prepared; in a sharp,

The Marquis of Santa Cruz, the veteran Spanish admiral, known as 'the never-defeated', Philip's first choice to command the Armada. However, he died before its departure and was replaced as commander by the Duke of Medina Sidonia.

well-conceived series of operations by land and sea his forces overran the country inside the year; Dom Antonio fled to seek support in France; Philip was crowned Philip I of Portugal.

At this high point of his reign the Spanish empire seemed to embrace the world. Apart from Philip's European possessions it included all the Portuguese trading stations and islands in the Indian Ocean and Africa, Portuguese Brazil southwards to Buenos Aires, established in 1580 on the banks of the Rio de la Plata; on the other side of the subcontinent it extended down the coast into what is now Chile and up beyond the isthmus of Panama into regions now named California, New Mexico and Texas to Florida; indeed the whole American continent was claimed. Across the Pacific his flag flew over the Philippine Islands, which were named after him. The threat represented by this colossus with apparently inexhaustible sources of wealth needing only to be hewed from the ground of the 'New World' was the major factor in European politics; the 'Protestants' of the north had to combine or they risked being swallowed one by one.

The risk became very apparent through the 1580s. Philip's latest army commander and Governor General in the Netherlands, Alexander Farnese, Duke of Parma, reconquered the southern provinces and in 1585 took Brussels and Antwerp. The Protestant leader, William of Orange, had been assassinated the previous year with Philip's active encouragement. Philip was known to have plotted Catholic risings in England and Elizabeth's assassination. The more immediate threat to England in 1585, however, was the prospect of Parma completing his reconquest of the Netherlands; then England would be facing the colossus alone; it was this that decided Elizabeth to send Leicester and his army to aid the rebel northern provinces, and Drake on the cruise which resulted in the insult to Philip on his own coast at Vigo and the sacking of Santo Domingo and Cartagena; these, of course, were the goads that persuaded Philip to make England his first priority.

The plan he received from his Admiral, Santa Cruz, was extremely simple: it was to gather together an irresistible fleet of some 560 warships (including 40 galleys and six galleasses), armed merchantmen and storeships of altogether 77,000 tons to carry an army of 60,000 soldiers and the necessary siege trains to England and put them ashore to march on London. Parma's plan was equally simple; it was for a surprise landing of his Army of the Netherlands on the English east coast, carried there in favourable weather by small craft constructed for the purpose. Both plans were impossible. Santa Cruz's demanded more men, more money and more ships than even the Spanish empire could command; Parma's demanded that neither the English nor the Sea Beggars who commanded all the rivermouths and sea coast of the Netherlands should get word of the construction and massing of the necessary small craft – nor when Parma got to sea attempt to stop him with their superior forces. Philip settled in principle for Santa Cruz's plan, but scaled it down to what was thought a manageable size. When during the course of 1587 it was realised that it was going to be impossible to gather even this force together and arm it, it was decided to combine both plans: Santa Cruz was to sail from Lisbon with a fleet sufficient to overcome the English fleet, and carrying some 16,000 soldiers and their supplies to rendezvous with Parma on the coast of the Netherlands; Parma meanwhile was to construct sufficient small craft to carry some 30,000 men of his Army across to Kent.

This was not the kind of plan to be expected of a prudent king. Perhaps Santa Cruz's optimism and the successful combination of sea and land forces in the conquest of Portugal seduced him and his advisors; but operations virtually on his own coastline were a very different matter from such a distant expedition. And nothing of such size and scope had ever been attempted before. Naval campaigns in the Mediterranean had been quite different in scale and purpose, relying as they did on the mutual dependence of galleys – essentially short-range warships – and seaside fortresses. The rules of the Mediterranean game were well known; campaigns were in the nature of annual ritual joustings in the fighting season. Here, however, there were Atlantic storms to batter and scatter the fleet, perhaps contrary winds to drive it off course, and off the French and Dutch coasts shoal water, strong tides and unpredictable weather even without the enemy forces. It was staking an immense amount of credit, in both senses, on an unpredictable outcome by an untried means. In a word it was imprudent. Without Philip's income from the New World and his command of Portuguese and Italian shipping resources, it would have been impossible. Was it the desperate throw of a basically insecure and therefore prudent man mimicking forcefulness? Had the flow of silver from the New World effected a transformation in his methods? Did he see himself, in his own words, as 'forced to take a stand as champion . . . of our sacred religion' which, even if it cost him his kingdom, would result in God receiving him in glory, 'truly the only goal worth striving for'? Was he simply ill-advised? He was tired and sick in the summer of 1587 and relying heavily on a small inner cabal of ministers who guarded their position jealously; neither of the principal members, Don Juan de Idiaquez and Don Cristobal de Moura, had any campaigning experience. But even those with experience seem to have been sanguine; most had been urging the 'Enterprise of England' for years.

Philip was not blind to all the risks; he made this clear to Parma in September. Santa Cruz had sailed to the Azores after Drake – vainly as it turned out – and it was now long past the campaigning season; nevertheless Philip was determined to proceed with the enterprise of England:

We are quite aware of the risk which is incurred by sending a heavy fleet in winter through the Channel without a sure harbour, but the various reasons which render this course necessary are sufficient to counterbalance this objection . . .[11]

These reasons were:

. . . the forces collected, and the vast money responsibility incurred, make it extremely difficult for such an expedition again to be got together if they escape us this time, whilst the obstacles and divisions that may arise (and certainly will do so) next summer, force us to undertake the enterprise this year or else fail altogether . . . On other occasions I have written to you, how all our prestige is at stake, and how much my own tranquility depends upon the success of the undertaking . . .

A week later he detailed the 'obstacles that may arise . . . next summer' when he sent instructions for Santa Cruz:

. . . trustworthy information has been received of the snares and plots the English woman is preparing . . . Moreover it is understood that peace talks between the Turks and Persians are proceeding apace, and the intention is, if peace be concluded, that the Turks should send a fleet in the summer to (attack) Italy . . .

Then we must consider the door that it would seem that God has opened for us in Flanders by our capture of Sluys whence the passage to England is short and secure; and also the many advantages secured with that place, among others the barges that can be brought together from the streams that debouch there; and the conveniences offered by the place itself and the lie of the land for the massing of an army speedily and secretly. Finally there are the forces now at His Majesty's disposal in many places. If they are considered separately none is sufficient for the task; yet if skilfully united they would assure us victory, if we do not delay to use them in view of the enemy's present unpreparedness . . .[12]

It seems that the opportunity he perceived now and the storm clouds ahead combined to produce a picture of utmost urgency. However, the opportunity was a chimera: the passage to England was *not* secured by possession of Sluys: an army and the necessary invasion barges could *not* be massed there secretly; above all, perhaps, it was precisely the junction of his two separated forces – 'which if skilfully united would assure us victory' – that made the odds so long against the enterprise succeeding.

These letters and others he wrote that autumn and winter suggest that a moment had been reached – one of those moments with which history is replete – when the principal figure had, or felt he had, no choice: events had conspired to overwhelm human judgement. On the one hand something had to be done about the English – whose goads were damaging his *reputacion* – thereby his credit – and who could only be encouraged to more dangerous exploits if allowed to go unpunished for another year. On the other hand it was necessary to strike before the political calm in the Mediterranean broke and the Turk, now negotiating for peace with Persia, was encouraged to attack Italy or even the Azores; the English ambassador at Constantinople was trying to embroil them in such schemes. There was Portugal, where discontent at the burdens imposed by the Armada preparations and Protestant assault by sea was reaching potentially dangerous levels; the English were harbouring the Portuguese Pretender, Dom Antonio, and encouraging insurrection; John Hawkins also had designs on the Azores, the hinge of the returning treasure fleets, hence, it was supposed, of Spanish wealth and power. Then there was France, now fortunately locked in civil war, but it would not remain so for ever. Above all, perhaps, was the acute financial strain of the Armada preparations. Everything in the political and financial constellation pointed to the need to take the initiative while it was possible and Philip's correspondence shows an increasingly desperate sense of time running to waste.

It was dangerous to go on, it was more dangerous to hold back. Looked at with the eye of hope, there was the chance of victory in the Channel; holding back meant certain humiliation and the waste of the millions already expended. It was a desperate gamble; Philip was by now an old, ill, self-willed, desperate man.

2

The Virgin Queen

In material terms Elizabeth I of England was a pygmy beside the King of Spain. It is this that gives the Armada campaign its enduring fascination. In a way littleness was a source of strength; Elizabeth had no distant possessions or spheres of interest to defend and distract her attention; she could concentrate on the main threat. Her priceless asset was the sea which surrounded her kingdom like a moat, leaving only one comparatively narrow land frontier with an even weaker kingdom, Scotland, in the north. The sea was far more than a moat, of course; it was the high road to trade and plunder; by strengthening her forces at sea England could increase her wealth and her defence at the same time. With the growth of the Atlantic system this happened quite naturally: it was a remarkable concentration of resources.

The sea was also an element which might have been designed for Elizabeth's method – or the method forced on her by weakness. It gave full scope to her suppleness, which could be called duplicity, and her refusal to commit herself to anything if it could possibly be avoided. This was illustrated soon after she came to the throne in an undeclared war with the French, who had built up an army in Scotland and were sending reinforcements. Ordering a squadron north to interdict them, she instructed her Admiral, William Wynter, to do nothing in the Queen's name, but 'as of his own head, do that enterprise he shall see most hurtful to the French'.[1] Wynter duly attacked a French convoy lying in the Firth of Forth, took two warships and some storeships and drove the rest ashore then disposed his squadron to blockade the Firth. Challenged two days later by the French party in Scotland whether he came as an enemy, he replied that he had been forced into the Firth by a storm: he had intended no hostility to anyone, but when fired on he determined to give the (Protestant) Scots all the aid he could, 'hereof the Queen's Highness, my mistress, was nothing privy.'[2] The treaty that followed this conflict provided for the withdrawal of all French troops from Scotland, removing the real threat from the north; it was a good instance of the economy of naval force operating on interior lines, and of the lies which could be used to absolve the Queen; while these convinced no one, they limited hostilities by preventing an open outbreak of war. This was the game Elizabeth's sea rovers, Hawkins, Drake and the rest, played as they ravaged Philip's ships and possessions in the Atlantic; the Queen was generally a major financial backer and drew a major share of the spoils as her share, yet she was 'nothing privy' to the enterprise. It is significant that the real break with Spain only occurred when she sent a land force under Leicester to the Netherlands in 1585: an army on land could not be disavowed.

Elizabeth had learnt suppleness in a hard school. She was the daughter of that robust monarch, Henry VIII, and his vivacious, dark-eyed mistress, Anne Boleyn, whom he married shortly after Elizabeth's conception. To free himself to do so he had to divorce his first wife, Catherine of Aragon, thereby provoking

Portrait of Philip II and Mary Tudor,
Elizabeth's half-sister, attributed to
Hans Eworth.

a break with the Pope and setting the country on the path of the Reformation or Protestantism in a rather English way, far removed from the thunderings of Luther or Calvin. His daughter by his first marriage, Mary, then 17, bitterly resenting the disgrace to her mother, regarded Elizabeth as illegitimate; two and a half years later Elizabeth was declared so officially. Anne Boleyn had failed to give Henry the son he needed, and had been tried for adultery, convicted and executed. Now that both royal daughters were of the same status Mary, senior by age, was reconciled, even affectionate towards her young half-sister.

Elizabeth was a lively child with a sharp, precocious intelligence directed by her tutors into the study of languages; in her early teens she spent her mornings on Greek, her afternoons on Latin and was already proficient in French and Italian; later she learnt Spanish. In this area she far outshone Philip of Spain, who was never at home outside his native Castilian tongue. Her father died when she was 13; after this she needed all her intelligence simply to stay alive, and so her adolescence coincided with her political apprenticeship.

Henry had succeeded in siring a son, Edward, by one of his later wives, Jane Seymour, but Edward was still a minor when he came to the throne and a succession struggle developed. Elizabeth became involved through the ambitions of Thomas Seymour, younger brother of the first Regent or 'Protector' of the young King. As Seymour's intrigues became known he was imprisoned in the Tower and Elizabeth, at the age of 16, had to use all her wit to distance herself from complicity. She succeeded and only Seymour paid the price with his head. Her next real test came after Edward died in 1553. Mary, her elder half-sister, succeeded to the throne, and the next year married Philip of Spain. Factional and religious antagonisms into which Henry's break from the Roman Church, his confiscation and sale of Church lands, and recently the struggles around the young King had plunged England, were given sharper focus by the Spanish marriage. Mary herself was a passionate Catholic; she sought to restore the True Faith and papal supremacy in England. There were still powerful Catholic families in the land, especially in the north, but more powerful interests had a stake in the Reformation, now 20 years old; the merchants of London and the southern and eastern ports, landed gentry, professional men and yeomen who had invested in former Church property confiscated, then sold off by Henry, clergy who had married under the new laws allowing them to do so, and younger spirits generally who had grown up with the reformed Church did not wish to come under the influence of Rome or a foreign king. Most important was the commercial interest which in its inherent opposition to feudal restriction was a natural supporter of protestant religion. Elizabeth was the obvious rallying point.

She was peculiarly sensitive to this mood, as she was to prove when she came to the throne. Her intellect was sceptical and pragmatic; extremes such as Mary's fanatic Catholicism were foreign to her; she could be swayed by passion, or appear to be, but ultimately never allowed herself to succumb; her head ruled her. Perhaps this was a lesson burned in by adolescent experience, particularly the affair with Thomas Seymour, a dashing and attractive gallant, whose fate must have affected her deeply; or perhaps she was simply, in A. L. Rowse's words, 'a woman at heart cold intellectually and emotionally.'[3]

At first she absented herself from Mass at Court but, with the mood of rebellion and conspiracy everywhere against the reimposition of Catholicism, this placed her in the gravest danger with Mary and her advisors. She acted the penitent, with tears in her eyes begging for books and tutors who would help her to correct the errors in which she had been brought up. Mary was pleased, but when Elizabeth's religious attendance still left much to be desired, she became deeply suspicious. Elizabeth assured her of the genuineness of her conversion. Her protestations were not enough. Mary saw heresy everywhere and, like Charles and Philip of Spain, linked it with rebellion. All Elizabeth's wit and dissimulation could not prevent others using her name for their attempts to overthrow Mary, and it was not long before she was taken to the Tower, protesting her innocence and loyalty to the Queen but scarcely expecting to emerge alive. Sufficient proof of her treason could not or would not be found, however, and it was considered too dangerous to execute her with the people very obviously on her side; she was removed into custody in a country house.

Meanwhile Mary set about reimposing her faith on the country. The first martyr went to the stake early in 1555, the year after her marriage to Philip, and over the three and a half years that followed before she died, unloved and childless, some 300 more were burned, including 60 women; it is significant that most of the victims came from London and the six surrounding counties, only one came from the north.[4]

'Bloody' Mary succeeded only in increasing the hatred of the papacy and foreign influence in the south of the country, and when Elizabeth succeeded her towards the end of 1558 England was as close to civil war as ever; it could be said it was closer, for in the eyes of the Catholic Church she was illegitimate, and therefore a usurper; moreover she was the last of Henry's children and had no heir; another succession struggle was bound to break out, if not before, then on her death, and both France and Spain, the great rivals for influence over England, were likely to back conspiracies for their favoured claimant. The French candidate was Mary Stuart, Queen of Scots, the daughter of Henry VIII's sister, Margaret, and James IV of Scotland; she was to Elizabeth what Elizabeth had been to the late Queen, the dangerous focal point for rebellion. Fortunately Elizabeth herself was Philip's candidate, and when he offered marriage she played for time and strung him along.

She did the same with religion, moving with the utmost caution to reinstate a moderate protestantism favoured by the ascendant majority in London and the south, teasing the Pope as she teased Philip. And while she steered between these twin dangers of internal anarchy and foreign domination, she courted her people. She was 25 years old, not beautiful in a conventional sense but with the freshness of young womanhood, with a fair complexion, expressive dark eyes, rich golden hair with reddish lights, 'of limbs and features neat'; she carried herself regally yet used feminine artifice to win her people of every class and condition, as one contemporary wrote, 'coupling mildness with majesty . . . and stately stooping to the meanest sort.'[5]

She used the same feminine arts at Court and in her council, encouraging favourites and factions, yet following her own course between them, at times temporising, more often wilful and imperious, never allowing her own instinctual feeling for the mood or interest of the country – at least those parts touched with the spirit of the Atlantic system – to be submerged by argument. In this she showed flair amounting to genius. She also had a sure judgement of men, their strengths and weaknesses, but never allowed even her most trusted councillors to gain an ascendancy; a contemporary wrote:

She was absolute and sovereign mistress of her grace and those to whom she distributed her favours were never more than tenants to will and stood on no better ground than her princely pleasure and their own good behaviour.[6]

There was more than artifice in her use of favouritism and sexual tension. She

Ambassador it made 60% on the capital invested. Cecil joined Elizabeth's other close advisor, the Earl of Leicester, in recommending Hawkins for a coat of arms.

Hawkins' third expedition of this type was commanded by Captain John Lovell since Philip, unhappy about the intrusions into his monopoly, had warned Elizabeth that his colonies were off limits. She and Burghley performed a typical charade, extracting a bond of £500 from Hawkins that he would neither go to the Indies nor send his ships there. Lovell duly went, but was less successful than Hawkins; the colonists had been alerted to Philip's displeasure at their trading with heretics. Before he returned Hawkins was preparing a fourth and larger expedition, six ships headed by two of the Queen's ships, backed by the usual London merchants, Navy Board officials and ministers, including Burghley who was a prime mover with Hawkins in promoting the venture; it was indeed a joint state/merchant project for forcing entry into the two Iberian monopolies.[11] Hawkins robbed the Portuguese successfully on the African coast, forcing his human wares on the Spanish colonists in the West Indies by burning their town, house by house, until they agreed to trade, but was then caught in a storm and driven to the anchorage of San Juan de Ulloa by Vera Cruz in the Gulf of Mexico. Here he had the misfortune to meet the incoming Spanish plate fleet carrying a new Viceroy for New Spain who attempted to surprise him after a flag of truce. In the ensuing battle Hawkins was forced to abandon all but two of his ships and was lucky to escape with his life.

San Juan de Ulloa, fought in 1568, marked a turning point in English relations with Spain. At the beginning of the series of voyages Hawkins had a network of commercial relationships with Spanish merchants and England was in the Spanish political orbit. Hawkins retained his Spanish connections after the battle, but neither he nor any other English sailor forgot the treachery practised on him by the Spanish viceroy nor the fate of those members of his expedition who were captured; two were burnt alive as heretics at Seville, four were consigned as slaves to the galleys, others were flogged; meanwhile Elizabeth and her ministers had moved into an area of undeclared, unacknowledged hostilities against the Atlantic monopolists. This would have happened without San Juan de Ulloa – had indeed happened with the despatch of the expedition – and the propaganda value of the English sailors burned by the Inquisition could have been gained from other similar instances; nevertheless the battle hardened attitudes on both sides.

The dates of the Hawkins' voyages are significant for an understanding of what lay beneath the religious – or in modern terms ideological – armour assumed. His first voyage coincided with the outbreak of civil war between the French Huguenots based on the Biscay and Channel regions and the French feudal centre in Paris; his second voyage coincided with the outbreak of revolt by the Protestant 'Beggars' of the Low Countries against their feudal centre, by an accident of succession located in Madrid. Atlantic wealth and the lure of wealth had caused the mercantile fringes of western Europe to break away from their feudal centres. Of course the breakaways were led by feudal nobles, the Bourbon Prince of Condé, and in the Netherlands Prince William of Orange; these hereditary leaders used the new spirit and the new wealth generated in the Atlantic system to further their own ambitions.

The significant difference in Elizabethan England was that the feudal centre, the Monarchy, was already enmeshed with the mercantile fringe; hence there was no break-away. Elizabeth and Burghley, Leicester and the officials of the Navy Board and the Admiralty Courts were linked with the merchants of

London and the Lords Lieutenants, Vice Admirals and merchants and officials of the southern counties in a web of piracy, smuggling and legal trade. 'Piracy' and 'smuggling' are of course charged with moral significance, as in the other direction is 'trade'. Viewed objectively there was no moral difference between the Portuguese and Spanish claims to monopoly won by conquest and supported by frightful exploitation and cruelty, and the 'Protestant' assault on those monopolies by force accompanied by equal exploitation and cruelty. This is not to take a Marxist view of history, but to take a historical, therefore non-Marxist view of human nature. Both camps were involved in the forcible exchange of wealth; neither would be termed moral by the standards of 19th- or 20th-century liberalism. The spirit of Elizabeth, the spirit of her 'Spirit', Burghley, was the spirit of merchant venture; it was in basic antagonism to the old feudal system of Europe, hence with its religious expression, Roman Catholicism. Elizabeth, with her practical intelligence, cool eye for men and remarkable flair for divining the true interests – in all senses – of her people, perceived this instinctively, as Burghley perceived it politically; both were led, step by step, via support for the Huguenots, via the exploits of Francis Drake, to the final defiance of Philip of Spain in the despatch of English forces to the Netherlands under Leicester in 1585.

By this time defensive preparations were well in hand. It was Burghley, working with John Hawkins, who initiated the preparations, and it is interesting that they began several years before Philip decided to send the Armada. The most important step was reform of naval administration; this arose from talks between Burghley and Hawkins in 1577; who initiated them is impossible to say; Hawkins' biographer, J. A. Williamson, suggests that personalities may have played a key role. Hawkins' father-in-law was the veteran Treasurer of the Navy Board, and he was at odds with other board members, notably the equally veteran Sir William Wynter, who was both Master of the Ordnance and Surveyor. In his discussions with Burghley, Hawkins accused Wynter of corrupt practices, grossly over-charging the Queen for naval stores, using timber bought for the Queen's ships to build ships for himself and associates, and similar abuses. This was the way things were run in all departments of state; perhaps Wynter was overdoing it. Hawkins told Burghley the fleet could be maintained at two-thirds the present cost of some £6,000 a year, and Burghley who was a good judge of men and had known Hawkins as a practical shipowner, businessman and voyager for 20 years, had him appointed Treasurer of the Navy in succession to his father-in-law in January 1578.

Hawkins not only kept his side of the bargain by cutting down the maintenance costs, but radically altered the composition of the fleet, changing it from an essentially defensive force of cumbersome floating castles packed with armed men to fight close-range boarding and entering battles into an ocean-going navy of low, relatively fast and weatherly ships described as 'race-built', designed to fight stand-off artillery battles. He was representative of what might be called the 'privateering' school of naval warfare; as always in periods of radical change, it was necessary to fight the old ideas represented in this case by the naval veterans on the board, in particular William Wynter, who could not conceive of warships without their high and 'commodious fights', however unmanageable these made them. Hawkins was supported by Burghley and won through in this and a complementary reform in manning: by reducing the complement of each ship and increasing pay by a third he sought to cut down disease consequent on overcrowding, and keep a better type of sailor, otherwise attracted to the merchant service.

It is certain that he and probably Burghley were thinking of more than defending the Channel; he had his eyes fixed on the treasure fleets from the Indies and was continually urging projects to attack them either on the isthmus or off the Azores or by blockading the Spanish ports themselves. One success would not only be a tremendous gain for the Queen, but would ruin Philip, whose loans were tied to the annual arrivals of the plate fleet. The Queen held Hawkins back, fearing that in the absence of a major part of the fleet, the Spanish army in the Netherlands might slip across the Channel.

The danger of such a project seemed to increase from 1580 as missionaries of the militant order of Jesuits landed in England; they had been trained in Rome for the express purpose of saving souls by winning the country back to the True Faith. Here a note of pure ideology enters the Atlantic struggle: for the alarm caused by the arrival of these Popish agents and the plots they were supposed to be hatching fanned the smouldering fires of English Protestant bigotry, and Elizabeth, ever sensitive to mood, was forced to abandon the moderation of her religious policy. She still refused to persecute ordinary Catholics – merely fining them for not attending Church of England services – but Jesuits and Catholic priests were now hounded down, imprisoned and executed in a campaign reminiscent of 'Bloody Mary's'.

There was substance to the rumours of Catholic plots for, at the same time as the Jesuits were arriving, the Pope was attempting to form a Holy League with Spain for an actual invasion of England. In 1582 hints of this were discovered by the Queen's chief of intelligence, Walsyngham, in letters hidden behind a looking glass belonging to a Spanish agent. Philip was still determined to clear up the Netherlands revolt before tackling England, but the content of the letters and the unrest stirred up by the Jesuits alarmed the council. Burghley ordered the executive head of the Navy, the Lord Admiral, to begin collecting information on which a plan of defence against seaborne invasion could be based, and the following year he ordered a census of the maritime population. The result of these initiatives was a detailed list of all English merchant ships and their tonnage, the names and places of residence of all masters, mariners, fishermen, and Thames wherrymen 'in all 16,255 persons who were in some sort accustomed to the water.'[12] It was a masterpiece of functional bureaucracy and enabled Burghley to provide for taking over merchant ships and impressing the required number of men in case of emergency. It is interesting that the detailed plans he made out in 1584, thus before Philip had decided to send the Armada, accurately predicted Philip's later design.

When the break with Spain came the following year, a programme of new building was taken in hand; Hawkins' chief lieutenants in the reconstruction of the fleet, the master shipwrights Peter Pett and Matthew Baker, each built a galleon to the new 'race built' pattern, *Vanguard* and *Rainbow*; Walter Raleigh built a similar rather larger ship, the *Ark Raleigh*, which was bought into the fleet as the *Ark Royal*; and two ocean-going pinnaces were added. By 1587, the Queen's Navy comprised 18 fighting galleons ranging from rather over 1,000 tons down to 300 tons, all except the three largest either new or rebuilt to the new long and low specification; seven smaller galleons of 100 tons or so and 18 ocean-going pinnaces for reconnaissance, despatches and supplies.

As important as the ships themselves were crews, their victuals and armament; these had been provided for with the same administrative efficiency, as had increases in taxation and customs duties to pay for them all; here Burghley had found a man as remarkable in his way as Hawkins; his name was Thomas Smythe and between 1570 and 1584 he doubled customs receipts on imports into London and subsidiary ports. While this was made possible by the rising volume

Sir Walter Raleigh (?1552–1618), Elizabethan explorer and adventurer, who stoutly defended Howard's strategy and tactics during the Armada campaign. Engraving by Simon de Passe (1595–1647), published as a frontispiece to Raleigh's *History of the World*, third edition, 1617.

of trade, Smythe's employment of more and better-paid customs officers turned haphazard collection and corruption into something approaching a modern service.[13]

The contrast between England and Spain in administrative and financial efficiency in these vital years leading up to the sailing of the Armada was as great as the distance between them in wealth. Elizabeth's ordinary annual revenues amounted to little over £200,000, yet by careful housekeeping – what Burghley termed 'parsimony' – and by making up deficits with the sale of Crown lands, occasional loans, and bonuses from overseas plunder, she entered the period of an open breach with Spain with a war reserve of £263, a population not unduly bowed by taxation, an efficient bureaucracy and no permanent debt. Philip on the other hand, whose revenues from Castile and the Indies amounted to over nine million Ducats – some two and quarter million pounds sterling, thus over 10 times Elizabeth's revenue – was deep in debt. Interest on the *juros* swallowed about a third of his revenues; much of the rest was mortgaged; his financial administration had been thrown into chaos by the shifts and turns needed to bridge the almost permanent gap between income and expenditure and worked on an *ad hoc* basis, meeting each emergency as it arose with whatever resources were to hand; the ordinary population of Castile had been taxed beyond the limit; the industrial base had ceased to expand; the treasury owed thousands to soldiers and suppliers; some of the arrears of pay went back over 20 years.[14]

While the differences can be explained by the differing status and roles, on the one hand of an imperial world power – a 'superpower' in today's terms – on the other hand of an offshore island, part primary producer of wool, part piratical predator, the cautious good judgement of the Queen and her 'Spirit' Burghley cannot be disregarded; when Burghley towards the end of his life came to reflect on the Queen's successses, he pointed to her 'parsimony' as one of the principal factors.

She was never in greater need of balanced judgement than in the final years leading up to the despatch of the Armada. With hindsight the outcome seems pre-ordained; at the time the issue was anything but clear-cut; she was beset by internal subversion, conflicting advice and her own doubts and fears. Fortunately she had in Walsyngham a master of counter-espionage: systematically intercepting, reading and redirecting the correspondence of Mary Queen of Scots – now Philip's choice for the throne of England – he uncovered a conspiracy to synchronise a Catholic uprising and the assassination of Elizabeth with the arrival of Philip's Army of England. Elizabeth had no qualms about punishing the conspirators; they were drawn through jubilant crowds in the City of London to suffer the barbaric fate reserved for traitors, hung, and, still alive, drawn and quartered in a public spectacle more ghastly even than the Inquisitors' human bonfires.

Where Mary was concerned Elizabeth hesitated; Mary was under her protection in England, having been forced to flee from Scotland almost 20 years before; since then she had been implicated in nearly every plot against Elizabeth; her ambition for the Crown and now Philip's ambition to use her for his own ends were beyond doubt. Burghley, Walsyngham, Leicester, her entire council, the Parliament, Lords and Commons, implored Elizabeth to have Mary executed. Yet she hesitated, sending back to Parliament 'an answer – answerless'.[15] Was it sentiment, revulsion against killing one of her own blood royal, or remembrance of the mortal dangers she had experienced under Mary Tudor? Was it in part calculation? While Mary lived and provided a focus for conspiracy, it would be easier to detect the plots. Was it fear that her death might

Mary Stuart, Queen of Scotland.
Portrait by François Clouet, 1559.

provoke hotheads into action, or finally decide Philip to send his armies against her, so starting an open war whose outcome was incalculable? She temporised, as she had temporised when earlier in her reign her Councillors and Parliament implored her to marry in order to secure the succession. She had always drawn back; 'In the end, this shall be for me sufficient, that a marble stone shall declare that a Queen lived and died a virgin.'[16]

In early 1587 another plot was discovered, this time involving the French Ambassador; pressure grew for her to sign Mary's death warrant. At last she did so, changing her mind immediately to sound out Walsyngham on the alternative strategy of an assassination that might not be traced back to her. Burghley and the council had her signature on the warrant, however, and they sent the second secretary Davison post haste to Fotheringay Hall, where Mary was held, to ensure its execution. On February 8th, 1587, Mary Queen of Scots died, as she had lived, sure in her Catholic faith and her right to Elizabeth's Crown. On Davison's return Elizabeth had him sent to the Tower and went into deep mourning; no doubt this, too, was a mixture of calculation and sentiment. Now the final break with Philip had been made.

Meanwhile reports had been coming in from Lisbon and Spanish harbours of great preparations for a maritime expedition, rumoured to be for England, and Elizabeth listened to advice that Hawkins, Drake and other exponents of a 'forward' naval policy – later called the 'blue water' school of naval strategy – had been pressing for years; the best place to defend the shores of England was on the coast of the enemy. The usual method of a part Royal, part merchant joint stock company was used to mount a large expedition, the largest so far. Elizabeth provided four warships and two pinnaces, Drake and his friends provided four merchantmen, the Lord Admiral, Howard of Effingham, provided a ship and a pinnace, London merchants provided eight ships including four fighting galleons of the Turkey Company and three pinnaces. Drake was given the command; Elizabeth soon changed her mind; revised instructions, forbad Drake to 'offer violence to any of his (Philip's) towns or shipping within harbouring, or to do any act of hostility upon the land . . .'[17] but to confine his plundering to the sea. By the time this message reached Plymouth, where the squadron was concentrating, Drake had sailed. 'The wind commands me away. Our ship is under sail. God grant we may so live in His fear as the enemy may cause to say that God doth fight for her Majesty as well abroad as at home . . .'[18]

So he wrote to Walsyngham. However much Elizabeth still tried to temporise it was too late for her to draw back.

3

The Sea Rovers

Drake, he was a Devon man; he was born by Tavistock, upstream from Plymouth, at some date in the early 1540s. His father was Edmund Drake, younger son of a yeoman farming family: whether Edmund farmed is not known; but it is known he was a convinced, perhaps even a fanatic Protestant and it is usually held that he was forced to flee Tavistock during a peasant uprising against the Reformation in 1549.

An alternative which seems more likely has been suggested recently by John Sugden, citing an entry from the *Patent Rolls 1547–1548* in which 'Edmund Drake, "sherman" and John Hawkyng "taylour" late of Tavistock, Devon', were indicted for having stolen a horse worth £3 from one John Harte on April 25th 1548; Edmund Drake was also indicted, this time in company with a William Master, 'cordyner', for assaulting one Roger Langisforde in the king's highway at Peterstavy, Devon, on April 16th and stealing 21s. 7d. from his purse.[1]

For whatever reason, Edmund Drake moved to Kent, where he lived in a hulk on the river Medway and preached his seditious doctrine – in Mary's reign – to sailors from the naval ports of Chatham and Gillingham. The young Francis absorbed all his Protestant ardour before being placed as a lad with the skipper of a coastal barque; in her he learnt the grammar of sailing in the winds and sluicing tides of the Thames estuary and East coast and from all that is known of him later he was a quick and capable pupil; it is evident his master thought so for at his death he left him the barque.

The Drakes were related to the Hawkins and it was perhaps through this connection that Francis was taken on in Hawkins' third slaving expedition to the Indies, which sailed under John Lovell in 1566. After this unsuccessful venture, the young Francis transferred into the flagship of the larger expedition which sailed under Hawkins himself in October 1567. He evidently impressed Hawkins for during the voyage he was given command of one of the smaller vessels, the *Judith* of 50 tons, and nearing Rio de la Hacha was sent ahead independently to reconnoitre with a pinnace in company.

In the fight at San Juan de Ulloa the *Judith* was one of the only two ships to escape; the other was the *Minion*, into which Hawkins had transferred with a number of men from the crippled flagship. The two vessels made their separate ways home, during which most of the 200 or so men aboard the *Minion* died of disease and starvation. In his report, written after reaching Plymouth, Hawkins stated that when the two ships escaped from San Juan de Ulloa, the *Judith* 'the same night forsook us in our misery.'[2] As Hawkins' biographer, J. A. Williamson, noted, 'It was a bitter thing to say of Drake, whose name he nowhere mentioned.'[3] No plausible explanation for Drake's conduct has been offered, for the Spaniards did not pursue and according to Spanish sources both English ships anchored for the night. It was an inauspicious prelude to fame on the world stage.

That summer he married. He had sold the old barque he had been bequeathed and had probably gained from his command of the *Judith* since Hawkins had instructed him before their flight from San Juan de Ulloa to take on board trade goods and perhaps some silver from the flagship as she lay crippled; it is even possible this was the cause of his hasty departure during the night.

Drake's name crops up next in the early 1570s, leading small expeditions to the isthmus of Panama, attacking coastal shipping and settlements and the mule trains bringing Spanish Peruvian treasure overland from the Pacific coast to Nombre de Dios, which he also attacked. After many disappointments, privations and dangers, not least from the fevers of the region which decimated his men, he succeeded at length, in alliance with a Huguenot privateer captain Le Têtu from Le Havre and a party of escaped black slaves, in surprising a treasure train and carrying off a quantity of bullion, estimated by the Spanish at between 80,000 and 100,000 gold pesos – approximately £40,000 – which was divided equally with the French. Le Têtu himself was left, wounded, at the scene and was put to death by the Spaniards when they arrived; no blame can be attached to Drake since he was responsible for the rest of his men. It was a hazardous game; many were playing it, French, English and Dutch; all knew the Spaniards showed no mercy to those they caught.

During his time in the isthmus Drake glimpsed the Pacific and the possibilities for surprising the ships bringing Peruvian silver up the coast to Panama naturally stirred him. It was almost certainly his chief goal when he set out from Plymouth in December 1577 to pass into the Pacific by the Straits of Magellan; the goals of the backers, an illustrious group including Leicester, Walsyngham, the Wynters, John Hawkins, Drake himself – for £1,000 – and the Queen, are less clear since secrecy and false information were used to put the Spanish off the scent, and the only known copy of his instructions seems to envisage a trading venture up the Chilean coast. In any case it was a well-armed and splendidly equipped expedition he led although the four ships were individually small; the largest was his flagship *Pelican* of probably little more than 100 tons, and perhaps 70 feet in length; later he renamed her *Golden Hind*, and so she is remembered, one of the most evocative names in naval history; for the voyage which started as a privateering venture on the undefended Pacific coast of Spanish America, and was certainly intended to return via the Straits of Magellan, turned into the first English circumnavigation of the world and netted a haul of gold pesos, silver bars, plate and other treasure such as legends are made of. The voyage has come down as an epic of daring and romance; daring it undoubtedly was, but desperate hardship, repeated frustrations and quarrelling to the point of incipient mutiny were more in evidence than the romance it naturally acquired in retrospect. It is a measure of Drake's exceptional self-reliance and strength of character that he brought it off as a triumph.

His navigational technique for crossing oceans unknown to the English was relatively simple: he captured Spanish or Portuguese vessels and stole their charts and pilots. It is from one of the pilots, Nuno da Silva, that we get one of the best descriptions of him in his prime: 'short, thick-set and very robust . . . of fine countenance with a fair/reddish beard and a ruddy complexion.'[4] Da Silva stated that he painted birds, trees and seals in his log; 'He is diligent in painting and carries along a boy . . . who is a great painter; shut up in his cabin they are always painting.'[5] He also described how the first thing Drake did on capturing a vessel was to 'seize the charts, astrolabes and mariners' compasses, which he broke and cast into the sea.'[6]

A Spanish prisoner described him as a strict disciplinarian, punishing the least

Sir Francis Drake.
Miniature by Nicholas Hilliard, 1581.

Contemporary view of Buckland
Abbey, Drake's house, now owned
by The National Trust.

fault in his men, but treating them otherwise with affection. For their part they treated him with great respect, as did the gentlemen aboard; none of these took their seat before him at table or covered their head before him after drinking a toast. Meals were served to a flourish of trumpets, accompanied by music and eaten off silver dishes with gold borders 'and gilded garlands in which are his arms'.[7] These may have been the arms of the family of which Sir Bernard Drake of Ash was head, since Francis, who liked to pretend to gentle birth, claimed kinship. The water in which he and the gentlemen rinsed their hands before meals and between courses was perfumed; many of the perfumes and other delicacies for the table had been given to him by the Queen, he said; he had the conceits of the archetypal self-made man. One Spaniard reported him 'so boastful of himself as a mariner and man of learning that he told them (his prisoners) there was no one in the whole world who understood the art of navigation better then he.'[8] On his return from the epic voyage Elizabeth knighted him on the quarter-deck of the *Golden Hind*; it must have given him as much gratification as his share of the enormous proceeds, and indeed his navigational accomplishment. He applied for a coat of arms and bought Buckland Abbey in Devon as his seat. To most English people he was, rightly, a hero, which was no doubt why Elizabeth risked the grave insult to Philip of knighting him; to the established gentry, envious of his legendary wealth and disliking what they heard of his jumped-upness and brag, he was, rightly, 'the Master theefe of the unknowne world'.[9] To the Spanish, he was 'El Draque', the dragon, and rightly feared.

There are many similarities between Drake and that other great English sailor, Horatio Nelson; both were extraordinarily vain but solicitous for their men; Drake seems to have brought the majority of the men home who started with him on the circumnavigation, a marvellous feat in that day. Both had a simple fervent faith in their Protestant God, an equally simple, fervent hatred for the Catholic enemy and all his abominations. Both were impatient of counsels and the accepted ideas of prudent men and had the moral courage to follow their own offensive instincts; both, having served a long apprenticeship in sea fighting, came to much the same conclusion about the prime factors; thus Drake: 'The advantage of time and place in all martial actions is half a victory'[10] and Nelson: 'Time is everything; five minutes makes the difference between a victory and a defeat.'[11] Above all, both had an instinctual eye for the right thing to do in a situation.

At no time did Drake display this more dramatically than when Elizabeth sent him to disrupt the Armada preparations in 1587; in the first place he sailed in great haste before her countermanding orders could reach him – or perhaps they had and he was forced to put out to deny them – before his victualling and manning was completed. Reaching the coast of Portugal and learning that the Spanish Admiral Santa Cruz was in Lisbon but that Cadiz was full of shipping with only galleys as protection he made for Cadiz; when he arrived with his leading ships he sailed straight in, against the protests of his Vice Admiral, one of the old school who tried to insist on a council; the galleys – the traditional Mediterranean warship – came to meet him but could do nothing with their bow guns against the broadsides of Atlantic sailing ships and he fell on the otherwise defenceless merchantmen in the outer harbour, destroying all the larger ones that could not flee to shallow water, then led a sortie of pinnaces into the inner harbour and burnt a galleon belonging to Santa Cruz. By the time he left, the Cadiz division of the Armada – chiefly store ships, it is true – had been wiped out.

He sailed down to Cape St Vincent after a squadron said to be there, and failing to find it, decided to establish himself ashore. Again his Vice Admiral protested; Drake confined him to his quarters, and after an unsuccessful sortie against the port of Lagos he personally led a storming party up to the castle at Sagres just to the east of the Cape. After the gate had been fired, the castle surrendered. No doubt the men had not been paid for some time. Drake now had a secure anchorage to water and refit, and he commanded the route by which the Mediterranean divisions of the Armada still to join and all supplies had to come to reach Santa Cruz in Lisbon. Beside the pulverising effect on Santa Cruz's preparations, these ravages on the very coast of Spain had a bad effect on the confidence of Philip's bankers, hence on the interest rates he had to pay. Their judgement was good; Drake had a grip on Philip's jugular, and had England been a developed naval power with reserves and organisation capable of maintaining the blockade – something which she did not manage for another two centuries – the Armada could never have sailed.

As it was, Drake's expedition had part strategic, mostly piratical aims since it had to show a profit for the backers, and it was this that drew him away from the Cape towards the Azores, where it must be assumed he had intelligence of a returning Indies fleet – either that or his provisions were running so low he could not delay in seeking a richer harvest than he was able to gather from the coastal trade. As it turned out, nearing St Michaels in the Azores, he chanced on a Portuguese carrack, the *San Felipe*, laden with pepper, other spices and exotic ware; he took her in short time and made straight home with her. The ship and her cargo fetched £115,000; his other plunder added another £26,000, making the gross profit on the expedition well over 100%; the Queen's share was £46,000, Drake's £18,000, a large fortune.[12]

The abandonment of the blockade had an unintended strategic effect; by threatening the Azores rendezvous for the homecoming treasure fleets, Drake forced Santa Cruz to follow him there with a fighting squadron and by the time the Spanish returned to Lisbon, weather-worn and in need of refit and provisioning, it was too late in the year to contemplate the Enterprise of England – not too late for Philip, but Santa Cruz, knowing better, would not sail.

Drake printed himself on the age; for the Spaniards his name was a synonym for English mischief, yet he was only the most fortunate and successful of a galaxy of Protestant sea rovers, English, French, and Dutch. His fellow adventurer in the isthmus of Panama, John Oxenham, was again in the isthmus at the start of his voyage of circumnavigation – it is often suggested they may have planned joint operations there – but Oxenham was captured and put to death by the Spaniards. The Suffolk adventurer, Thomas Cavendish, followed Drake's route into the Pacific in 1586, completing a similar circumnavigation of the world in the Armada year, without however making a similar profit. Drake as first to surprise the Spanish had reaped 'the advantage of time and place'. The Huguenot captain Jean Ribault planted a colony in Florida on the strategic flank of the route taken by the treasure fleets homeward bound from the Havana. When this was abandoned – in part due to the perfidy of the English pirate and turncoat, Thomas Stukeley, whom Ribault unwisely sought as a partner – it was re-established by another Huguenot, René de Laudonnière; this was at the time of Hawkins' second voyage. The following year the Spanish Admiral in charge of the defence of the treasure fleets, Pedro Menéndez de Avilés, forced the surrender of the little settlement and Ribault who was there again learned – if he did not already guess – that the word of a Spanish aristocrat was worth as little as that of an English pirate; he and the rest of the survivors were massacred.

Of the English who tried to colonise in North America, Sir Walter Raleigh and Sir Richard Grenville are best known for the Virginia settlement. To the Spaniards Grenville was 'that great pirate'; to later generations of Englishmen he is best known for his epic defence of the *Revenge* against an overwhelming Spanish force in 1591. Their forerunner in the colonising venture was Sir Humphrey Gilbert, who claimed Newfoundland for the Queen in 1583; in the same year he was lost while returning to England in the smallest of his ships, a mere 10 tons. His last words to anxious observers aboard the larger ship in company were immortalised in Hackluyt's *Divers Voyages*, 'We are as neere to heaven by sea as by land.'[13]

Of others who made their name sailing to America, Martin Frobisher stands out. A Yorkshireman, he came to London as a boy after the death of his parents and sailed on an expedition backed by his kinsman, Sir Thomas Yorke, to the Gold Coast of West Africa. The majority who sailed, including the leader, Thomas Wyndham, succumbed to the fevers of the area, and young Frobisher – or as he signed himself Frobiser or Forbiser – was one of only 40 to return. The

Drake's Leat. Drake devised a scheme to bring water to Plymouth from Dartmoor. This map of 1592 illustrates the scheme, and also shows Drake's home, Buckland Abbey, and an Armada beacon.

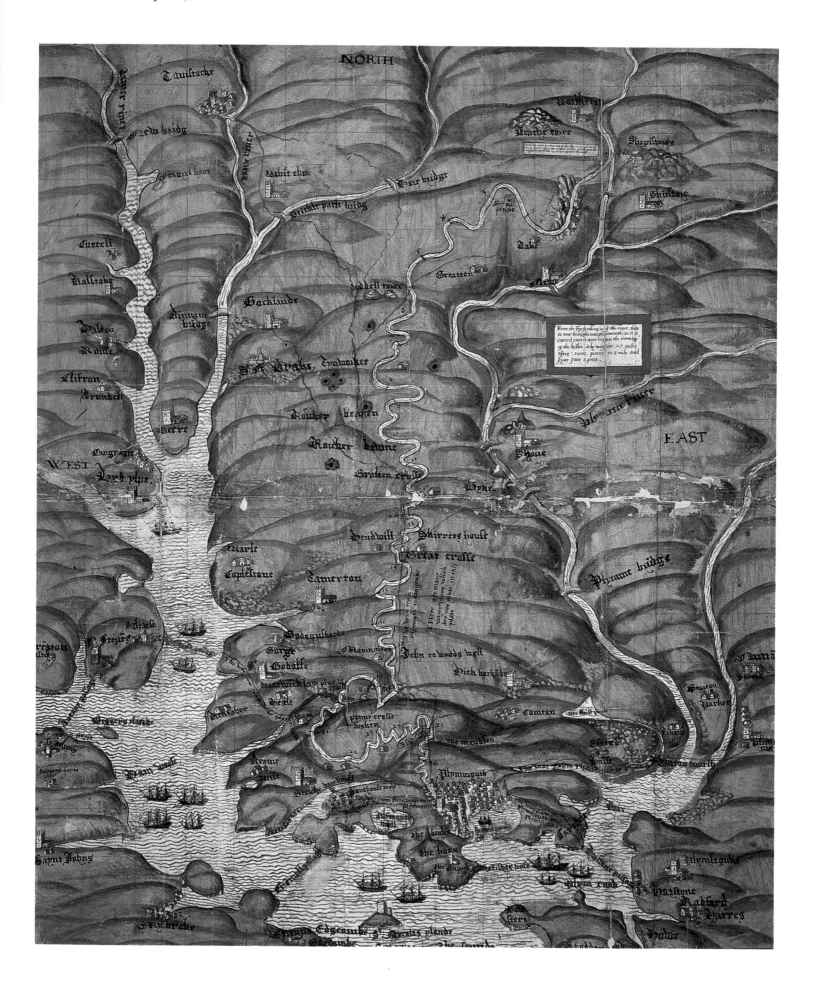

Sir John Hawkins (1532–95),
merchant adventurer and radical naval
administrator, who gave Elizabeth the
most effective navy of the day.
    Sixteenth-century English school.

next year, 1554, he sailed on a second expedition to the Gold Coast under John Lok; while ashore he was captured by natives and taken to the Portuguese slaving station at Elmina, from where he was sent to Europe; no doubt Sir Thomas Yorke was made to pay for his release. Afterwards he seems to have served for a while as a merchant's agent in Morocco, then in the 1560s he came home and started a career on his own account as a pirate working with other Protestant privateers on the western end of the English Channel.

Frobisher established his fame with attempts to find a North West Passage around the top of North America to Asia. He may have been inspired by Sir Humphrey Gilbert, whom he knew, or his former leader to the Gold Coast, John Lok, who promoted the venture; alternatively he may simply have been chosen by Lok as a suitable commander for the expedition. Ideas for passing around America into the Pacific either southabout by the Straits of Magellan or by a presumed strait northabout were in the air; Frobisher sailed on his first voyage northwards in 1576, the year before Drake departed southwards for the Straits of Magellan. He passed Newfoundland and the Labrador coast and sailed into a broad, deep inlet at the southern end of Baffin Island, which bears his name today. He brought back an Eskimo whom he passed off as an Asiatic to show that he had found the North West Passage – which of course he had not – and a sample of black ore glittering with mica, which he passed off, despite negative assays, as gold. The double lure of gold and the expected route to Cathay (China) allowed Lok to found a Company of Cathay backed by the usual royal and merchant investors, headed by Elizabeth herself. How far this was a confidence trick on Frobisher's or Lok's part, how far they themselves were victims of a collective gold hysteria will for ever remain cloaked in the mists of the northern seas. Frobisher led two expeditions for the company and brought back further samples of the ore, which was at last recognised as worthless.

Elizabethan judgement on the merits of their most famous sailor-explorers may be gauged from the fact that it was Drake who was chosen to command the 1585 expedition to the West Indies heralding the open break with Spain, Frobisher who was made his Vice Admiral. He was a large, extraordinarily powerful, truculent man as rough as the age and profession which formed him and a harsh disciplinarian who frequently antagonised his subordinates; captains were wary of serving with him. There was no question of his ability as a sailor or his courage but he was not a man happy to be second in command. He vented his feelings of frustration and envy after the Armada campaign in 1588, sounding off against Drake in the company of John Hawkins and others and characterising Drake's service to the fleet as that of a 'cowardly knave or traitor', accusing him of trying to cheat others of their share of the spoils, and of slandering.

'He hath', he said, 'used certain speeches of me which I will make him eat again or I will make him spend the best blood in his belly. Furthermore, he reporteth that no man has done so good service as he. But he lieth in his teeth; for there are others that hath done as good as he and better too.'[14]

Besides the leading names there was a wealth of experienced sea-captains and merchant venturers who were either not granted a chance at fame, or who have been largely ignored by historians – the Chichester shipowning family, the Fenners, for instance, who were as active as the Hawkins of Plymouth in breaking into the Portuguese and Spanish monopolies. George Fenner fought a famous action off the Azores in 1567: in command of the *Castle of Comfort* with two smaller consorts he held off a Portuguese squadron of seven ships for a day, and the next day forced them to leave him. Thomas Fenner was a favourite of

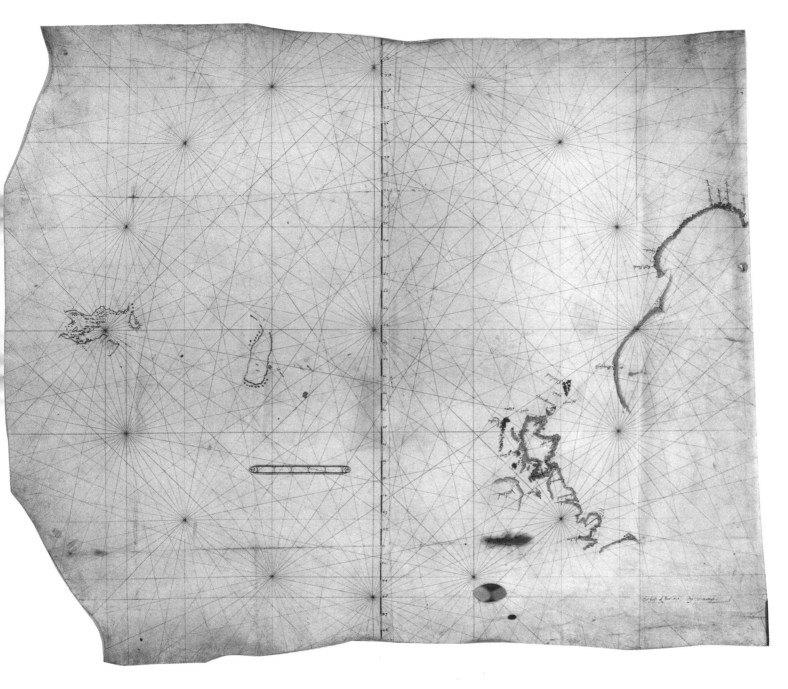

Map used by Martin Frobisher on his voyage in search of a North-West Passage to the Indies, 1576, showing Frobisher Bay in Canada which he discovered.

Drake's; he sailed with him in 1585 and 1587 and again in the Armada campaign; there is little doubt that in the meantime he and his brothers, William and Edward, cruised as pirates under the colours of the Portuguese pretender, Dom Antonio. Besides the gentleman adventurers and men of means was a host of plain sailors of fortune ready to lend themselves to any scheme of plunder and indulging in petty larceny from small craft when the chance offered – the lawless, sordid reverse side of the courage and enterprise and opening visions of the world for which the Elizabethan sea rovers are remembered.

The Dutch 'Sea Beggars' were an equally lawless menace. They had emerged from the rebellions of 1566 and 1567 against Alva's repressive policies in the Low Countries; their first leaders, middling to minor nobles – more country squires than noblemen – and chiefly from the northern provinces, Friesland and Holland, were dedicated to avenging their fellows executed or burnt alive at Alva's hands. They were also dedicated to piracy – if for no other reason than to

Charles Howard (1536–1624), 2nd Baron Howard of Effingham: Elizabeth's naval commander-in-chief, who knew his advantage and held it.

Miniature attributed to Rowland Lockey (pupil of Nicholas Hilliard), 1605.

support themselves – and to the Protestant religion, hating Catholicism, which was identified with Spanish oppression. Calvinist ministers were carried aboard the ships and prayers said morning and evening, as indeed in English, and Huguenot and Spanish ships. They were a band of ruffians nonetheless, better known for ruthlessness than Christian piety.

William of Orange joined them to his cause by issuing them letters of marque; since he was a sovereign Prince at war with Spain, this legalised their attacks on Spanish shipping, making them 'privateers' or privately owned warships rather than pirates. They operated from wherever they could find shelter outside Alva's reach, chiefly at first from Emden and Delfzyl near the mouth of the river Ems in the northern province of Groningen, but increasingly from the English, southern Irish or French Atlantic ports where they could dispose of their booty. For use in their shallow coastal waters they had developed a type of gunboat known as a 'cromster'. This was adapted from the ordinary coasting 'hoy', generally a two-masted lugger, but carried an exceptionally heavy armament of eight culverin, six demi-culverin and two lighter pieces. They were so effective for inshore operations that they were later adopted by the Queen's navy. The combination of English pirates and Huguenot and 'Sea Beggars' privateers disrupted Channel trade, including the staple English wool trade to the Netherlands; it was as much for this reason as for her ever-temporising policy towards Spain that in 1572 Elizabeth decided to ban the Beggars from her ports and prohibit English subjects from supplying them or buying their booty. It is evident that this was a genuine response to the frustrations of the English merchant community since she also sent a Royal Squadron on a serious cruise against Channel pirates.

A large body of Beggars under their leader, William van der Marck, Lord of Lumey, was in Dover at the time and Lumey had asked Elizabeth if he could continue to use this strategic harbour as a base, offering her the services of his 'fleet' in exchange. She ordered him to leave immediately. He did so, and after cruising about for several weeks until desperate for fresh water and provisions, fell on and took the port of Brille near the Hook of Holland, whose Spanish garrison had been withdrawn. This was the turning point of the Dutch rebellion, for from this base the Sea Beggars spread out through Holland and the web of Zealand islands, radicalising the burghers with their own fierce spirit, and taking the ports at the head of the great rivers, most importantly Flushing, which commanded the Scheldt, hence all the trade to Antwerp, the commercial and financial capital of Philip's empire. Soon the northern provinces, from being a beleaguered enclave, were in the strategically commanding position of being able to draw supplies of arms, provisions, money and men from outside by sea, while denying these advantages to Alva and his successors who had to use the slow and immensely costly overland route from the Mediterranean, the so-called 'Spanish Road' from Genoa and Milan up through Savoy, Franch-Comté and Lorraine.

Such was the position in 1587 when the latest and most successful Spanish commander-in-chief in the Netherlands, the Duke of Parma, received Philip's instructions to prepare an army to act in concert with the Armada he was sending from Spain to invade England. Parma sent back messages that he had no deep-water ports where such a rendezvous could be effected; his forces were concentrated in Flanders; the shoals off the ports of Dunkirk and Nieuport would prevent the galleons approaching, while the barges and other flat-bottomed craft he was assembling to transport his men would be at the mercy of the shallow draft vessels of the Sea Beggars. His protests were ignored.

4

The Reluctant Commander

Philip's mind was overwhelmed by urgency. Since Santa Cruz's return in September 1587 from the chase to the Azores after Drake, Philip had been urging him to sail on the Enterprise of England. He hoped to achieve surprise while the English were unprepared, but this was completely to underestimate Walsyngham's intelligence system, while to hazard the ships and men collected at such expense to North Atlantic gales and the rock-bound coasts of the Channel entrance and the shoals off Flanders in the short days of late autumn and winter can only be ascribed to desperation, ignorance, bad advice from his inner council or the corrupting effects of power, age and illness. Santa Cruz found reasons to postpone his departure.

So the main body of the fleet remained off Lisbon, straining to the strong tides of the Tagus while the damages of the late voyage were made good, more provisions, stores and armaments trickled in and were taken aboard, others deteriorated alongside the men. At the best of times the life of sailors in the royal service was little different from that of the slaves or convicted criminals serving in the galleys. They lived in noisome, cramped conditions between decks whose seams, swollen in the sun, leaked in the rain, were provided with food of inferior quality – biscuit containing straw for the greater profit of the contractor and frequently old and maggoty – and were treated by the King's officers, as they complained, 'like dogs'.[1] One of the few things making life endurable was a daily allowance of wine; like the beer issued to northern sailormen, it blurred the rough edge of their existence. Both food and wine became scarce that winter as money dried up and contractors' debts mounted. Hunger and contagious disease spread between decks; two pilots are said to have died of starvation; if so how many men must also have wasted away and succumbed to the unhealthy, overcrowded conditions? The Commander-in-Chief himself was not spared. When in January 1588 Philip sent an emissary to Lisbon to find out how things were with the fleet and why Santa Cruz still reported himself unprepared to sail, he found the great man on his sickbed. Probably run down with anxiety, he had caught typhus and was dying.

Directly he heard the news, Philip cast around for a successor. The report he had on the state of the fleet and men made it clear that what was needed urgently was not an admiral or fighting general so much as an administrator who could pull the force into shape in quick time. He did not have far to look for such a man. Don Alonso Perez de Guzman, seventh Duke of Medina Sidonia, premier noble of Andalucia, who had long experience in organising expeditions, both naval and military, was already taking a leading part in the procurement of ships, men and provisions for the Armada, and had been a technical advisor since the plans for the expedition had taken shape early in the previous year. In addition he was the wealthiest grandee in Spain, an important qualification at that time when leaders of expeditions and even captains of troops were expected to oil the uncertain machinery of the exchequer with their own resources – particularly important at this time when the Paymaster to the Armada was in debt to the tune of almost 300,000 ducats.[2] Besides money, Medina Sidonia disposed of men; by virtue of his position as traditional war leader of Andalucia, virtually Philip's viceroy in this southern corner of the peninsula which was the major recruiting ground for soldiers, he could raise levies from his own and neighbouring estates – had indeed raised an army of 6,000 for the recent Portuguese campaign; he was also assured of a following of young nobles, eager to win *reputacion* if not wealth as well in an overseas expedition.

A great deal of Medina Sidonia's income came from the customs house at San Lucar de Barrameda, the port at the mouth of the Guadalquivir which led up to Seville, the centre for the New World fleets. The ancestral seat of the Guzmans was at San Lucar; he had been born there and had taken an interest in the shipping anchored or passing up or down on the tides of this main artery of Atlantic trade since his youth; for the past five years at least, he had been concerned with the fitting out of the annual *flotas* for the Indies, and was now seeing to the final fitting out and manning of the escort galleons known as the Indies Guard, which were soon to sail around for Lisbon to form with the Portuguese galleons the fighting core of Santa Cruz's fleet. The contacts and credits he had with the merchants of Seville, the centre for provisions and naval stores, were as important recommendations as his personal wealth and following.

Besides all this Medina Sidonia had the necessary personal qualities; this had been apparent throughout his life: as a 24-year-old, he had bid for a contract to maintain the Royal galleys; his offer had not been accepted, but the recommendations he received in council indicate that even at that early age he was regarded as eminently trustworthy: 'the Duke, being the person he is, will keep (the galleys) in very good order . . .'[3] He had acquitted himself well during the Portuguese campaign, making use of connections in the Algarve to smooth the occupation of southern Portugal. More recently in his capacity as military leader of western Andalucia, he had led the levies to the relief of Cadiz when Drake attacked the port; he was popularly believed to have forced Drake to withdraw; Philip had been impressed by the speed and determination with which he had met the crisis, and created him Captain General of Andalucia – the position he had already in all but name – as proof of his favour. Now 38 years old, in the prime of life, he, if anyone, would be able to bring order and method to the chaotic conditions in the fleet over which the dying Santa Cruz was still attempting to preside. His only drawbacks were his lack of experience at sea and in command of fighting operations – as opposed to the military promenade of the Portuguese campaign. Nevertheless he would be able to call on the experience of his squadronal commanders, who were fighting men with experience in naval warfare. As for the campaign in England, Parma would be in command there.

In fact, doubts have been raised whether Philip really intended the invasion of England – whether he did not expect the mere show of force to overawe Elizabeth and bring her to terms. Thus Professor I. A. A. Thompson: 'The *first* task of the Armada was to parade, to sail up the Channel and beat its chest before England's gates.'[4] Preliminary soundings for peace negotiations were already under way, and on January 30th Parma had written to Philip that all intelligence seemed to 'prove that the Queen of England really desires to conclude peace; and that her alarm and the expenses she is incurring are grieving her greatly.'[5] Philip had not received this before he decided on Medina Sidonia, but Parma was only expressing the trend of all reports reaching Philip from the spy net in London.[6]

Of course he had sufficient experience of Elizabeth to know that she would play for time in any negotiations until the immediate danger was past, then relapse into her former policies. It was against this knowledge he was preparing the Armada: if once it could be launched on its way, it was unlikely the English navy could seriously damage the ships. With the inaccuracy of guns, very slow rate of fire and small batteries mounted at that time it was virtually impossible to wreck Atlantic vessels by stand-off gunnery, while if it came to a boarding contest – which Philip knew the English would avoid if they could – Spanish superiority in numbers and discipline would tell. He had every reason to believe, therefore, that if the Armada could reach the Channel and flaunt its size and impregnability – better still if its presence could inspire the English Catholics to rise up against Elizabeth – she could be forced to concede to his terms; these would alter the religious balance in England, and keep her fully occupied within her own borders, as will appear. Fearing, as he did, the huge costs and uncertainties of war, there is no doubt this was his preferred alternative; it is significant that he gave precise instructions about the terms he would accept. To take this a stage further and suggest he expected such an outcome is not permissible on the evidence.

In any case the burning imperative was to get the Armada to sea, thus gaining the initiative which could easily be lost yet again if Drake were to get out first and repeat his exploits of the previous year. For this purpose there was no one better suited than Medina Sidonia; accordingly on February 11th Philip had his minister Idiaquez write to advise the Duke he had 'fixed his eyes' on him to succeed to the command. Medina Sidonia was horrified, and responded with a celebrated letter pleading unfitness for the post:

I first humbly thank His Majesty for having thought of me for so great a task, and I wish I possessed the talents and strength necessary for it. But, sir, I have not health for the sea, for I know by the small experience I have had afloat that I soon become sea-sick and have many humours. Besides this . . . I am in great need, so much so that when I have had to go to Madrid I have been obliged to borrow money for the journey. My house owes 900,000 ducats, and I am therefore quite unable to accept the command. I have not a single real I can spend on the expedition.

Apart from this, neither my conscience nor my duty will allow me to take this service upon me. The force is so great, and the undertaking so important that it would not be right for a person like myself, possessing no experience of seafaring or war, to take charge of it. So, sir, in the interests of His Majesty's service, and for the love I bear him, I submit to you . . . that I possess neither aptitude, ability, health, nor fortune for the expedition . . . But besides all this, for me to take charge of the Armada afresh, without the slightest knowledge of it, of the persons who are to take part in it, of the objects in view, of the intelligence from England, without any acquaintance with the ports there, or of the arrangements which the Marquis has been making for years past, would be simply groping in the dark . . . So sir, you will see that my reasons for declining are so strong and convincing in His Majesty's own interests, that I cannot attempt a task of which I have no doubt I should give a bad account. I should be travelling in the dark, and should have to be guided by the opinions of others, of whose good or bad qualities I know nothing, and which of them might seek to deceive and ruin me . . .[7]

And so it went on. Philip thought his excuses stemmed from modesty. He knew him well; he was probably right. Santa Cruz was a world-renowned Admiral who had distinguished himself in command of a division of galleys at the Battle of Lepanto, which had passed into legend; he had distinguished himself again at the capture of Tunis in 1572; more recently as Admiral of the Ocean Sea he had trounced a Protestant, chiefly French Huguenot fleet

The Duke of Medina Sidonia, commander-in-chief of the Spanish fleet.

The Duke of Parma (1545–92), Philip's most successful Governor-General of the Netherlands and one of the finest soldiers of the day.
Engraving by a Spanish artist, ?18th century.

attempting to take the Azores for the Portuguese Pretender, Dom Antonio. He was known as the 'Never defeated'. What man lacking all experience in command at sea could follow such an Admiral without the gravest misgivings?

There were other reasons; as Professor Thompson has pointed out, the Duke thought the whole idea a mistake and had no chance of success;[8] moreover, it was bound to cost him a great deal of money – as Philip intended, as indeed it did – some three quarters of a million ducats. Against this certain loss and the probable, more important loss of *reputacion*, there was no advantage: his wife is supposed to have said while urging him to stay at home, 'It is enough to be the Duke of Medina'.[9] Indeed it was. He had nothing to prove; the roving ambitions of his youth had been replaced by care for his vast estates; he was comfortable and busy and of a pensive and diligent rather than adventurous disposition; some years before, Philip had appointed him Governor of Milan, but he had managed by repeated excuses and postponements to avoid taking up the post. Now personal inclination and a sound estimate of the consequences led him to try the same tactics.

Philip would have none of it: 'It is I who must judge of your capabilities and parts,' he wrote, 'and I am fully satisfied with these . . .' As for health, one had to believe that God would grant it since he would be sailing in His great cause. 'You have shown your good intentions by your diligence and care, and since these qualities were never so necessary as they are now, prepare and steel yourself to the performance of this service.'[10]

Contemporaries agreed with Philip's estimate. Parma, with whom the Duke was to co-operate, wrote that the choice was a good one.[11] The Venetian Ambassador in Madrid, who was well informed and knew Medina Sidonia, reported on him as 'a prince of many parts, in spite of his never having been to sea' and in a later despatch, 'he has excellent qualities and is generally beloved. He is not only prudent and brave, but of a nature of extreme goodness and benignity.'[12] The French Ambassador reported on him as one of Philip's most capable subjects.[13]

Realising from the tone of Philip's letter that he could not escape the commission, the Duke set out on the road to Lisbon, leaving his beloved estate, one must assume with a heavy heart, resigning himself to his duty to God and his King. It is a poignant moment: the forces driving Philip, who feared war, to gather a huge force against a Queen even more afraid of war, had drawn in this reluctant nobleman – while off Lisbon thousands of the less fortunate, for the most part conscripted or simply held to the service when their ships were commandeered, suffered hunger and disease in the wet and cold of an evil February. The Duke was as much a prisoner as they, as the King, as Elizabeth in England, bright coloured threads in a seamless tapestry stretching back in time and space. They saw God's design; we might point to human aspirations for power and wealth, fame and spiritual satisfaction, or lower in the scale simple subsistence, and to the laws by which systems once formed for the gratification of these desires grow and perpetuate themselves until opposed by other systems formed for the same ends under different conditions, forcing inevitable conflict. Attempting to analyse the systems, we might reach conclusions about the importance of money as both goad and constraint, hence the extraordinary influence of national and international moneymen and the rates at which they thought it prudent to loan; it could be argued that Philip was forced into this desperate venture chiefly in order to keep up his credit rating. Yet the moneymen were themselves cogs in the system; their wealth had accumulated from a thousand exchanges by piracy or trade, and they lent it out to others desirous of gaining more in the same ways; they regulated the system, defining success or failure with their artificial but most potent tokens, fixing the odds by the rate of interest, but the impetus came from individuals who, in a world of relative scarcity, inevitably desired more than any system could provide. We might deplore the results but we are woven into the same system with threads stretching further back than Philip and Elizabeth and have no more hope of escape by applying to reason than Medina Sidonia by praying to God as his horses' hooves clacked on the stony way to Lisbon.

Arriving at the beginning of March, he was appalled by what he found. The lack of an overall commander, lack of money, villainous contractors, rotting food, foul weather, disease, death and the long-enforced stay had contributed to a collapse in morale and sense of purpose and responsibility. He gathered a small staff of experienced officers, including a gunnery expert, studied Santa Cruz's plans and began to create material and spiritual order; he set the example himself, visiting every ship and climbing down to inspect the orlopes and holds, a sturdy, pale-bearded figure of middling height with high forehead and thoughtful eyes and the velvet aura of wealth and hereditary rank. Whatever his private doubts – and these were amply outlined in letters to Philip – his energy, quiet purposefulness and evident knowledge of what he was about impressed his advisers and the prickly senior commanders; a new mood began to spread and catch light in the early spring sun.

One of the first things that concerned him, apart from the condition and uneven distribution of provisions and the loss of men from disease and desertion, was a shortage of artillery and ammunition. From his intimate knowledge of the Indies *flotas* he knew the Protestant interlopers' tactics of standing off if it came to a fight and using their broadside guns rather than risking a boarding contest; he had warned Philip the previous year that this was what the English would do, and knew that in such a contest he needed more guns and more powder and shot for those he had; the galleons of the Indian guard he had been overseeing had 60 shot for each piece, and he sent urgent appeals to Philip in an attempt to obtain something like this proportion for all his fighting ships; he also appealed for more heavy guns and gunpowder.

These shortages reflected Spain's industrial failure. And since the industry of the Low Countries, the chief source of manufactured goods from textiles to the most modern ordnance, had been disrupted by war and the Sea Beggars' naval blockade, guns had to be procured from wherever they could be found. Some had come from the former centres of gunfounding in Italy, many by expensive covert dealings with the Protestant enemy through the agents who thrive in such conditions. One Royal ordnance foundry remained to Philip in Malaga and another in Lisbon, the only permanent factories left in the peninsula; these were pressed into an emergency programme to try and meet the Duke's demands.

The ships for which armament was needed were as motley a collection as the guns. Philip's naval administration was concerned with the galley fleet; this had been the instrument of command in the Mediterranean. To protect the treasure convoys across the Atlantic a squadron of fighting galleons had been built; these could not be large however since they had to be able to clear the bar at the mouth of the Guadalquivir; they were rated some 530 tons Spanish measurement, which may have been up to a third less by English measurement,[14] thus probably under 400 tons or rather smaller than the average English first line warship. The necessity for more and larger Atlantic warships had been urged on Philip for a long time; with the conquest of Portugal and the need to defend her Atlantic islands and sea routes as well, the question became pressing and a programme for building a regular Royal navy had been taken in hand, the construction farmed out to private yards on the Biscay coast where Spanish shipbuilding was concentrated. The usual things happened with the financing of the programme; the builders were not paid; sums earmarked for them were diverted to other suddenly more pressing needs, and eventually, towards the end of 1584 – just one year before it was decided to mount the Enterprise of England – Philip wound up the contracts. This occurred at the end of the fourth successive year during which the unsatisfactory and expensive system was employed of hiring and converting merchantmen for Atlantic campaigns; it is a telling indication of the desperate strait into which the Spanish financial administration had been driven by war and debt.

When it came to gathering the Armada for England the only warships were ten galleons of the Indies Guard and the same number of mostly larger Portuguese galleons. There were also four galleasses from Naples; these were a hybrid attempt at marrying the best points of the oared galley and the sailing warship; they were to prove a failure; the banks of rowers got in the way of a useful broadside armament; they were too heavy to compete with a galley in calm conditions, not as seaworthy as a galleon in heavy seas.

For the rest Philip had to make up his fighting force in the usual way with large merchantmen hired or simply taken over in Spanish ports, fitted with ordnance and extra decks to the fore- and aftercastles to accommodate light guns and soldiers and give them the high platforms important in close-range sea fighting. It is probable that most of these ships were of Mediterranean build and more lightly constructed and broader for their length than the Atlantic galleon type. Colin Martin, who has dived on several Armada wrecks and verified their construction by observation, believes that a policy decision was made in 1587 to substitute large Mediterranean *naos* – as these merchantmen were called – for the original smaller, more weatherly ships built on the Biscay coast. He attributes this to a realisation that the 40 galleys which Santa Cruz intended to take as a fighting core were no use against broadside galleons; Drake had proved it at Cadiz that year. Most of the galleys were dropped from the force, therefore, and broadside-fighting ships substituted; in order to mount guns large enough to be effective against the English fighting at a distance – as Medina Sidonia had suggested they would – beamy Mediterranean cargo-carriers were called for.[15] This is probably how it happened. If so, it demonstrates the short-sightedness or the desperate exigencies which had caused Philip to abandon his naval construction programme, for these tubby vessels were inevitably slower and clumsier than purpose-built warships and quite unsuitable against the 'race-built' galleons developed by the northern sea rovers; they were made even clumsier by the addition of the high 'fights' for the soldiers at bow and stern.

This was realised by the experienced commanders and no doubt by Medina Sidonia. A special emissary sent by the Pope to Lisbon that April to find out how matters stood with the expedition quizzed 'one of the highest and most experienced officers' of the fleet about his expectations if it came to a fight in the Channel. He was told the English had faster and more manoeuvrable ships, many more long guns, and knowing their advantage, would hold off and knock the Armada to pieces without allowing effective reply. Nevertheless, since they, the Spaniards, were fighting in God's cause he was confident God would send a miracle – 'some freak of weather, or more likely just depriving the English of their wits' – allowing them to close, when Spanish superiority in numbers and quality of soldiers would bring victory. They were sailing, this officer concluded, in the confident hope of a miracle.[16]

Tactics did not trouble the majority of military officers, nor the upwards of 400 young caballeros and hidalgos who had joined the expedition to make their names and perhaps their fortune in the fighting. The Castilian-Spanish system was the creation of a landholding military caste, stamped, like all such, with notions of honour, *reputacion* and pure blood. The sea was outside their interest; ships were transport, sailors in the same class as merchants or the landless vagabonds to be seen everywhere on the roads, and beneath their concern. Such views were to be found in their rawest state among the lowest orders, the hidalgos, virtually the proletariat of the nobility, especially exaggerated in those whose land was barely large enough to support them, or whose ancestry was not beyond suspicion of taint by Jewish blood. A grandee like Medina Sidonia could interest himself in ships and mix with merchants and financiers; a hidalgo was more likely to scorn both. Those who had attached themselves to the expedition had no idea of defeat or even the necessary miracle at sea; in their youthful ardour and pride as Spaniards, they were as impatient as Philip for the sailing date.

The spiritual aspects of the enterprise were looked after by nearly 200 friars aboard the various ships. It was, after all, a crusade; Philip made this his first point when he sent Medina Sidonia instructions at the beginning of April:

. . . the cause you are defending is so peculiarly His as to give us hope of His help and favour if it is not made unworthy by our sinfulness. For this reason you must take particular care in the Armada against sin of any kind, but especially the sin of blasphemy, by providing heavy penalties to be rigorously carried out if any err in this way. This so that the crime of the sinner should not be visited on the heads of those who tolerate the sin, and also because, since we are fighting for Our Lord and for the glory of His name, that name may be venerated by all . . .[17]

The Duke carried out this instruction faithfully; his own sailing orders stressed that the object of the expedition was to regain for the church countries oppressed by enemies of the True Faith:

In order that this aim should be kept constantly before the eyes of all of us I enjoin you to see that, before embarking, all ranks be confessed and absolved, with due contrition for their sins . . . I also enjoin you to take particular care that no soldier, sailor or other person in the Armada shall blaspheme or deny Our Lord, Our Lady or the Saints, under very severe punishment to be inflicted at our discretion.[18]

This was not mere ideological propaganda, although it served that purpose. Faith was always a personal need or conviction, and in that age when privation, disease and death were the everyday stuff of life, it was especially necessary to believe; in the closed society of Spain there was only the True Faith; it was as much a part of being a Spaniard as pride in honour and pure blood.

Work slowed in Holy Week during the usual religious processions and services, and on April 25th a great service was held in the Lisbon cathedral to dedicate the voyage. Philip's Viceroy of Portugal, the Cardinal Archduke, rode out with Medina Sidonia from the gates of the palace, and followed by the commanders and officers of the Armada and the gentlemen volunteers in brave and colourful array '. . . a blue cloak of rash with a gold lace round it' . . . 'jerkin of wrought velvet lined with taffety' . . . 'leather jerkin perfumed with amber and laid over with gold and silver lace' . . . 'jerkin embroidered with flowers laid over with gold lace' . . . 'breeches of yellow satin drawn out with cloth of silver' . . . 'breeches of rash laid over all with gold lace and blue-stitched taffety hat with a silver band and a plume of feathers . . .'[19] and clattered past the guard of honour and through streets crowded with onlookers to the cathedral. There a huge standard, embroidered with the Royal Arms flanked by Christ crucified

LA FELI
CISSIMA AR-
MADA QVE EL REY
DON FELIPE NVESTRO
Señor mandó juntar enel puerto
de la Ciudad de Lisboa enel
Reyno de Portu-
gal.

El Año de mil y quinientos y
ochenta y ocho.

HECHA POR
Pedro de Paz
Salas.

Title page and specimen page from a general summary of the inventory of the Armada published in Lisbon where the fleet had assembled. It details 130 ships, 27,365 men and 2,431 pieces of artillery.

and the Virgin Mary, had been laid out on the altar. When Mass had been sung and the Holy enterprise had been blessed by the Archbishop of Lisbon, the Viceroy led Medina Sidonia to the altar; as the Duke knelt the Viceroy lifted a corner of the standard to place it symbolically in his hands. Outside the guard of honour fired a salute, echoed after a short interval by the thudding of guns from the fleet in the river. It was grand theatre. It could be seen when the standard bearer held the banner aloft that it bore the words *Exurge, domine et vindica causam tuam* – 'Arise, O Lord, and vindicate thy cause'. After the months of confusion and delay, who could doubt the grand fleet would now be sailing; who could doubt it would be victorious?

Informers jostled among the crowds outside in the Plaza. There was never any lack of intelligence about the Armada; the trouble was, as always, to disentangle genuine reports from spurious 'clutter'. In this Walsyngham was well served in his two principal agents for Spain; one, Anthony Standen, who used the code name Pompeio Pelligrini, had the Tuscan Ambassador to Philip's Court in his net, and the previous year had used the brother of Santa Cruz's secretary. It had been his reports that the fleet would not be ready to sail in 1587 that had enabled Elizabeth to pluck up courage to send Drake out. Now 'Pompey' reported the Armada would sail in the middle of May. Again he was accurate.

The ships started dropping down on the tide to the mouth of the Tagus during the second week in May, but then a spell of unseasonable storms prevented them sailing until almost the end of the month; as the wind eased and came round to the nor' nor' west, Medina Sidonia gave the signal to weigh and led out in his flagship, *San Martin*. For the spectators, watching from both shores as their ancestors had watched the departure of Vasco da Gama's little squadron in the very early days of the oceanic adventure 91 years before, it was an unparalleled spectacle. There were 150 vessels,[20] large and small, bright with paint and multi-coloured pennants and ensigns bearing the different devices of the squadrons to which they were attached, and displaying the cross of the crusade painted red on their ballooning sails. Noble as they must have looked as they leant to the breeze and moved out towards the deeper blue of the open ocean, the best were unhandy by the standards of even the next century; the most sluggish could not weather the rocks and shoals off the southern shore without the aid of a tow-rope from a galley or one of the small despatch vessels and it took two days for them all to clear the river; such was the scale of the problem in sheer seamanship confronting the Duke.

He appears not to have been disturbed. Perhaps it was a result of encouraging discussions with a friar named Antonio de la Concepcion. 'He is certain that Our Lord will vouchsafe a great victory to Your Majesty' he had written to Philip on the 14th.[21] More probably it came of satisfaction at having imposed his order on this huge expedition, and the knowledge that everything, humanly speaking, that could be done, had been done; the guns had been distributed to the ships on a rational plan, the shot had been increased to an average of about 50 for each piece and powder in proportion, sailing and fighting instructions, rendezvous and passwords had been prepared and issued to the captains, every detail of small arms and ammunition, provisions, pioneers' tools and wagons, the great guns of the siege train for use in England, the mules to draw them, even rope-soled sandals for the muleteers had been attended to systematically; perhaps it was relief at the end of his labours; now it only remained for the Lord to grant a fair passage. Perhaps the spirit which his presence and high sense of responsibility had caused to spread through the expedition was reflecting back on him. At any rate he seemed for the moment confident enough.

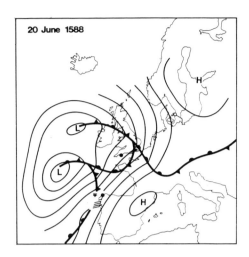

20 June 1588

Map produced by the Climatic Research Unit, University of East Anglia, showing the Atlantic weather system on 20 June 1588 when the Armada was scattered off Corunna. Positions taken from Spanish and English accounts are indicated by roundels, the observations of the Danish astronomer, Tycho Brahe, by the hollow circle.

The mood did not last long. The wind stayed in the north or thereabouts and it was impossible for the unwieldy mass of ships, restrained as they were by the worst sailers, to make way against it. It was not until June 9th that the wind settled in the west sou' west, enabling them to run before it and make distance in the right direction. By then, almost a month since they had left their berths off Lisbon, the casked drinking water was green and the victuals 'so rotten and stinking' that much had been thrown overboard to prevent it spreading 'pestilence' among the men.[22]

By June 13th the south-westerly weather had brought the Armada up to Cape Finisterre, the departure point for the Biscay crossing; then head winds set in again, and the Duke's pilots advised him to enter Corunna. He decided against it because of the difficulty of preventing men deserting 'as usual', but by the 19th, as the wind came round again into the south west, the deterioration of the food stocks, particularly water, caused him to change his mind. He led in to the harbour, followed by a part of the fleet; the rest, unable to work in before darkness fell, stood out to sea for the night. The wind backed and freshened, blowing up into a gale that forced them to run before it into Biscay. On the 21st Medina Sidonia wrote to Philip:

The people of the country say that so violent a sea and wind accompanied by fog and tempest have never been seen; and it is very fortunate that all the Armada was not caught outside, and particularly the galleys, which would certainly have been wrecked, and the whole Armada endangered . . .[23]

He had, he continued, shipped fresh stores of meat and fish aboard the ships with him, and had almost completed watering. He was not in good health, but was looking after everything as carefully as he could 'with sorrow, as Your Majesty may imagine, at the misfortune that has befallen the Armada. Notwithstanding all my efforts not to enter port, I find myself here, with the rest of the Armada out at sea.'

The men were confined to the ships, and only those going on special duties ashore were granted passes, signed by himself, which enabled them to get through an infantry company stationed on the quay by the local commander, the Marquis of Cerralbo. The system and the severe punishment threatened by his provost marshals worked well. Nevertheless, by the 24th, with the weather still bad, a large part of the fleet still missing, and sickness spreading in those ships inside Corunna, he had become thoroughly pessimistic about the whole enterprise; he unburdened himself to Philip: up to this point, he wrote, he had delayed saying anything lest it be thought he was moved by personal interest; now he felt impelled by duty to submit certain points for consideration: he reminded Philip that originally he had declined command of the Armada:

This was not because I wished to refuse to work, but because I recognised that we were attacking a kingdom so powerful and so warmly aided by its neighbours, and that we should need a much larger force than Your Majesty had at Lisbon. This was my reason for at first declining the command, seeing that the enterprise was being represented to Your Majesty as easier than it was known to be by those whose only aim was Your Majesty's service . . .

To undertake so great a task with equal forces to those of the enemy would be inadvisable, but to do so with an inferior force, as ours is now, with our men lacking in experience, would be still more unwise. I am bound to confess that I see very few, or hardly any, of those on the Armada with any knowledge of or ability to perform the duties entrusted to them. I have tested and watched this point very carefully, and Your Majesty may believe me when I assure you that we are very weak . . .[24]

He pointed to Parma's weakness also, then to the great force Philip had collected for the conquest of Portugal, a contiguous land. 'Well, Sire, how do you think we can attack so great a country as England with such a force as ours is now?' Finally, he advised 'making some honourable terms with the enemy' rather than continuing with the plan.

When he wrote this, he was still missing 35 vessels, including two galleasses; many had put into ports along the southern Biscay coast as far as Santander, but a large body, including many of the store ships known as 'hulks', had been driven up to the western approaches to the English Channel, and were awaiting him at the next rendezvous position off the Scilly Isles.

Despite all, Philip was not to be dissuaded:

No blame attaches to you for what happened in the storm . . . Stir yourself then to do your duty, since you see that, pressed as I am by financial and other difficulties, I am resolute to overcome them all with God's aid.[25]

He wrote this on July 1st. Four days later, he reiterated his intention on no account to desist from the enterprise, but 'to carry forward the task already commenced, overcoming the difficulties which may present themselves', and sent detailed instructions, which he summarised at the end:

The men and stores are to be kept intact by feeding the men on fresh provisions. The ships are to be united in Corunna, or at least so many of them that those missing shall not be of importance; and you are then to prepare with all speed, so as to be ready to sail on your voyage as soon as you receive my further orders . . .[26]

Frail and ill, the old King performed his part by continual prayer at the Masses sung in the great chapel of the Escorial, a worn figure with only the white of his hair and ruffs at neck and sleeves and the badge of the Golden Fleece hanging at his breast to offset the overall black in which he dressed.

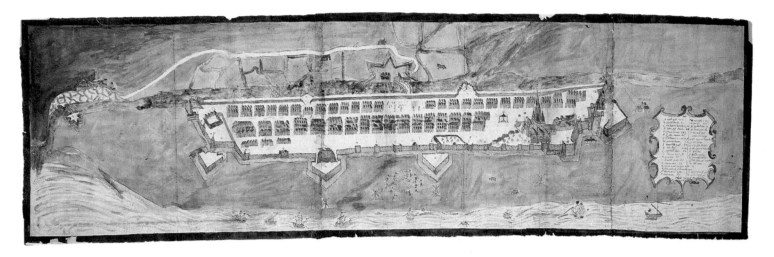

Maps of East Coast military defences
were hurriedly drawn up in the early
summer of 1588, in anticipation of
possible invasion. Here are maps of
Yarmouth, and Weybourne on the
North Norfolk coast.

5

The Lord High Admiral

From the English viewpoint, the problems appeared as great. There was no doubt the Armada had sailed. There had been varying reports of its strength crediting it with up to 500 sail; the most recent and reliable was a list, actually prepared from Medina Sidonia's report to Philip before leaving Lisbon, which had been printed and distributed no doubt to alarm Elizabeth and encourage her Catholic subjects. This showed 130 sail, including four galleys and four galleasses, carrying altogether over 19,000 soldiers, more than 8,000 sailors, 2,080 galley slaves, besides gentlemen adventurers and unattached officers, servants, 85 hospital staff for the 580-ton 'hulk', *San Pedro el Mayor* – which was fitted out to receive sick and wounded and supplied with 6,000 ducats worth of 'drugs and pothecary stuff' – nearly 200 friars of various religious orders, 22 gentlemen of the Duke's household and 50 of the Duke's servants, paymaster's staff and officers of justice. The number of guns and shot and the quantity of powder and match was listed for each ship; altogether there were 2,477 guns, but the sizes were not stated. Discounting a squadron of 23 store 'hulks' and some 33 small scouting and despatch vessels, it was still a formidable force of some 70 mostly large, armed merchantmen and warships, apart from the galleasses and galleys.[1]

In addition to this threat, known to be carrying a siege train for operations ashore, there was Parma's army believed to number some 30,000 men in Flanders. Parma had been making extraordinary preparations: he had assembled or had built over 200 small craft of all descriptions including barges designed to transport horses, with ramps for the animals to embark and disembark, had employed thousands of workmen digging canals from Antwerp and Ghent to Bruges and so to the sea coast in order to bypass the Sea Beggars' hold on the Scheldt and had collected some 20,000 casks, it was said, for joining together to form the basis of floating bridges. It was supposed he intended to take his force across to the Thames estuary, or perhaps Harwich or even Yarmouth higher up the East Anglian coast – it was not known where he might choose. At one time in February Walsyngham was convinced he would make for Scotland. Then there were French Catholics under Henry, Duke of Guise, subsidised by Philip; Medina Sidonia might be intending to put in at a Channel port to carry a French army across to England. Alternatively he might be making for Ireland or Scotland or the Isle of Wight. Walsyngham and Burghley assumed – rightly – that he would attempt a junction with Parma, so that their combined forces could cross under cover of his warships and be put ashore somewhere in the Thames estuary. But for Elizabeth, corrupted by her years of power and grown querulous and vindictive towards even her most faithful counsellors, it seemed the blow might fall anywhere.

The naval Commander-in-Chief responsible for parrying it at sea and ensuring it could not land was her Lord High Admiral, Charles Lord Howard of

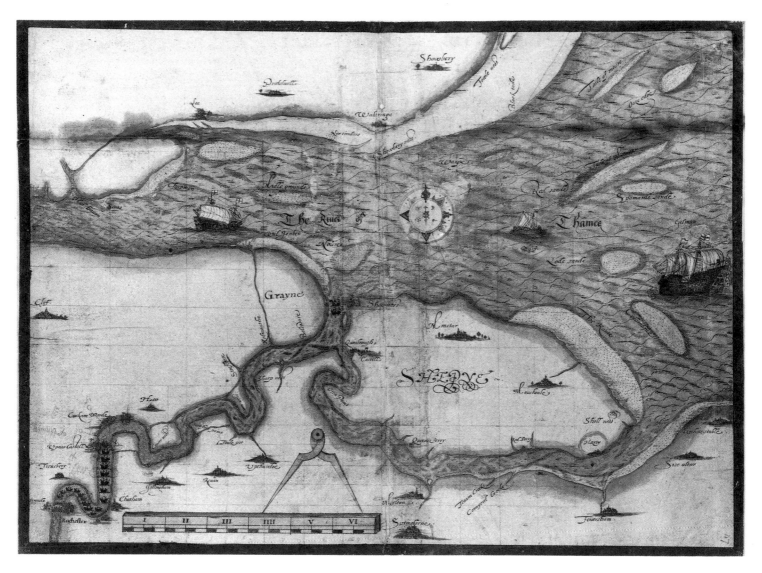

A sixteenth-century map of the Isle of Sheppey and Thames Estuary. Ships of the English fleet can be seen laid up in the River Medway.

Effingham. Like Medina Sidonia, Howard had been called for political, administrative and personal reasons rather than experience in sea fighting or command of fleets. He came from a family which had worked its way up from minor Norfolk gentry to distinction at Court and on the battlefield under successive English Monarchs. One of the secrets of the Howards' hold on power had been success in rearing households of healthy children and marrying them well; if one branch of the family backed the wrong side, there were sufficient kinsmen on the right side to pull the erring relations back into favour; and in the small world of those who counted in Elizabeth's England, Howard was either related or connected by marriage to most; he could claim kinship with Elizabeth herself from his grandfather, Thomas Howard, 2nd Duke of Norfolk, one of whose daughters had married Sir Thomas Boleyn, father of Anne, Elizabeth's mother.

He was in appearance and manner the popular archetype of an English aristocrat; a tall figure with a grave face and powerful nose, he prided himself on his prowess at sports; he won prizes riding in the lists, hunted with dogs and falcons and retained an athletic figure all his life. He was also something of a dandy, paying close attention to the cut of doublet and cape, the fit of the hose over his calves, the plumes and jewels in the gorgeous hats he wore at Court.[2] He affected contempt for men of letters and lawyers possibly because his own education had been poor; his spelling was bizarre even by the standards of the day, his sentences often as difficult to unravel as Drake's, who could have had little or no formal education. Nevertheless he had an intensely practical, non-speculative, cautious commonsense very English intelligence, as his conduct of the Armada campaign was to prove. He was also responsible and loyal – as a contemporary put it, 'such a one as the Queen . . . knew to be a fit instrument for her service, for she was a proficient in the reading of men as well as books.'[3]

As a young man he had been under the shadow of his father, Lord Admiral in Mary's reign, and had had to wait until almost 50 with only occasional official appointments before Elizabeth made him Lord Admiral in 1585. In this great office, probably the most lucrative of all in perquisites, he was responsible on the one hand for the operational control of Elizabeth's navy, on the other hand for the Admiralty Courts which sat to adjudicate on prize goods and other maritime affairs. In this role he issued commissions to owners of ships allowing them to attack and plunder Spaniards provided they could put up a bond of usually £3,000 and prove they had suffered losses at Spanish hands; by the time Howard was appointed the Spanish war was open, if not declared, and there was no requirement to prove loss; anyone who could fit out a privateer and put up the necessary bond received a 'Letter of Reprisal'. In return the Lord Admiral received a tenth of any plunder. He also had a right to pirate goods seized, and half the value of the 'Royal fish', whales, sturgeon, porpoises. He seems to have been as diligent in protecting this minor interest as in the major matter of his 'tenths' of captured booty; in one barren year for sturgeon he ordered inquiry made so that if any persons were found to have taken fish and not presented them, 'I myself may see them punished.'[4] In addition to his perquisites of office, he adventured privateers on his own account and took shares in joint stock expeditions; his share of Drake's capture of the *San Felipe* in 1587 was £4,338. He was, like all ministers at Elizabeth's court, professionally and financially bound up with the English assault on Spanish treasure and had been a strong supporter of Burghley's arguments for expanding the fleet in 1585.[5]

Now he was enjoying the benefit. The fleet had been mobilised in the Autumn of 1587 after a scare that some ships of the Armada had been sighted off Cornwall. The measures Burghley had been perfecting over the years had worked smoothly; merchantmen had been detained in port, and those selected as suitable for conversion had been sent round to the Thames by the various ports as their contribution to the national effort. The Vice Admirals of the maritime counties had impressed the number of 'expert seamen' expected from them by virtue of the lists drawn up in 1584 and despatched them to the fleet. The Surveyor of Marine Victuals, authorised to draw £24,500 on the Exchequer 'for the victualling of 10,000 men of the navy for three months',[6] had purchased the necessary supplies of beef, flour, butter, cheese, fish, peas, biscuit and ale and the rest from sources previously listed, and had them transported to the dockyards to be put aboard the ships. By the end of November Howard, overseeing preparations at the dockyards in Deptford and the ships in the Medway, had felt confident enough to return to discuss matters with Elizabeth and the council; at the end of December he had been commissioned by the Queen as 'our lieutenant general, commander in chief and governor of our whole fleet and army at sea' and given the widest scope 'to invade, enter, spoil and make himself master of the kingdoms, dominions, lands, islands and all other places whatever belonging to the said Spaniards . . .'[7]

His powers to do anything of the sort had been removed within a month.

Letter from Sir William Wynter, Elizabeth's veteran naval commander and administrator, to the Earl of Lincoln, Howard's predecessor as Lord High Admiral, dated 21 October 1578. The letter is concerned with problems of ships' ballast and rotting timbers, and how to combat the problems. The following is a transcript:

The unloked for decayes that have fallen out uppon searchinge of the shippes (which have ben latelie repayred at woolwich and Deptford in their drie dockes) is not unknowen to your Lordshippe both for that you partelie sawe hit your self and alsoe hit haith ben shewed to your L: by me and other my fellowes in offyce, And haveinge considered what haith ben the cause thereof I doe finde that it is the ballaste beinge gravell which could not be trenched by reason of the Cooke roomes that were made uppon the same, and of the often lecadge of beere with the sheadeinge of water uppon the saied ballast which did bryede suche a dampe therein as it did taynte both tymber, plancke, tryenayle, and the yron worke that laye neare unto hit: for remedie whereof (from hence forewardes) it is thought good that there be cooke roomes devised uppon the overloppes in the best wise that may be for saffetie, and that the shippes be ballested with stones which will suffer ayere to goe throughe: The quantitie of stones that moste serve for the Navye would growe to a rounde charge if it should altogeather be had frome the Quarryes neare Maydestone, for the easeinge whereof if it might be your good Lordeshippes pleasure to conferre with

Walsyngham's reports and common sense indicated that the Armada would not be sailing during the winter months, and to cut down the wages and victualling bills, a large number of the seamen were discharged, leaving only skeleton crews for the fleet. This was an example of Elizabeth's 'parsimony' which must have saved hundreds of lives, for however efficiently the victualling organisation worked, the food once aboard ship was stowed and prepared in the holds in conditions which might have been designed to contaminate it and cause disease which the crowded and unhygienic state of the berth decks of a fully manned warship might have been designed to propagate. Statistically the sailor took a far graver risk eating, or drinking the casked water after a few weeks aboard, than he faced in action.

This did not stop the work of the shipwrights, caulkers, sailmakers and riggers fitting out the ships under John Hawkins' overall direction; by early March a great part of the fleet was ready. Howard's enthusiastic reports provide a striking contrast to Medina Sidonia's lists of complaints to Philip; thus on March 2nd:

. . . this much I will say to your Lordship. I have been aboard of every ship that goeth out with me and in every place where any may creep and I do thank God that they be in the estate they be in; and there is never a one that knows what a leak means . . . there is none that goeth out now but I durst go to the Rio de la Plata in her . . . [8]

A few days later he transferred his flag from the *White Bear*, one of only three of the English Royal ships retaining the traditional lofty castles, to the new, race-built *Ark Raleigh*, bought into the service as *Ark Royal*. In her he led a squadron – less the four largest ships still fitting out – from the Thames estuary to the anchorage known as the Downs, inside the sandbanks off the east Kent coast. The short cruise confirmed all his good opinions of Hawkins' work:

I protest before God and as my soul shall answer for it, that I think there were never in any place in the world worthier ships than these are, for so many. And as few as we are, if the King of Spain's forces be not hundreds, we will make sport with them . . . [9]

As for the *Ark*, he asked Burghley to tell Elizabeth her money had been well spent, 'for I think her the odd ship in the world for all conditions . . . we can see no sail, great or small, but how far soever they be off, we fetch them and speak with them . . .'[10]

Elizabeth, meanwhile, had sent commissioners across to Flanders to open discussions about peace with Parma; it is unlikely she expected anything to come of it. Howard certainly did not, and in what looks like an act of defiance, he took his squadron across to France, and thence on a westerly wind up to Flushing to encourage the rebels. He arrived on March 13th, and was received enthusiastically; 'Beggar' captains and sailors there, seeing his ships bright with fresh paint and flags, in Sir William Wynter's words, showing themselves 'like gallants . . . I assure you it would do a man's heart good to behold them',[11] came and offered their services at any time he or Elizabeth should call for them. He reported to Burghley that Elizabeth could be as sure of Flushing and all the towns in the island of Walcheren as she could be of the Isle of Sheppey itself.

Drake, too, was cynical about the peace talks. He had been given a small squadron headed by the *Revenge* (flag), *Hope* and *Nonpareil*, all Royal ships of 500 tons and upwards, and the rather smaller *Swiftsure*, and was at Plymouth with the three Fenner brothers, Thomas, Edward and William, waiting impatiently for the chance to sail on another pre-emptive cruise against the Armada on its own coast. Elizabeth was apprehensive, and he was forced to wait all that month and the next. He fired off urgent letters reminding her of the great preparations at my L. Threasurer that a lettre be directed to the keeper of the Castle of Rochester commaundeinge hym to suffer us that we might digge uppe and carrie away the stones which lie in the old fundacions within the saied castle without toucheinge anye parte of that which standeth above grounde, hit would helpe muche towardes the ballesteinge anewe of the navie, and soe the provicion which we should have from Maydestone would not (I suppose) be great, This I ame of opynion would doe well, and therefore I beseche your L. that I may understande what shalbe your pleasure to doe herein, soe that I might take order to set forewardes the same before my departeinge herehence: I would have wayted uppon your L erre this at the Courte, but it haith soe happened with me as I could not without geveinge of offence. And thus moste humblie takeinge my leave I desire god to keepe you in healthe.

Upnore the xxjth of October 1578.
Your honorable Lordeshippes
to commaunde
W. Wynter

I have drawen adrawght of a letter to bee writen from your L. & the rest which I seande herein enclozed. yf hit shall lieke your L. then hit maye bee engrossed at your pleasure.

[Addressed]

To the rt honnerable & my verie good L. the Erell of Lyncolne L admyrall of yngland

[Docketed]
21 octob. 1578 Sir William Winter to my L. Ballasting of ye L. shippes with stone.

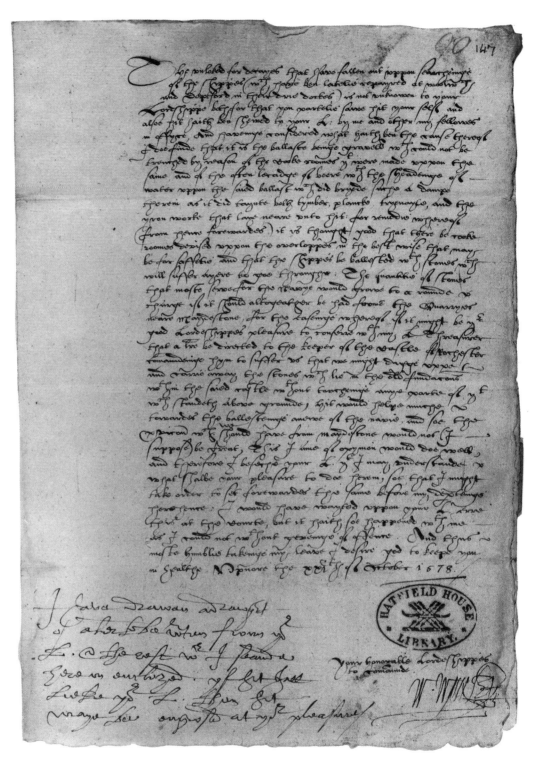

Lisbon and of his own depredations the previous year which had prevented the Spaniards from sailing; if she would send him four more Royal ships and the 16 merchantmen being fitted out on the Thames, he would sail immediately for Spain:

. . . and if the fleet come out of Lisbon . . . they shall be fought with, and I hope through the goodness of our merciful God, in such sort as shall hinder his quiet passage into England; for I assure your Majesty I have not in my lifetime known better men, and possessed with gallanter minds, than your Majesty's people are for the most part, which are here gathered together, voluntarily to put their hands and hearts to the finishing of this great piece of work; wherein we are all persuaded that God, the giver of all victories, will in mercy look upon your most excellent Majesty and us your poor subjects, who for the defence of your Majesty, our religion, and our native country, have resolutely vowed the hazard of our lives.

The advantage of time and place in all martial actions is half a victory; which being lost is irrecoverable. Wherefore, if your Majesty would command me away with these ships which are here already, and the rest to follow with all possible expedition, I hold it in my opinion the surest and best course . . . for this I surely think; there was never any force so strong as there is now ready against your Majesty and true religion; but that the Lord of all strengths is stronger and will (defend) the truth of his word for his own name's sake.[12]

Howard, riding in Margate Roads, was as eager to be off: 'I think there was never a more willing company to venture their lives in Her Majesty's service than be here,'[13] he wrote. Earlier Burghley had intended him to take the main body of the fleet round to Portsmouth by the first week in April, thence to join Drake at Plymouth, but delays in fitting out the four large ships and the merchantmen had prevented him, and it was not until towards the end of April that Elizabeth finally made up her mind that he should go. By then he was waiting for more provisions. He was not able to sail until the last week in May and then had to wait until the 31st before he found a fair wind to take him westward down the Channel. He left his kinsman, Lord Henry Seymour, with a squadron of smaller Royal ships to guard against a descent by Parma and liaise with the Sea Beggars.

Arriving in Plymouth on June 2nd, Howard made Drake his Vice Admiral. He was, perhaps, surprised at the grace with which the great sailor accepted subordination: at any rate he wrote to Walsyngham later describing 'how lovingly and kindly Sir Francis Drake beareth himself; and also how dutifully to her Majesty's service and unto me, being in the place I am in . . .' and asked that Drake be sent a private letter of thanks for it.[14] The advice he received from Drake, Thomas Fenner and the experienced commanders he had brought with him, John Hawkins and Martin Frobisher, was unequivocal and urgent: '. . . the surest way to meet with the Spanish fleet is upon their own (coast), or in any harbour of their own, and there to defeat them.'[15]

Boisterous westerlies, which would have driven the ships back up Channel if they had emerged from the Sound, held him in; the same weather prevented victuallers beating down to him, and within three weeks he was again low on provisions; he wrote to Burghley:

I will never go again to such a place of service but I will carry my victuals with me, and not trust to careless men behind me. We came away with scarce a month's victuals . . . We think it should be marvelled at how we keep our men from running away, for the worst men in the fleet knoweth for how long they are victualled; but I thank God as yet we are not troubled with any mutinies, nor I hope shall not; for I see men kindly handled will bear want and run through fire and water.[16]

Despite all frustrations he still retained his enthusiasm for his ships and men, telling Burghley that if the wind had been favourable they would have been on the enemy coast long since:

They should not have stirred, but we would have been upon their jacks . . . yet we were and are resolved to go whensoever the wind shall serve, and to be as near as we can where we may meet with the King's fleet, which I pray God to send us to do; for, Sir, since the world began, I think there was never a willinger company to do their prince service than these be.

Visscher's engravings of the English warships *Ark Royal*, Howard's flagship of about 800 tons, *Tiger*, 200 tons, and *Golden Lion*, about 500 tons. All three were part of the English fleet.

This was written on June 23rd, as Medina Sidonia, in Corunna, was feeling the deepest misgivings about his own prospects, and steeling himself to state them openly to Philip.

Howard's enthusiastic letter alarmed Elizabeth. She had intelligence of the Armada's departure the previous month, and the thought of her fleet sailing for the Spanish coast, missing Medina Sidonia at sea and leaving him free run of the practically undefended coasts of England, Ireland or Scotland was too much; she immediately instructed Howard to confine himself to cruising off and on between England and Spain. It would probably have been better to have cut down the cruising area even further to the western approaches to the English Channel; it was there two centuries later in the heyday of fighting sail that England's main fleet cruised so that with the prevailing westerlies it could gain the advantage of the windward position against a hostile fleet attempting to enter the Channel. However that may be, Howard wrote back with obvious reluctance 'I must and will obey . . . and I shall most humbly pray her Majesty to think that that which we meant to do was not rashly determined . . .'[17]

So far he had had no firm news of the whereabouts of the Spanish fleet, for as he wrote, 'there was never any such summer seen here on the sea',[18] and all the small craft he had sent off as scouts had been driven back by the weather without being able to gain intelligence. Then, on July 1st, a small barque out of Ireland fell among the group of Spanish vessels which had been caught by the gale off Corunna and driven north to the Scilly Isles. She was captured, but by luck parted the tow-rope and escaped to bring in the news of 18 great ships with red crosses on their sails – all very full of Spaniards. At about the same time one of the scouts Howard had sent out reported sighting others of the Spanish fleet off Ushant. It seemed clear the Armada had been scattered; Howard waited nevertheless in case he heard of landings anywhere, then on July 15th, re-provisioned at last and with no untoward news, he put out and took up station at the entrance to the Channel, between the Scilly Isles and Ushant, spreading his fleet in three squadrons:

. . . so as, if any of us do discover the Spanish fleet we give notice thereof presently the one to the other, and thereupon repair and assemble together. I myself [Howard] do lie in the middle of the Channel with the greatest force. Sir Francis Drake hath 20 ships and 4 or 5 pinnaces, which lie towards Ushant; and Mr Hawkins, with as many more, lieth towards Scilly.[19]

They were not much more than a day in this position when the wind went round to the north and it was decided to make for the Spanish coast; barely into the Bay of Biscay another change forced them back, and since provisions were again becoming short and men going down sick they returned to Plymouth. It is a measure of the constraints imposed by food and the way it was stowed and prepared aboard that by the time they were back in harbour after a summer cruise of not much more than a week they had 'cast many (men) overboard'[20] and now had to land so many sick that it was necessary 'to discharge some ships to have their men to furnish others.'[21] This made little difference since the discarded ships were the smallest and least useful. Howard, Drake and Hawkins remained supremely confident about the condition of the main units on which the outcome would depend, and were anxious to put out again directly they had taken on fresh water.

The time for meeting Medina Sidonia on his own coast was past, though; he had sailed from Corunna on July 22nd, and the same weather which had forced Howard back to Plymouth had wafted him northwards across the Bay. He had

Visscher's engraving of the *White Bear* of about 900 tons, originally Howard's flagship.

Seal of Lord Howard of Effingham as Lord High Admiral. This shows an Elizabethan warship: within the Garter on the mainsail are the Howard arms.

Part of a list of 123 ships that served
against the Spanish fleet, and received
pay from the Queen, 1588.

61

1588.

The names and number of shipps that
served against the Spanishe flete and
receyved pay from her mate ao 1588

152
83

1	The Beare	29	Hawkyns	57	Delyght
2	Tryumphe	30	Argus	58	Vigaru
3	Eliz Jonas	31	Gally bonavolia	59	Gallyon Leycster
4	Whitebere	32	Brigandyne	60	Geo: bonaventure
5	Arke Ralegh	33	Nyghtyngale	61	Salamon
6	Golden Lyon	34	Revenge	62	A new pynnes
7	Dredd nought	35	Nonperille	63	Susan a new pynnes
8	Bonaventura	36	Hope	64	pynnace
9	mary Rose	37	Swyftsure	65	Sannet
10	Swallowe	38	Ayde	66	Jane bonaventure
11	Foresyght	39	Mousse	67	mary rose of Lond
12	Eagles	40	Jesus Bradd	68	Galyon of Frobysher
13	Moone	41	E Bonaventure	69	Hasard of Feversham
14	Defyance	42	golden noble	70	Ruben of Sandwch
15	Elin of Malden	43	Hope Hawd	71	Eliazar of Dover
16	mary gold	44	Oxygfry	72	Beare of yarmouth
17	Rainbowe	45	Eracke	73	willm of Colchester
18	Vanntguard	46	Jacque talbot	74	willm of Rye
19	Antelope	47	mynion	75	prymrose of Harwch
20	Bull	48	Espus	76	wm of Feversham
21	Tyger	49	Jacque bond	77	mynion of Bryghtelm
22	Scoute	50	Jacque bonus	78	Brygdyne of Bryghtelm
23	Tramontana	51	Jacque gardyns	79	handmayd of Bryghtelm
24	Argatt	52	Eliz flower	80	Ayde of Bryghtelm
25	Sonne	53	pryze	81	new bonaventure of Hastyngs
26	marlyn	54	Eliz Drak		
27	Grey	55	Beare Young		
28	George Hoy	56	Galte Dorse		

lost some 40 ships and the galleys when a storm blew up on the 27th, but found them two days later, all but the galleys; the same day he raised a headland in the north-east, pronounced by the pilots to be the southernmost tip of Cornwall, the Lizard.

It is not possible to make more than an estimate of the relative strengths of the opposing fleets now about to meet; armaments have to be extrapolated from incomplete lists of the types and sizes carried; ship types have to be deduced from inconclusive evidence buttressed by nautical archaeology on those Spanish wrecks which have been found; ship sizes are complicated by different rules used by the English and Spanish to calculate tonnage. None of this matters except to the purist: the two fleets were never comparable; they were assembled for different objectives and, despite all Medina Sidonia's attempts to find more guns and shot they were not equipped to fight the same kind of battle.

In numbers and sizes of useful ships Medina Sidonia had a clear advantage; of his two main battle squadrons, that of Portugal had seven great galleons of 800–1,000 tons and three of 350 to 500 tons, that of Castile had seven 530-ton Indian Guard galleons, two rather larger galleons as flag- and vice-flag-ships, one small galleon and four large armed merchantmen of 650–950 tons – in all therefore he had 20 purpose-built warships and four armed merchantmen of a size to give a good account of themselves. In addition he had a squadron of four heavily armed galleasses, useful – or so it was supposed – for their extra mobility in light airs and calms to bring a concentration to bear where required. He had no galleys; all four had been dispersed by the latest gale and forced to seek shelter.

To oppose this main battle, Howard had in Plymouth four great ships of some 800–1,000 tons, the *Ark Raleigh* sometimes listed 800 tons, often less, seven middling ships of 400–600 tons, three of 300–400 tons – in all 15 warships which could mount a useful broadside. Lord Henry Seymour had one middling and two 300-ton warships with him in the Narrows, but since Howard had no means of calling him quickly nor Seymour any way of beating down Channel to him if the wind was in the west – which it usually was – there is no reason to include these unless and until the Spanish fleet succeeded in forcing its way up Channel to the Narrows.

It is usual to reduce Spanish tonnage by about a third to find the equivalent English tonnage, although a document found by Colin Martin showing the measurements and tonnages of six Mediterranean ships requisitioned in Lisbon for the Armada campaign suggests that there may not have been such a great difference, or indeed much difference at all.[22] Even reducing the given Spanish tonnages by a third, one is still left with 21 warships or large auxiliaries of 350 tons and upwards in the squadrons of Portugal and Castile. There is no doubt that – apart from the three English great ships which retained their high castles – the Spanish vessels *looked* more imposing; all contemporary evidence agrees on this. There is also no doubt that because of these lofty sides acting like sails they were extraordinarily clumsy to handle by comparison with the English ships.

Besides his warships, Medina Sidonia had four squadrons of 10 armed merchantmen – less the flagship of the Biscay squadron which had not returned since the storm – of a size sufficient to mount heavy guns and carry a considerable number of soldiers; there were over 17,000 soldiers all told in the various ships. The eight larger store 'hulks' also carried a few heavy guns, a defensive light armament and 150 to over 200 soldiers each. Against these Howard had perhaps four armed merchantmen of size; the majority of his 25 auxiliaries were under 200 tons – although again the English ships were more manoeuvrable than the roundish Mediterranean cargo carriers probably in the majority on the Spanish side. In terms of numbers of sizeable vessels, therefore, Medina Sidonia had an advantage of about 3:2 in warships – excluding the galleasses – and something like 10:1 in useful armed merchantmen; since all his main units were crowded with soldiers there can be little doubt that if it came to a static boarding and entering contest Howard would stand no chance.

Everyone knew, of course, that the English would not fight like this; therefore the relative strengths in broadside armament was important. This is not known in detail, but estimates have been made which are probably accurate enough: for the Spanish fleet, Professor Thompson has used four inventories which between them list sizes and types 'of 1,770 of the total 2,411 guns' aboard the ships which reached the Channel.[23] From these he has extrapolated on a squadronal basis to obtain the probable sizes and types of the remaining guns. Previously Professor Lewis had done much the same thing for the English Royal ships;[24] simplifying and confining the results to guns throwing balls of eight lb or over which might do serious ship damage, we get:

		Spanish		English	
Cannon-type 30-pounders and upwards		26	} 95	55	} 55
12–29-pounders		69		—	
Culverin-type 16-pounders and upwards		16	} 172	130	} 330
8–15-pounders		156		200	
Perier-type 22-pounders and upwards		5	} 197	38	} 38
and misc. 12–21-pounders		113		—	
8–11-pounders		79		—	
		464		423	

If we wish to add to these totals guns throwing shot weighing between four and seven and a half pounds, which could damage rigging and men behind superstructures, we find the total number of Spanish guns, four-pounders and upwards, 735, English 683 – in fact much the same proportions as heavier guns alone.

These figures need interpretation. If it is assumed that the 'Perier type and miscellaneous' group were, like the 'carronades' of the 18th century, chiefly suitable for very close-range work, and that the real ship-damaging guns in a stand-off contest were cannon, demi-cannon, culverin and demi-culverin, then the English had an advantage of 385 to 267 pieces. If however all guns heavier than eight-pounders, or even all guns heavier than four-pounders, are included as useful broadside guns, then the Spanish had a small advantage in numbers, but the English a small advantage in average weight of shot.[25]

This again needs interpretation: at the effective range of 16th-century ship-borne guns concentration of gun-power in each hull was more important than total gunpower in the fleet. The distribution of the Spanish effective pieces is not known precisely but can be estimated from the fleet list Medina Sidonia prepared for Philip at Lisbon, which shows the number of guns, shot and the weight of gunpowder carried by each ship.[26] The smaller vessels which could only mount small pieces had an allowance of one quintal (c. 100 English pounds) of powder per gun or less. The flagships of the effective squadrons on the other hand carried from two to three quintals of powder per gun mounted – the average about 2.25 quintals. Medina Sidonia's flagship, *San Martin*, carried 2.9 quintals per gun, the galleons of the Indian Guard two quintals. From this it may

Sir Francis Drake (?1540–96).
Unknown artist, c. 1580–85.

be assumed that all ships listed as having two quintals of powder or more per gun had their share of effective pieces. There were 42 such ships with Medina Sidonia off the Lizard. However, on the English side the effective guns were mounted in fewer than 20 Royal ships. It can be assumed, therefore, that in general the English had an advantage of rather more than 2:1 in weight of broadside ship to ship; this is what counted. Since it was believed by contemporaries that the English had far the better gunners and – as will appear – all their guns were well mounted on ship-board carriages whereas a proportion of the Spanish heavy pieces were not, this advantage can at least be doubled.

While it is impossible to arrive at precise comparisons of the weights of shot thrown by the opposing fleets or ships, or the exact gunnery advantage, what seems quite clear is that the English had superiority both in weight of broadside, effective ship to effective ship, and in speed and manoeuvrability – particularly to windward – and could dictate the tactics. The commanders on both sides knew they would do so. It is not clear that this would allow them to win; given the inaccuracy and slow rate of fire of cast guns and the relatively small numbers and calibre of those mounted, it would be impossible for them seriously to damage the Spanish fleet if Medina Sidonia took up and held a defensive formation. Like the Spanish commanders, Howard and Drake entering the Channel should have been praying for a miracle – changes of wind or weather to scatter the Armada, as had happened already several times, or the Spanish commander losing his wits and dividing his squadrons or leaving his store ships unprotected, being misled by incompetent pilots – or, as happened, that he should have been given instructions virtually impossible to fulfil, from which he was not allowed to deviate. Here, at any rate, is an analysis of the situation by a contemporary, Sir William Gorgas, who served in the campaign and later wrote these 'Observations' for the instruction of others faced with the same threat of Spanish invasion. Dealing first with the 'hugeness and numbers of their (Spanish) vessels as for multitude of soldiers and mariners', he went on to list the naval advantages enjoyed by the English fleet:[27]

. . . as namely for our swiftness in outsailing them, our nimbleness in getting into the weather of them, our little draught of water in comparison to theirs, our stout bearing up of our sides in all huge winds when theirs' must stoop to their great disadvantage many ways, our yawness in staying well and casting about twice for their once and so discharging our broadsides of ordnance twice for their single, we carrying as good and great artillery as they do and to better proof and having far better gunners, our knowledge and pilotage of our own coasts, channels, sands and harbours, and soundings being far above theirs . . . I say, setting the one against the other for a seafight (we) are more powerful to annoy them and guard our coasts than they of force to offend and invade us if we use the benefit of our shipping right, and God give us grace to employ these gifts to best purpose . . . For without his grace, his gifts do little avail in any human course whatsoever . . .

6

The Craft and Mystery of the Sea

The ships about to be joined in battle were the most complex human creations, untouched by science, the products of centuries of natural evolution by trial and error, and over the past hundred years the challenge of more distant seas. A few master shipwrights boasted mathematical knowledge, but like everything about their craft the formulae they used were rules of thumb handed down over generations as craft secrets. In the past few years, a few, like Elizabeth's chief shipwright, Matthew Baker, had begun to draft plans before they built but for the majority it remained a matter of fixing the principal dimensions by rule as proportions of the main members and filling in the rest by eye. A naval captain wrote in 1604 that he had never found two ships alike though built by the most experienced and skilful shipwrights 'because they trust rather to their judgement than their art, and to their eye than their scale and compass.'[1]

There were two European shipbuilding traditions, northern and Mediterranean; in the northern tradition the hull planks were overlapped along their whole length one on the other 'clinker'-fashion with comparatively light frames inside to stiffen them transversally; with the Mediterranean 'carvel' tradition the frames were stouter and the planks around them were butted against each other to provide a smooth hull surface. It is believed the systems derived more from the tools employed than from other local peculiarities; the saw was in common use in the Mediterranean from at least the time of the ancient Egyptians; shipwrights were able to saw the straight edges necessary for carvel planking; in the north, however, in the early days the saw was virtually unknown; the tools used were axes and adzes; logs were split down the grain, then hewed with the adze into planks.

The two systems continued side by side into the 16th century; many Elizabethan merchantmen, probably most of the smaller ones, were 'clinker'-built. But for the larger warships and merchantmen for long voyages the 'northern' had everywhere given way to the Mediterranean methods of framing and planking – probably because 'clinker' build was less suitable for the immense weights and strains imposed on ships' hulls by the mounting and discharge of heavy artillery; alternatively, it may be that with the increase in size of ships clinker construction had grown too complex and time-consuming, therefore too expensive; the remains of one 15th-century English great ship, the *Gracedieu*, show an extraordinarily complicated construction, each clinker plank built up in three layers, the two outer layers 12″ wide and tapered in thickness, the inner 8″ wide to butt on to the outer two layers of the next plank below, leaving a 4″ overlap for its own outer layers;[2] as in all clinker construction the frames inside were notched in steps to conform to the overlaps, something that was unnecessary with carvel planking.

However it came about, the change from clinker to carvel in England can be dated to the reign of Henry VIII at the beginning of the 16th century. Henry was a great gun enthusiast, who provided his warships with as many of the largest pieces as he could find; to accommodate their weight below decks and at the same time mount a powerful broadside, his shipwrights fashioned gun ports with hinged lids in the hull planking between the frames. English merchantmen designed for the dangerous Levant trade began to show hull gunports at the same date. By Elizabeth's reign carvel build with rows of lidded gunports along both sides and in the stern was standard for warships and sizeable merchantmen.

The first step in building one of these ships was to lay her keel, a massive baulk of oak or elm formed in medium and larger ships from two or more lengths of timber joined with a long diagonal interface, or 'scarph', throughbolted. In one surviving contract of 1583 for a vessel in the 200-ton range, the keel was to be 58 feet in length, 14″ square, and made from two lengths joined with a six foot long scarph.[3] In a warship of the largest size the keel would be anything up to 110 feet long. This was laid on baulks or stocks in a drydock or more usually a slipway slightly inclined towards the water of a river. Similarly massive stem- and stern-posts – the stem wedge-shaped in section and placed to cut the water with its narrower edge – were erected at bow and stern. The stem-post was scarphed to the forward end, the stern-post mortised to the after end of the keel, and both were bound to it at the correct angle by timber 'knees'; these were roughly triangular in shape and cut from trees where a thick branch entered the trunk; the grain thus curved in conformity with the angle to be supported.

The stem-post which was shaped in a convex curve was inclined – or 'raked' – forward to give an overhang; the sternpost was given a rather smaller 'rake' aft, both together generally being equal to or rather more than the maximum breadth or 'beam' of the vessel to be; the waterline and 'overall' lengths of a ship were therefore considerably greater than the keel length. A typical Mediterranean or Portuguese cargo carrier might have a maximum beam of almost half her keel length, about a third of her length overall;[4] in a typical Elizabethan man-of-war the proportions were closer to one-third of keel length, one-quarter of length overall: Howard's paragon of sailing virtue, the *Ark*, is listed as having a beam of 37 feet on a keel length of 100 feet – rather over a third; the *Rainbow* and *Vanguard*, built at the same time, were considerably slimmer, the latter with a beam of 32 feet on a length of 108 feet.[5] After the keel and stem- and stern-posts, the lowest sections of the 'frames', known as 'floors', were laid at right angles across the keel and bolted to it with iron bolts, or hardwood dowels known as 'trenails'. In the 1583 contract for a ship with a 58-foot-long 14″-square keel the 'floors' were to be 11″ deep and 8″ thick. The flat lower edge of the 'floors' before they turned up into the round of the bilge might be anything from less than a tenth to a third of the eventual maximum width of the vessel at that point. This formed the flat bottom of the ship. The next sections of frame known as 'futtocks' were joined to the floors at the turn of the bilge, either scarphed or simply overlapped side by side and bolted; the latter system gave double framing at the bilge, indeed the frames were placed so close that overlapping the futtocks and floors gave almost solid timbering at this important point.

The frames were extended up around the curve of maximum breadth and inwards to the topmost decks with 'navall' and 'top' timbers similarly joined with scarphs or overlaps. Thus the vessel took shape. The sternmost frames either side of the sternpost were of heavier curved timbers known as 'fashion pieces'; these formed the shape of the flat transom stern.

Although no two vessels had quite the same shape, all had full rounded bow frames and reached their maximum breadth rather over a third of the keel length from the stern-post,[6] leaving a long, narrowing run to the stern – the underwater fish shape portrayed literally in one well-known drawing by Matthew Baker. The maximum beam was designed to be just above the water line when fully loaded so that leaning to the wind a greater area of hull was immersed on the leeward side, tending to greater resistance to further heeling. Nevertheless, scientific principles of stability had not been discovered, and many ships, overmasted perhaps, or with towering superstructures, or built too deep for their breadth – or simply badly loaded or ballasted – were excessively tender, or 'crank', meaning they could not carry their canvas in anything of a blow without heeling too far or even going right over. According to Sir William Gorgas, as previously quoted, English warships had a great advantage over the Spaniards in this respect. The frames were stiffened transversally by cambered beams running from one side to the other; these were supported by longitudinal timbers known as 'clamps' and by vertical knees hewn – like the knees for the stem- and stern-posts – from 'grown' or curved-grain timber and bolted to the frames. In the 1583 contract, the beams were to be 12″ square. The deck planking was laid and fastened over these beams like floor planking over the beams of a house, but rather more strongly since hardwood 'trenails' were used for the purpose. In the 1583 contract 2″ oak planks were stipulated for the upper deck, but 2″ spruce was perhaps more generally used. The lower or 'orlope' deck was formed of thicker plank, 3″ or for large warships 4″; in combination with the hull planking this made the lower section of the vessel into a strongly framed and stiffened hollow girder.

The lower beams were supported at the centre by stout pillars, or 'stanchions', rising from a baulk of oak known as the keelson, running from end to end over the keel and bolted to it above the 'floors'; in larger vessels there was an additional line of stanchions rising either side of the centre-line from the 'floors'; there were double or treble lines of stanchions between the orlope and upper decks.

Externally the frames were stiffened by the hull planking – 3″ thick nearest the keel in the 1583 contract, 2½″ for the rest. For larger vessels of 400 tons and upwards the skin planking would be at least 4″ thick up to the line of the upper deck; usually in English ships those bottom planks which were under the water the whole time were of elm or beech, those above the waterline of oak. Curves were steamed into the planks before they were laid over the frames by placing them over hot coals and swabbing them with water while gradually forcing them round to the required shape. The ends of the planks at the bow were let into rabbeting at the edge of the stem-post; at the stern the 'fashion pieces' had similar rabbeting to receive the after planking. Where each plank abutted the next it was generally fastened to the frame with iron bolts; between, 'trenails' were used for fastening since in time the iron affected the timber around it. Spanish shipbuilders were known for using more iron bolts than the English as a consequence of which the timbers of their vessels were more liable to 'iron-sickness'.

Additional longitudinal stiffening was provided by heavier timbers known as 'wales' bolted outside the frames. In the Mediterranean tradition these followed the lines of the decks since originally the deck beams came through the outer skin and rested on the 'wales'; as vessels became larger this practice was discontinued in favour of supporting the beams on the frames with internal 'clamps' and 'knees'; still the two main 'wales' ran around the hull at approximately deck level.

The lines of the 'wales' and the lighter stiffening pieces above, known as 'rails' and 'ribbands', and the exterior planking followed a sweet curve or 'sheer' rising rather steeply at the bow, even more steeply at the stern; inside the decks might follow this sheer for most of the body of the hull or take a somewhat flatter line; in either case they were stepped down to a lower level at both ends; there were probably several reasons; at the bows the arrangement allowed the hawse holes for the anchor cables to be sited at a convenient level below the beakhead but above the deck; it also lowered the weight of the bow chase guns; in the stern the lower level provided a space at a proper height for the tiller, which was mortised and bolted to the rudder head and came in through a port above the main transom beam; again stability was assisted since there was a considerable weight of guns mounted here to fire out of both stern and side ports; these were probably the heaviest pieces the ship carried, and this space was known as the 'Gun Room'. The positioning of the side gun ports also probably influenced the deck level since the sheer of the hull planking brought the lower wale up to gunport height at both ends, and it was a cardinal rule not to cut ports through these main strength members.

The evolution of the galleon design is not known in detail; the introduction of the type has been claimed for the ancient city state of Ragusa – Dubrovnik in modern Jugoslavia – a centre of shipbuilding in the 15th and 16th centuries which provided several ships for the Armada; it is also claimed for the even greater mercantile and shipping centre, Venice; on the other hand, it may have evolved from the cargo-carrying carrack in the new conditions of Atlantic trade and fighting or more probably from the fast Portuguese 'caravels'; the terms 'galleon', 'barque' and 'caravel' seem to have been interchangeable at this date.[7] Wherever and however it evolved, the galleon had slimmer proportions than the traditional 'carrack' and was distinguished by a flat stern, forecastle set back from the stem and a ram-like projection forward: this was called the beakhead; probably in early galleons it was intended as a ram. By the second half of the 16th century it remained only as a design feature, usually carrying a grotesque head or figure of some sort at the end. No doubt it served a useful purpose when the ship was pitching in heavy weather by breaking the force of the seas; in ordinary weather the triangular space formed between the two side arms of the beakhead forward of the stem was used by the crew to relieve themselves; the 'heads' has come down the centuries as the nautical term for a lavatory.

The side arms of the beakhead butted on to the forward wall or 'bulkhead' of the forecastle; in English race-built galleons this was only one deck high; it had been a fighting platform in the earlier Royal ships and remained so on Spanish galleons. It was comparatively short, soon dropping to the 'waist', which extended aft to the mainmast at about mid-length. Aft of the mainmast a raised deck known as the 'half deck' continued to the stern; in Spanish galleons, this was the lowest deck of a high aftercastle; in English warships there was nothing raised above it save a short poop deck at the very stern. The larger galleons had an open gallery around the stern, entered from the great cabin in the after part of the half-deck.

The main hatch through which ballast, cargo, guns and stores were loaded was a long opening in the upper deck between the foc's'le and the mainmast; it was bounded by a raised coaming, and when not in use was closed by portable transverse beams and gratings; these allowed air and light below and gave the name to this area of the waist, 'the gratings'. The boats were carried on the gratings; in some ships there was a gangway above leading from the half-deck to the foc's'le. A similar hatch in the orlope deck below gave access to the hold. In most English Royal ships the depth of hold was about half the breadth but in the more modern vessels it was rather less; the *Ark* had a 15-foot-deep hold and a breadth of 37 feet, the *Rainbow* and *Vanguard* 12- and 13-foot holds respectively and a breadth of 32 foot suggesting an evolution in the design of English ships more comprehensive than a simple increase in length and removal of upper-works.

The 'orlope' deck was situated at or just above the load waterline at mid-length, thus at the widest section of the ship, and seems to have had some six feet headroom. It was here the main battery of guns was carried. When cruising they were lashed at the ship's sides with 'breeching' ropes to rings bolted in to the frames; going into action the gun ports were raised and the gun-carriages manhandled into position so that the muzzles of the pieces extended outboard; there, no doubt, they were lashed. Whether in use as the berth deck or in action the gun deck, this long, slightly sheered, cambered, heavily-beamed and rather dim space must have been severely congested. Down the centre, the main hatch, secured by tarpaulins, was flanked by stanchions; forward of the hatch were the massive riding bitts for the anchor cables and the inner end of the bowsprit coming in at an angle to starboard of the foremast which rose through the deck from its step on the keelson; forward of this the deck stepped down to the 'fore peak', the forward section of which was divided off by a raised coaming known as a 'manger' whose purpose was to contain water coming in at the hawse holes and divert it to the 'scuppers' cut through the ship's sides.

Aft of the hatch on the orlope was the great trunk of the mainmast, the pump handles on either side, and aft again the capstan, its spindle also disappearing through the deck above. Beyond that was a transverse timber partition, or 'bulkhead', where the deck stepped down to the 'Gun Room'. In action the guns and gun carriages occupied most of the corridors of space between the stanchions beside the hatch coaming and the massy timber knees projecting in from the ship's side. The deck – in warships – was strengthened below for the great weight of the guns by timbers known as 'carlings' fixed between the beams; transverse pieces known as 'ledges' connected them to the 'clamps' on which the beams rested at the ship's side.

Ships were provided with stability by loading ballast on planks lining the floors at the bottom of the hold; this could be gravel or stones or even sand. The Spanish wrecks which have been found were ballasted with stones. The cooking space or 'galley' was built of bricks and mortar about midlength of the hold, thus a more or less permanent part of the ballast here; in larger ships this structure was probably supported on a 'false orlope' of unplanked beams running across between the futtock timbers. Above the brick firebox with its bronze or iron cauldrons and 'cob-yrons' hung on the bars of the range to support the spit there was – to judge by indications from the wreck of the English warship, *Mary Rose* – a lead-lined hood to carry the smoke up through the orlope and the upper decks. The orlope beams above the galley were also probably sheathed with lead to protect them from the heat. Although the hold was considered the safest and steadiest place for the galley, there were obvious disadvantages; smoke and cooking odours must have permeated the berth decks and provisions while the noisome odours and gases from putrid water and rats' droppings in the bilges and ballast, the gloom and lack of air below all worked against cleanliness in the preparation of food; as remarked, the sailor was at greater risk eating his meals aboard than fighting. In merchant ships where the hold was given over to cargo, the galley would more probably be found in the foc's'le. Forward of the warship's galley in the hold the heavy anchor cables were flaked, aft was the main storage space for the casked provisions and ammunition; there was also a decked 'false orlope' here in the more recent English naval ships, with small cabins for the bo's'n, surgeon, gunner and carpenter,[8] probably also the sailing master in a flagship with numerous officers to occupy the upper cabins. In the smaller and older ships this space would have been occupied by the powder magazine, bread room and steward's room, all reached through square 'scuttles' cut in the deck of the 'Gun Room'. The carpenter and bo's'n had their store rooms forward below the orlope, and reached in the same way by square scuttles cut in the deck.

Except for the hatchways, there was scarcely a right angle built into a ship; the keel, keelson, floors, stanchions, masts, deck planking and portions of the framing, especially the upper parts where they sloped inwards to give a 'tumble home' to the ship's side, were straight; everywhere else sweet, natural curves met and crossed, defying calculation or mass production; the timbers were selected and complex joints fashioned by eye, with the use of only saw, adze, chisel and wooden mallet, or awl to bore the holes for the iron or hardwood bolts with which the parts were fastened to each other. The snug jointing and the rabbeting of main members to receive the edges of the outside planking, the precise balance of size, hence strength, of different members with functional shapes were the product of highest craftsmanship; for it was not a house standing on firm ground the shipwrights were creating, but a free-moving structure liable to stress in every direction; at one moment the hull might be poised on a swell at mid-length with bow and stern virtually unsupported; the swell would pass to the bow while another lifted the stern, leaving the weight at mid-length with ballast, cargo, guns and provisions temporarily suspended. Waves would buffet and heel her, inducing diagonal stresses on the frames and beams; pressure of wind in the sails would be transmitted through the standing rigging to the sides and through the shaking masts to decks and keelson. No-one who has ever heard the creaking protests of a wooden ship in a seaway, and felt her living, quivering timbers beneath his feet, the masts whipping like alders in a gale as she rides and hangs and swoops and leans, could fail to appreciate the supreme skill of the shipwright's craft.

The seams between the hull and deck-planking were rendered watertight by 'caulking' with tarred fibres known as 'oakum' unpicked from old hemp or manila rope. This was wedged between the planks with a caulking iron of wide blunt end shape beaten with a hammer; hot pitch was poured in on top of the oakum along the seam. Several preparations were used on the timbers of the underwater hull to keep them sweet. The Portuguese and Spanish used tallow, mixing it with lime, sulphur or fish oil in a vain attempt to poison the wood-boring teredo worms active in tropical waters; the English and Dutch used a coating of pitch or tar mixed with goat's hair, which was quite as ineffective either for preventing barnacles, weed or worms. Experiments were made with lead sheathing for explorers' vessels quite early in the century, and it is interesting that the Belgian marine archaeologist, Robert Sténuit, found pieces of lead sheathing from the wreck of the Armada galleass, *Girona*.[9] By the 1580s the English used a light wooden sheathing over the coat of pitch or tar for foreign-going warships, an innovation generally credited to John Hawkins; this probably delayed, but could not prevent, the worms boring through the bottom timbers nor, of course, the accumulation of external growths. Thus ships had to be drydocked or more usually beached and heeled artificially with tackles to the mastheads – 'careened' – every few months so that their bottoms could be scraped, repaired and given another coating. On occasion fires were lit beneath to hasten the anti-fouling process, sometimes with fatal results.

It does not seem likely that Howard's ships were sheathed; he reported in April

Detail of mast included in title-page drawing for the first English manual of navigation (see illustration on page 78).

after the *Ark* had been sent back to the dockyard for repairs that she was now:

mended of her leak, which was a bolt forgotten to be driven in, and the outside covered with pitch so it could not be seen; and when the sea had washed it off, then brake in the leak; and she was not well caulked in any place but now most perfect.[10]

Above the waterline the side timbers were 'paid' with a preservative mixture of oil, turpentine and resin, all, like pitch and tar, products of the Baltic; above the upper wale the sides were painted in bright coloured patterns; in the English Royal ships the Tudor colours white and green might be interspersed with contrasting reds, yellows and purples usually in geometric designs. The Royal arms were painted – probably also carved – on the flat after end of the sterncastle, probably also adorned with Tudor roses and fleur-de-lys; a carved and painted head or beast, usually a lion or dragon, was fixed at the end of the beakhead, and there might be light, domestic carving around the small arched ports along the sides of the forward and after superstructure, around the gallery, and on the arched entrances to the half-deck and foc's'le from the waist; elsewhere there was little decoration. Even the Spanish and Portuguese galleons, which had marginally more elaborate and gilded sterns, were remarkably plain by the standards of the following century. The converted cargo-ships which formed the bulk of the Spanish fleet would have had even less adornment.

All the final fitting and decorative work was done after the ship had been launched down the slipway, as also, of course, the masting and rigging. The standard sizeable cargo carrier or warship was a three-master; the largest were four-masters; there were ten of these in Howard's fleet, how many in the Spanish fleet is impossible to say, but judging by the numbers of large ships there were probably many more than 10. The three- or four-master had evolved in the latter part of the previous century from vessels with a single square driving sail set on a central main mast assisted by balancing and manoeuvring sails on short poles at bow and stern, the forward sail also square, the after one a triangular 'lateen' sail set on an angled spar. By the end of the 15th century the foremast had grown taller and set a sail which was not as large as the 'main' but was nonetheless a powerful driving sail with perhaps a small 'topsail' on a 'topmast' extended above; the balancing function forward had been taken over by a square 'spritsail' set from a boom hung beneath the angled bowsprit. The mainmast had also been extended by a 'topmast' which set a 'topsail'. The after or 'mizen' mast with its lateen sail remained small; indeed with the high aftercastles of the time it could not have grown much without unbalancing the ships. Four-masters appeared early in the 16th century and Henry VIII's great ships boasted 'topgallant' extensions above topmasts on fore, main and mizen and even a topmast extension on the aftermost 'bonaventure mizen' mast. The topsails and topgallant sails set on these high spars were narrow and tapering, and no doubt only used in the gentlest weather; ordinary trading and overseas vessels did not carry so much canvas, and it is probable it soon fell into disuse in the English royal navy too.

By Elizabeth's reign the average merchantman and medium-sized three-masted warship set a square spritsail under the bowsprit, a square foresail or fore 'course' on the foremast and fore topsail above, a square main course and main topsail on the mainmast and a lateen on the mizen; Elizabeth's larger four-masters also set topgallants on fore and main and some, like the *Ark*, appear to have set a small triangular mizen topsail.[11] The fourth, or 'bonaventure mizen' mast set a lateen sail. Carrying these high spars was made considerably safer by another innovation attributed to John Hawkins after he became Treasurer of the

Terrestrial globe of 1541, made by
Gerhard Mercator of Duisburg.

73

Navy in 1578; this was a design which allowed topmasts and topgallants to be lowered to the deck – or 'struck' – at sea. Since all the yards holding the sails could be lowered, a ship could be reduced to bare lower masts in a gale. Reefing was as yet unknown; however, the area of fore, main and mizen sails was altered by means of canvas 'bonnets' and 'drabblers' – usually spelled 'drablers' – laced along the lower edges of the sails; in very light weather both 'bonnet' and 'drabler' were added; as the wind rose, first the 'drabler', then the 'bonnet' were taken off to reduce canvas. The yards were lowered to allow this to be done from the deck.

The two chief masts, the fore and main, were stepped in a square timber frame on the keelson; the mizen, bonaventure mizen and bowsprit were stepped on strengthened deck beams. The mastheads were supported by stays leading forward to the base of the next mast ahead – in the case of the foremast to a point on the bowsprit – and by multiple back stays, shrouds and 'tackles' leading aft on both sides to 'chain wales' bolted outside the main 'wale' to take these ropes clear of the ship's side. Each backstay and shroud was set up taut by means of lanyards passing through two blocks known as 'deadman's eyes' – later 'deadeyes' – so called because instead of the usual rollers, or 'sheaves', they merely had three holes through which the lanyard was rove. The lower end of the shroud was spliced around the upper 'deadeye'; the lower 'deadeye' was attached to a chain which led down from the 'chain wale' to an eye bolted through the side frame below. Since rope stretched under strain and in differing weather conditions, it was necessary to attend to the tension in the shrouds throughout the voyage. Small tarred lengths of line called 'ratlines' were made fast across the spread of the shrouds to provide footholds for climbing. The topmast shrouds were spread out from the mast by transverse timbers bolted to the lower mast just below its head and forming part of the base of the fighting 'top' there; the shrouds were set up in the same way with deadeyes and crossed with ratlines for climbing.

The yards which spread the square sails were held to the mast by a 'parrel', a triple necklace of hardwood rollers threaded on line; vertical timber 'ribs' separated and held the three tiers in place. The parrel was a comparatively loose attachment which allowed the yard to be hoisted or lowered and angled in both vertical and horizontal planes by 'lifts' and 'braces'. The 'lifts' led from the yard ends – or yardarms – to blocks at the masthead, thence down to the deck, the 'braces' which angled the yard for the wind direction led from the yardarms aft; those from the main yard led down to blocks at the side of the poop, those from the fore yard which did not have such a clear run because of the spread of the mainsail were taken to blocks on the main stay, thence to other blocks on deck. The angle a yard could be 'braced' round – thus the angle the ship could 'point' into the wind – was restricted by the shrouds which it came up against when braced hard for either tack. Obviously the further the yard could be held out forward of the mast, the more it could be braced round before coming up against the rigging, but whether the English had such a device which might have contributed to their evident ability to sail closer to the wind than the Spanish is not clear.

Indirect leads and tackles were necessary for much of the intricate web of rigging which had been evolved for the fine adjustment and control of the sails – the 'sheets' and 'tacks' which led from the lower corners or 'clews' of the square sails to restrain the lifting, ballooning canvas, the 'bowlines' attached to the sides, or 'leeches' to hold the leading edge up into the wind when sailing close-hauled, the 'clew garnets', 'buntlines' and 'martlets' to gather up the canvas when sail was being taken in, and a score of lines whose names and purposes once familiar to every sailor are now virtually forgotten. These were led to wooden pegs or 'pins' along the side rails abreast of the mast they served and there made fast – 'belayed'. Every sailor knew by long practice which line belonged to each pin.

Galleons were neither particularly fast nor manoeuvrable except by comparison with previous round ship types, some of which, like the carrack, were still very much in use. In a fresh breeze they might make four knots if the bottom were free of growth, probably six knots in a strong breeze[12] with the sails wetted to make them draw better; above that they had to shorten sail and the heavy pitching they were subject to by virtue of their short keel length slowed them. In a gale they generally took in all sail, except the fore course, lowered the other yards to the deck, struck the topmasts – and topgallants if fitted – and ran under the foresail or a part of the foresail with the yard lowered to half mast. It was advisable to carry some head canvas since the high stern structure acted like a sail tending to bring them round into the trough of the seas; it seems, however, ships could and frequently did run under bare poles without any canvas. If running was not possible because of land or rocks downwind, or if a rising gale made it dangerous to continue, ships were brought round beam on to the wind to lie 'a-hulling'; this meant lashing the tiller down to leeward and lying with bare masts so that the force of the gale acting on the after superstructure was counter-balanced by the force of the waves on the bluff bows. Some ships refused; then it was necessary to raise some balancing canvas.

In 1957 Alan Villiers decided to test the ancient practice of lying 'a-hull' in a gale in the replica early 17th-century barque *Mayflower II* whose lines were similar to those of an Elizabethan galleon. All sail was taken in; the wind was on the starboard beam and the wheel was put hard down – thus the rudder hard a-starboard. The author, on the wheel at the time, recorded:

We lay like this for some minutes and the wind on the high after-structure held the bluff bows up into the seas and possibly gave us fractional headway. Then I was ordered to lash the wheel hard over as it was, and we stayed like that all night, very snug and secure while the gale howled in the rigging and beat up against the solid Devon timbers.[13]

There was no wheel in 16th-century ships. Northern vessels were steered by a long lever made of ash known as a 'whipstaff', which extended from the inboard end of the tiller – to which it was attached by a loose iron ring – vertically up into the space below the half deck where the helmsman stood, able to observe something of the sails through gratings or perhaps a specially arranged hood in the half deck. The staff was pivoted on an iron spindle as it came up through the 'whipscuttle' in the deck, thus when moved to starboard the tiller was swung to larboard – or port – and vice versa. The helmsman's compass was housed in a panelled stand known as a 'bitakle' fixed just before the whipstaff; it was furnished with a light for use by night.

Spanish vessels, perhaps because of the several decks aft which would not have permitted the helmsman to see out, seem to have been steered by means of purchases rove from the tiller to the side frames; northern vessels used such 'relieving tackles' in heavy weather. In both cases the officer of the watch out on deck had to keep his eyes lifting to the wind in the sails, for although a ship's canvas was trimmed to a fine balance to enable her to hold her set course with scarcely a touch on the helm, there were many occasions, sailing close-hauled, running before a quartering sea or in changeable conditions when helm was very necessary.

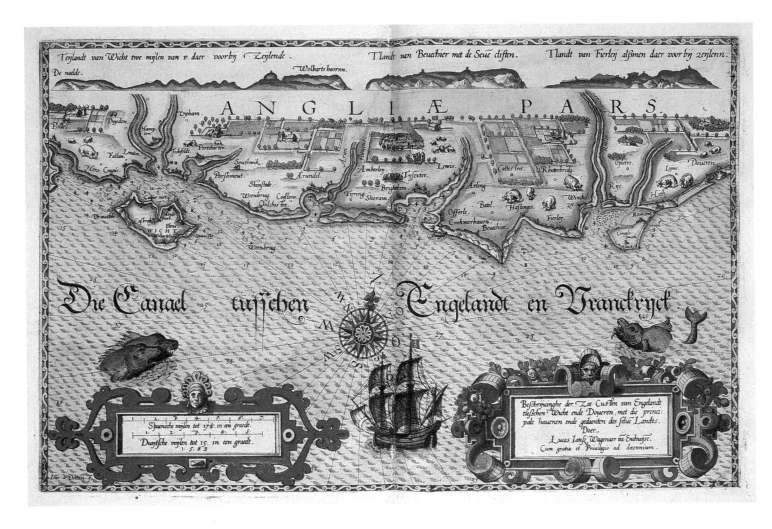

The Dutch pilot Lucas Janszoon Wagenaer published the first atlas of charts and sailing directions for the coasts of North-west Europe in 1584 and 1585. An English translation, *The Mariner's Mirrour*, appeared in 1588 shortly after the Armada campaign. This spread delineates the South Coast of England and Isle of Wight.

The baggy shape of the flax sails which stretched in strong blows scarcely permitted making way into the wind; with the weather leeches hauled forward by the bowlines a ship might be able to head within about six points (67½°) of the wind, but her drift to leeward would lose her at least a point so that she could make good at most 10 degrees; since she would not travel at much over five knots even with a clean bottom it can be seen that if tide or current were against her she would lose ground.[14] For this reason tidal streams were the most important factor in coastal navigation and knowledge of the tides was a basic for shipmasters.

The contrary winds and tides inevitable at some time in a voyage of any length meant that while a vessel might make five or six knots on good days – certainly while running down the trade winds or in the band of westerlies south of the Cape of Good Hope – it could not hope to average much more than two or three knots for an ocean voyage as a whole, and on Mediterranean voyages from northern waters frequently as little as one knot.[15]

The same baggy, ballooning shape of the sails which made it impossible to point well into the wind, made going about by 'tacking' a slow and cumbersome manoeuvre. There are no records of how long it took to tack a sizeable vessel – perhaps quarter of an hour, but that is guesswork based on the time taken by ships of a rather different shape in succeeding centuries. It seems from Sir William Gorgas' account that if an English warship took this length of time a Spanish galleon must have taken half an hour at least; it is by no means impossible: an English shipmaster in the early 1600s wrote of 'the loss of time in hawking of (ships) crosse by the wind.'[16] At one point in the evolution the ship would be making sternway with her tiller reversed to bring her head round. Of course she might not come round; the terms 'in irons' and 'dead in the wind upon a stay' were long in use to describe a failed tack.[17]

There is much more that could be said about the relatively primitive performance and materials of ships despite the complex craftsmanship and ingenuity that went into them. Their shapeliness has probably never been surpassed: the three-dimensional curves of the sails full of wind, the round and sheer of the bulwarks narrowing to the poop, the bend of topmasts framed in the swing and spread of the rigging transformed them into living works of art. But they were frail works, subject to all the uncertainties and hazards of the elements they rode, virtually becoming a part of them. Given the vulnerability of all ships, there seems little doubt that English ships enjoyed a reputation above all others at this date; when William Harrison – like Sir William Gorgas – recorded 'that for strength, assurance, nimbleness and swiftness of sailing, there are no vessels in the world to be compared with ours',[18] he was not merely indulging insular conceit; there is much evidence to suggest he was right.

As for navigating vessels from one place to another, there were two distinct branches of the art, coastal and oceanic; the first was acquired by long experience of shore marks and the positions of shoals, the direction of tides, times of high water at ports at different stages of the moon, depths of water and the nature of the bottom brought up on the sounding lead; if a shipmaster could read he probably had a notebook called a Rutter compiled from his own and others' observations of the compass courses to be steered between the headlands on his usual routes. There were also printed Rutters, in which the Dutch were by this date predominant: in 1584 an English translation of two of the Dutch northern waters' Rutters was printed under the title *The Safeguard of Sailors*; besides 'Courses, Distances, Depths, Soundings, Floods and Ebbs', this was illustrated with woodcuts showing the coastline and hills in silhouette as they appeared from seawards. It was dedicated, with some foresight, to Lord Howard of Effingham.

Voyages were made from headland to headland – known as 'caping' – finding somewhere to shelter if it seemed a storm was blowing up, making an offing from the land if there was no safe haven. It was a craft whose only instruments were the magnetic compass, the sounding lead and line, a sand glass to tell the hours of the watch and perhaps keep a rough account of the courses made good, and a wooden board attached to a length of line known as a 'log'; this last was for measuring speed through the water. The board was hove over the stern and the line allowed to run out freely for a certain time. The length which ran out was measured, then scaled up to give the speed.

Charts had been printed from copperplate engraving since the 1540s, but were chiefly used by Mediterranean, Spanish and Portuguese pilots and particularly for oceanic navigation; they were not necessary for 'caping' voyages, and northern seafarers, if they bothered with them at all, had manuscript 'Sea Cartes' which were small outline maps of sections of the coast showing the ports and marked with lines of compass bearings emanating from various useful points.

The accuracy of some of these may be gauged from Howard's comment that July when spreading his fleet to watch the mouth of the Channel: 'Whatsoever hath been made of the S(leeve, it) is another manner of thing than it was taken for; we find it by experience and daily observation to be an hundred miles over.'[19] Two years earlier Howard had convinced the Privy Council that a

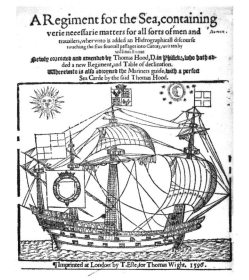

Title-page of *A Regiment for the Sea*, a navigation manual by William Bourne of Gravesend, first published in London in 1574.

compilation of charts and sailing directions published in 1584–5 by the Dutch pilot Lucas Janszoon Wagenaer, should be translated into English and printed; but this work was not completed until a few months after the Armada campaign.

Those masters who found it useful to keep a reckoning of their position out of sight of land because of the distance from one cape to the next, or who were forced away from the land by the weather, probably used a traverse board. This was marked with lines radiating from the centre to each of the compass points. Holes were bored at regular intervals along these lines and the helmsman, each time he turned the half-hour glass, put a peg in the hole corresponding to the course he had been steering. At the end of the watch the navigator chalked the courses on a slate, together with an estimate of the distance run which he may have gained by heaving the log or more probably guessed by eye and experience; after making allowances for leeway and tide he entered the resultant course and distance made good in his journal or log book. Mediterranean and Iberian navigators were more advanced in the use of calculation and pre-worked 'traverse' tables than the majority of English shipmasters.[20]

Oceanic navigation was a different matter; it too depended on estimation for longitude, but the plotting of latitude was scientific. The method had been pioneered by the Portuguese during their campaign of discovery down the African coast and into the Indian Ocean during the previous century. At the beginning of the African voyages the Portuguese pilots had determined their latitude in the customary way by observation of the angular height of the Pole star above the horizon, making an allowance by rule for its distance from the celestial pole. As they reached further down the coast they could no longer see the Pole star, and it was their drive to substitute a method using observations of the sun that led to the production of volumes of tables known as *The Regiment of the Sun*. These listed the sun's declination – that is, its displacement from the plane of the equator – for every day of the year.

To find his latitude, the navigator used a sea astrolabe to observe the sun's highest altitude at noon. The astrolabe was a brass instrument in the shape of a circle graduated in degrees of arc with an arm pivoting at the centre; there were two flanges on the arm, each with a sighting hole. To use the instrument, the navigator suspended it at about waist height from a lanyard through a ring at the top, then rotated the sighting arm until the ray of sunlight through the hole in the top flange fell on the hole in the lower flange; he then read off the altitude where the pointer at the end of the arm cut the scale. This needed a great deal of experience and skill on the unsteady deck of a ship, probably with a wind disturbing the alignment of the instrument; in hazy weather when the outline of the sun itself had to be observed through the sighting holes it needed steady assistants, and at all times great patience, since without any accurate means of telling the time, observations had to start well before noon was expected. Having found the highest altitude, the navigator consulted his 'Regiment' to find the declination that day and either added it to his observed altitude or subtracted it to find his latitude.

There was no way of finding longitude since the only method of time-keeping was by sand glass or sundial corrected for season and latitude, and neither were in any sense accurate. Estimates of the course and distance run allowed a reckoning to be kept, but after several days with varying courses and speeds this became very approximate; consequently ocean voyaging was commonly completed by 'latitude sailing', that is getting to the latitude of the destination then steering east or west along the parallel until land was raised. If this was not convenient because of the prevailing winds, a landfall might be sought above or below the

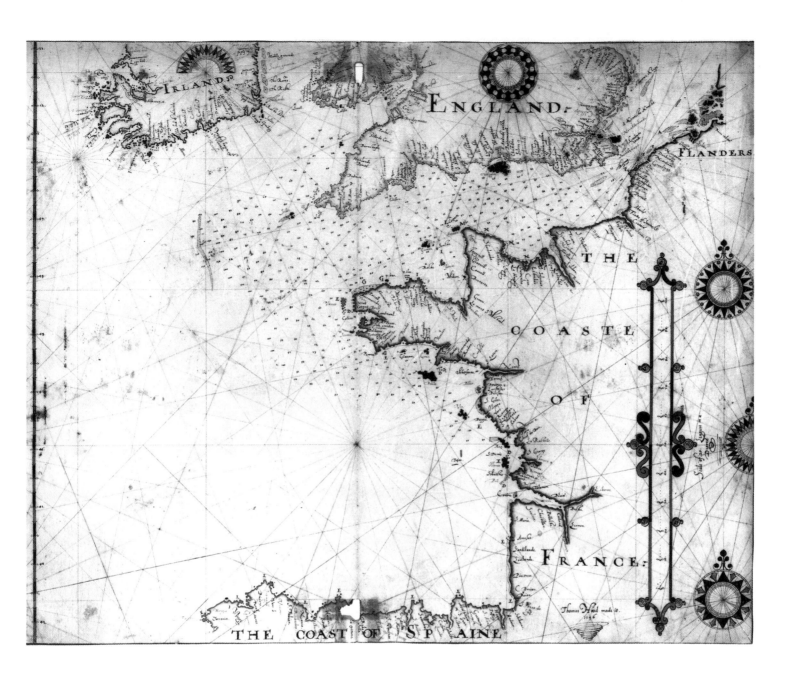

Chart of the Bay of Biscay and English Channel, drawn by Thomas Hood in 1596. Hood was a shore-based mathematician; this chart shows the increasingly scientific approach to navigation exhibited by the English at this time.

destination and the voyage completed with a coasting passage. Medina Sidonia's pilots did not have any difficulty finding the entrance to the English Channel since they were able to hold northerly courses with the prevailing westerly weather, then steer northeasterly as their observations of the sun told them they were in the latitude to make a landfall on the southwest corner of England.

7

The Guns, the Gunner and the Crew

Ships' armament was in the same mid-way evolutionary stage as the vessels themselves, similarly non-standard and diverse. Guns were of two chief types, cast or forged; there was a bewildering variety of classes within each group, however, and an almost infinite variation in the size and shape of individual pieces. The most powerful were cast from iron or bronze – an alloy of copper and tin also defined as 'brass'. They were categorised both by the size of shot they threw and by the ratio of their length to the diameter of the bore, or 'calibre'. The longest in relation to calibre, hence to size of shot, were known as culverin – Spanish *culebrina*; they varied from about 24 to over 30 calibres in length. A full culverin might be anything from 10 feet – sometimes less – to over 13 feet long – the average perhaps 11 feet – with a bore of 5–5½″, and throwing a 17½–18 lb iron ball. Next in this class, demi culverins, might be from eight to 12 feet long with a bore of 4½–4¾″, throwing a 9 lb ball; next down in size, sakers, threw a 5 lb ball and minions – seven and a half to eight feet long – threw a 3–4 lb ball.

The cannon – Spanish *canon*-type was rather shorter for the size of bore – a ratio of anything from 16–22 calibres. A full cannon might be 11 feet, the same as an average culverin, with a bore of 8″ instead of the culverin's 5–5½″; it threw a ball weighing from 40 lb upwards; the gun itself weighed 3 tons upwards against the culverin's 2 tons. Few whole cannon were carried by either side. A demi cannon was 10 feet long with a bore of 6–7½″ and threw a 30 lb ball. This was closest to the type which came to be standardised in the 18th-century heyday of fighting sail as the main battery gun of a ship of the line. The Spaniards also had a quarter cannon – *cuarto de canon*, Colin Martin has found two pieces answering to this description in the remains of the *Gran Grifon*, the flagship of Medina Sidonia's squadron of store ships which was wrecked on Fair Isle; they are eight feet long with a bore of 4″, throwing a ball about the size of a demi culverin's, but with a length to bore ratio of 22:1 putting them into the cannon category.[1]

None of these measurements or ratios were absolute; there were greater varieties within each category than between the two categories; as a contemporary put it 'the founders never cast them so exactly but they differ two or three hundredweight in a piece'.[2]

Besides these two main battering categories for a stand-off artillery duel there were lighter-metalled, shorter and wider pieces known as Periers with a length of less than 10 times their bore – generally throwing a stone shot – and mortars which might have a length as little as one and a half times their bore. These were designed for a very much smaller powder charge, indeed most Periers were cast with a short section of smaller bore or 'chamber' at the extreme inner, or breech end of the barrel for the powder charge. They were carried for short-range work, the smaller varieties as anti-personnel and anti-rigging weapons throwing a scattering of small shot.

All these guns were cast in one piece with a closed breech end, hence had to be loaded from the muzzle end. The powder was inserted first and rammed down to the breech with a long-handled rammer; at sea the powder charge was made up below decks, and before the action if possible, into canvas cylinders because of the obvious convenience, and the dangers and difficulties of ladling powder into a long barrel on a rolling deck, probably in some wind. Long-handled ladles were carried, nonetheless, for every gun. After the cartridge and a 'wad' of old rope junk, the ball or other projectile was rolled in and also rammed home with a wad of junk to keep it in place. Next the gunner took his powder horn containing fine powder and filled the 'vent' – a hole drilled down through the breech of the piece into the bore where the cartridge was. The gun was ready to be fired.

The pieces were mounted on timber carriages, in the English service traditionally elm. The guns' 'trunnions' – spindles projecting horizontally from either side of the barrel slightly forward of the point of balance – rested in slots cut for them in the two vertical side pieces, or 'cheeks' of the carriage, and were prevented from jumping out by iron bands across the top. The cheeks, which extended towards the breech end in the familiar pattern of descending steps, were mortised into a flat, rectangular bed. Two axletrees crossed this bed and were similarly mortised; timber wheels or 'trucks' turned on the projecting ends; the trucks at the forward end of the carriage were rather larger than the trucks at the rear to compensate for the camber of the deck down towards the ship's side.

The weight of the breech may have rested on a baulk of timber placed across the steps of the two cheeks with wedges, or 'quoins', used to alter the elevation of the gun; alternatively the weight may have been taken on blocks and quoins placed on the flat bed of the carriage. In either case the piece would have been 'laid' for elevation during the ship's run in towards the enemy; as the ship came round to deliver the broadside the angle of heel would have changed; no doubt the gunners allowed for this when they laid their pieces. Aiming – or 'training' – involved levering the carriage with crowbars across the direction of travel of the wheels, hence was neither quick nor precise; there is no doubt from contemporary English accounts that it was practised; however, the art of pointing the piece consisted in allowing the ship itself to bring the gun on target, even to the extent of calling out directions to the helmsman; thus the Elizabethan sea officer, William Monson:

a principal thing in a gunner at sea is to be a good helmsman, and to call up to him at the helm to loff or bear up to have his better level and to observe the heaving and setting of the sea to take aim at the enemy.[3]

Whether Monson was using the word 'level' to indicate the elevation of the gun or its aim at the target, as in the small arms drill of the time 'level your piece', is not clear. The method is plain, though, and it was a method that did not alter; towards the end of the following century, a gunnery manual instructed the sea gunner to stand to the left of his piece with his right foot on the carriage; then: 'looking over the Peece . . . give fire . . . when you see from the Breech of your Peece to the Muzzle and so to the Mark.'[4]

A length of line impregnated with combustible material, known as a 'match', was used to fire the guns; this was lit before the action and secured in the end of a staff called a linstock, some of which have been found with their lower end finishing in a spike for free-standing. When the gunner saw his piece lined on the target, he blew the smouldering end of the match to a brighter glow and placed it to the powder in the 'touch hole' or vent; there was an appreciable spluttering interval while the fire passed down the train of powder to the charge inside, then

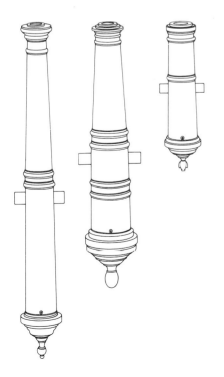

Culverins (left) were from 25 to over 30 times longer than the diameter of their bore, cannon (centre) some 18–22 times and cannon-perier (right) less than 10 times longer.

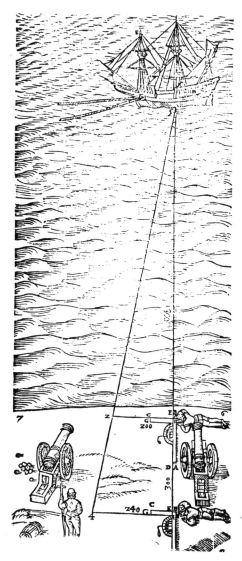

Illustration from Lucar's Appendix to the gunnery manual, the *Colloquies of Tartaglia* (1588). This illustration shows the type of sixteenth-century field gun-carriage on which a number of the Spanish Armada heavy guns were probably mounted.

the slamming roar of the explosion, a spurt of fire and smoke from the vent and the ball emerged from the muzzle wrapped in swathes of grey-white smoke.

Did these great cast guns leap back in recoil as they did in Nelson's day? There is no certainty on the point; the probability – it might be said the overwhelming probability – is that they did not.[5] In the first place there was the little space; the extreme breadth of the gun deck of a sizeable English naval ship was 30–35 feet, leaving at the most 28–33 feet from side to side between the gun port sills, thus 14–16½ feet from the port sill to the centre line over the keel. Yet the main hatch, its coamings and the stanchions there must have occupied four feet at the least either side of the centre line, leaving 10–12½ feet of clear deck to the port sills; a culverin was 10–13 feet long, hence the culverins here – and seven years after the Armada it was proposed that 12 culverins should be carried on this gun deck, six a side – must have been brought up – if allowed to recoil – with their muzzles either still outside the port or just inside.

Turning to documentary evidence, a pamphlet by one John Montgomery drawing the lessons of the Armada campaign, states that in action mariners should work with the gunners 'to traverse, run out and haul in the guns'.[6] This suggests that the guns were *hauled* in to be loaded after firing. In the 18th century, when guns were allowed to run themselves in with their own recoil momentum, they were brought up at the desired limit by stout 'breeching' ropes which passed around the breech and were made fast to rings in the ships' side frames. The first English nautical dictionary, by Henry Mainwaring, published early in the 17th century defines breechings as used to 'lash fast the ordnance to the ship's side'; it continues, 'these we do not use in fight.' If these heavy ropes were not used to restrain the guns in recoil what method could have been used? The pieces weighed two tons. The same dictionary defines gunners' tackles as purchases used 'to haul in and out the ordnance.'[7]

There are three possibilities: either the guns were allowed to recoil after firing, and were brought up somehow short of the stanchions, pumps, hatch-coaming, or they were lashed fast in the firing position by their side tackles, and were hauled in with the same tackles after firing so that they could be loaded from the deck; or they were lashed fast in the firing position throughout the course of the action and were loaded from outboard – that is by men clambering out and having the sponge, cartridge, rammer, balls and wads passed out to them through the port. There is documentary evidence to show that guns were loaded from outboard in the Portuguese and Danish services in the 17th century, and there is a drawing by W. van de Velde showing this happening on a Dutch ship in port; one man is sitting astride a projecting gun barrel, another is perched on a wale and both appear to be using rammers to load their piece. Recent tests by Major J. G. D. Elvin, however, have indicated that loading while sitting astride a gun barrel is not possible; the weight of the long staves of sponge and rammer proved too much for the strongest who attempted it: Elvin's conclusion was: 'it is absolutely impossible to sponge and ram cannon as Van de Velde has shown.'[8]

There is no question from documentary evidence that outboard loading *was* practised; perhaps the loading number went over the side with a bowline around him and perched beneath the projecting barrel; perhaps lines were made fast to the staves of sponge and rammer and he was assisted from on deck.

However this may be, it was perfectly possible to fire a heavy gun on a non-recoil principle since this is known to have been done with 32-pounder carronades in the early 19th century. Assuming contemporary range tables more or less accurate these would have had a recoil energy of some 9,600 foot/lb against only 5,100 foot/lb for a 16th-century culverin.[9] In view of the dangers

These sketches by William van de Velde surely substantiate the practice of loading great guns from outboard.

inherent in allowing guns weighing two tons apiece to charge about on the cramped and pitching decks of an Elizabethan warship, it seems highly probable that they were lashed hard against the port sill before firing, and only loosed and hauled in in a controlled manner by their side tackles afterwards; those guns in really tight positions at bow and stern were probably loaded from outboard.

Against this supposition there is a remark by Sir William Wynter in a letter written during the Armada campaign about 'a hurt that I received in my hip by the reversing of one of our demi-cannons in the fight.'[10] This sounds extremely like a recoil. Perhaps different gunners practised different methods; there is little doubt this was the case. However, the argument remains very open.

The documentary evidence for Spanish and Portuguese methods of mounting and firing their guns is equally difficult to interpret. There is no doubt that they used field carriages aboard ship rather than the special shipboard carriages described above well into the next century. Moreover, spoked, field-carriage wheels have been found by Colin Martin in the wreck of the *Trinidad Valencera* of the Levant squadron of the Armada, and from their position hard by a 7¼" calibre bronze cannon he has concluded that the piece was mounted on the carriage of which the wheels formed a part.[11] Since they are five feet in diameter, and the cannon and carriage together might have measured up to 20 feet from the muzzle to the end of the trail, it is clear that it could not have been allowed to recoil; it is difficult even to imagine such a cumbersome and potentially top-heavy monster being hauled inboard to load. It must have been lashed fast at right-angles to the ship's side and aimed by the ship's helmsman bringing it on target. However, inventories of guns aboard Spanish ships captured by the English suggest that the majority were mounted 'on their carriages a-shipboard'.[12] It seems, therefore, that there might not have been very much difference between the Spanish and English gun mountings so far as the more modern effective pieces were concerned.

For both sides the process of reloading these great cast pieces, whether from outboard or by hauling them in, was a long business with due interval left for the piece to cool. It is for this reason that the other chief category of gun, forged, or 'built up' was important. These pieces were constructed on an entirely different principle; their barrels, or 'halls' were simple tubes, open at both ends, formed from bars or strips of wrought iron typically 1½–3½" wide, ¼–½" thick, arranged lengthwise like the staves of a barrel and forged and welded under the hammer over a mandrel. Heated rings of iron, often in groups of three, were placed around the tube so formed, usually at close intervals of 3–6" and burred down at the edges while still hot; as they cooled, they 'shrank', gripping the tube and reinforcing it against the pressure which would be built up inside as the gun was fired. The ends of the strips beneath were then hammered up over the muzzle and breech rings. That was the traditional way of making these 'built-up' barrels. However, technology had advanced to the stage where they were also formed from a single sheet of iron forged into a tube, then similarly bound with reinforcing rings.[13]

The 'chamber' containing the powder charge was a separate forging or casting, in shape like a beer tankard on its side, whose open end was formed to fit snugly into the breech end of the barrel. Originally both barrel and chamber were held in a wooden bed or 'stock' carved out of a single log of oak or elm to take them. A solid 'butt' at the breech end was left above the hollowed section so that the chamber could be wedged into place against it and retained when the piece was fired. The barrel was held in place in the stock by broad iron straps bolted to the timber or by square projections mortised in.

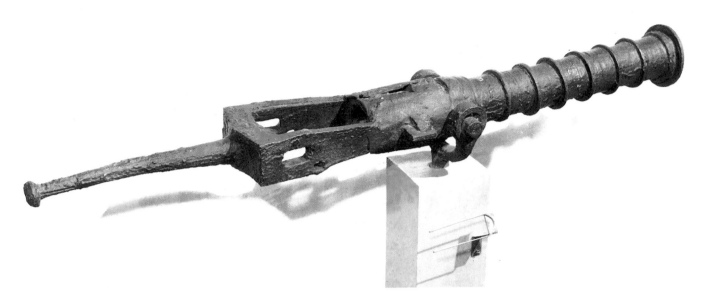

Wrought iron, breech-loading swivel gun (from the first half of the sixteenth century) mounted on a wooden post. Chamber and forelock to hold the chamber in place are missing.

Compared with the thickness of metal at the breech end of a cast gun where the explosion of powder took place – 1⅛ times the diameter of the bore – the chamber wall of a built-up gun was thin; and since the joint between chamber and barrel was always a source of gas-escape and the wedge or bolt holding the chamber in position against the force of the explosion was a frequent source of weakness, breech-loaders could not compare with cast guns for power. They did have a tremendous advantage in speed of loading however; each was provided with at least two chambers, so that one could be charged below decks and brought up ready for insertion directly the other had been removed after firing and a wad and ball placed in the breech end of the barrel. For this reason, although the heavier breech-loaders were perhaps obsolescent, the lighter pieces of this type, known in England as fowlers, slings, bases and murderers – in Spain *esmeriles*, *versos* or *peteraras* – were the preferred armament for close-range, clearing an enemy's decks before boarding, or defending against enemy boarders. They were loaded with iron 'dice shot' which spread like shotgun pellets. John Hawkins' son, Richard, who was as active at sea against the Spaniards as his father, extolled fowlers, bases and murderers 'for that their execution and speedy charging and discharging is of great moment.'[14]

There were a few of these smaller pieces still with wooden stocks, but by far the majority were all metal, the chamber held in a wrought iron extension with an open top shrunk or welded around the breech end of the barrel; a horizontal slot from side to side at the rear of this chamber-holder allowed an iron slide, known as a 'forelock', to be inserted to wedge the chamber in position. This was generally put in from the right hand side; since it was apt to be ejected with killing force when the piece was fired, the vent was generally placed on the left top of the chamber so that the gunner might be clear of the danger – not, of course, of the danger from an adjacent piece.

In action these guns were mounted with a simple swivel attachment consisting of an iron spike which dropped into a vertical hole bored in the ship's side rail or a port sill of the fore or after castle; the upper end of the spike branched into a stirrup-shaped fork whose arms came up either side of the barrel to support and enclose the 'trunnions'; the 'swivel' gun thus mounted could be pointed and elevated over wide angles with one hand by means of an iron tail piece welded to the rear of the chamber holder; many swivel guns show sighting marks notched at the muzzles. With its rapid rate of fire the breech-loading swivel was undoubtedly a potent weapon at close quarters, and a great number of the 2000 or so small Spanish guns must have been of this type.[15]

The English, of course, did not intend to allow it to come to close quarters; they put their faith in the heavy cast guns of the cannon and culverin type, in which – as shown – they probably had an overall superiority, almost certainly a huge superiority ship for ship. In theory the culverins with their greater length/bore ratio had a greater range than cannon and demi cannon; this has been disputed by one recent authority on the grounds that the black powder in use in the 16th century was fast-burning and as a result gave no additional impulse to the shot beyond a length of travel of 12 to 18 times the diameter of the bore; guns like the culverin with a length of barrel some 30 times their bore gained no advantage over cannon, therefore, because the shot had reached its maximum speed within the cannon length of 18 times the bore; according to this argument both cannon and culverin balls emerged with precisely the same 'muzzle velocity', hence travelled much the same distance for any given angle of elevation. The reason for making the culverin type so long, it is asserted, was to increase the pressure on the molten metal at the breech end while casting – since guns were cast in vertical moulds, breech down – and so produce a denser, stronger metal in this vital breech area where the explosion of powder took place.[16] This argument has been challenged, as has the argument about the rate of burning of 16th-century powder, which of course cannot now be tested. The Elizabethan officer, Monson, certainly believed that longer pieces shot further 'as the shorter piece will spue her powder'.[17]

Fortunately the discussion is largely academic; with the inaccuracies cast into the bore of the guns of the time, together with the inaccuracies due to the spin imparted to the ball by the last part of the barrel it happened to touch on its way out – for it was always cast considerably smaller than the bore so that it would not get stuck – and the greater inaccuracies inherent in fixing the elevation and aiming the pieces from heeling and moving ships – the difficulty indeed in allowing for the time lapse between putting the lighted match to the powder and the charge going off – there is no need to discuss ranges outside, say 300 to 500 yards so far as sea battles are concerned. Since both cannon and culverins could fire over 2,000 yards the only point at issue is whether the culverin had an advantage within the effective ranges out to 500 yards or so.

Muzzle velocity is a factor here since the higher the velocity the flatter the trajectory of the ball and the greater the 'point blank' range at which the gun could be levelled at its target instead of being given an angle of elevation. In the heyday of fighting sail this horizontal range was of the greatest importance; when the skill of guns' crews was equal, ships armed with the longer horizontal range broadside almost invariably beat their shorter-range opponent; this was demonstrated especially in a few cases when frigates armed with carronades – the latter-day Periers – were defeated by vessels armed with cannon throwing a lighter ball but with a flatter trajectory.

Elizabethan gunners certainly believed that culverin and demi culverin had a longer range and a longer point-blank range than cannon and demi cannon; few range tables agree but the point-blank ranges of the two were listed as about 400 and 340 yards respectively, an advantage to the culverin and demi culverin of 60 yards.[18] This cannot have been tested with the precision one would expect for modern range tables; no two guns were alike; the 'windage', or difference between the diameter of ball and gun bore, would have been different, so would the weight of powder charges. However, there is no doubt there was sufficient experience of artillery by that date for gunners to know whether or not longer

Lionel Willis' representation of an English 'race-built' warship of 1586–88. For the sake of clarity various features have been omitted: these include the boats over the gratings in the waist between the fo'c'sle and the half-deck; the substantial bollards known as the 'knights' – since they were often carved with head and helmet – used to secure the halyards and top ropes for hoisting and lowering the yards, topmasts and t'gallantmasts; the pin-rails for 'belaying' the running rigging, either by the mast or more probably secured to the side timbers; and the tackles and 'breeching ropes used to manoeuvre and secure the great guns on their wheeled carriages. The carriage guns on the upper deck would probably be minions or sakers, on the 'orlope' deck below, which was both main gun-deck and berthing space, culverin and demi-culverin or even demi-cannons would be mounted where the ship was widest, and perhaps as bow- and stern-chasers. The 'orlope' deck at mid-length would lie about two feet above the water line, the lower ledge of the gunports there about five feet above the water when the ship was on an even keel, hence in blowing weather it could be hazardous to use the main battery guns. Below the 'orlope' was the hold; the huge 'tuns' used to transport wine – the theoretical stowage capacity of which was used as a measurement of a ship's size – are shown here with the ship's fresh water supply, stowed below the main hatch directly on top of the stone ballast and forward of the galley, here fitted on a 'false orlope'.

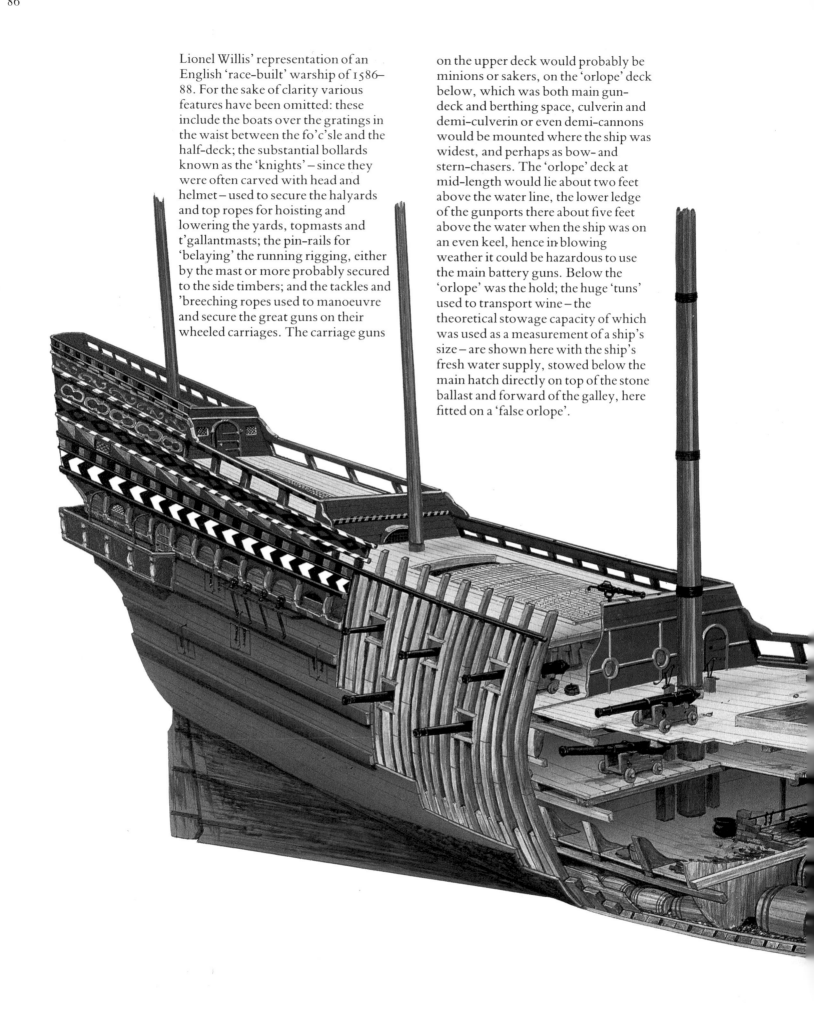

Just abaft the mainmast a bulkhead rose to close off the space below the half deck. There were no exposed companionways up to the half deck as in later sailing men of war since this was literally a castle to be defended if the ship was boarded and entered. A breech-loading swivel in the illustration does duty for the many that would have been mounted along the rails here. The half deck was reached by a pair of companionways just forward of the mizen; another pair of companionways went down to the 'orlope'. There were other companionways forward in the waist by the break of the foc's'le. The carpenter's and bosun's store rooms and powder magazine below the fore-peak were reached by vertical ladders through square 'scuttles' in the orlope, as were the breadrooms and captain's and officers' store-rooms below the gun-room aft. There is some doubt about the exact arrangement of the accommodation aft, but the main features are described on pages 90–91 with Lionel Willis' illustration of a Spanish warship.

The rigged version shown in the inset is illustrated again on page 114 where a description of the sails and rigging appears.

Iron demi-culverin, English c. 1570–
80, length 11 feet.

guns reached further, or more probably could be charged with sufficient powder to reach further; the probability must be that with the powder and charges of the time the culverin could achieve a longer point-blank range – therefore did have a higher muzzle velocity. Of course there is a possibility that this was an error repeated in different gunnery manuals, so attaining the status of Holy Writ.

Accepting that the Elizabethan gunners were practical men, not quacks, the culverin's higher muzzle velocity would have had some importance at the extreme ranges for effective gunnery; a modern gunnery computer fed with data from 16th-century range tables and programmed to simulate the flight of balls from a demi cannon and a culverin, both elevated five degrees, shows that the cannon ball – reaching 500 yards in three seconds against two seconds for the culverin ball – would have dropped 115 feet below a line extended out from the bore, the culverin ball only 53 feet below the line;[19] in other words the culverin only needed about half the cannon's angle of elevation above the target at this range. Whether this difference would have had much significance given the clumsy arrangements for elevating the guns, and the shifts in wind pressure, thus heel, during the moments before firing, must be doubtful. Nevertheless, it does suggest that the culverin-type had a marginal advantage at the extremes of effective range; the closer the vessels came to real effective range inside 200 yards, where the shot might expect to hit rather than fly over, or short of the enemy hull, the less the culverin's advantage; indeed at this distance the inaccuracies of the guns and elevating apparatus would have cancelled out any possible advantage.

This theoretical conclusion is borne out by the evolution of naval armaments: the culverin enjoyed great popularity in the immediate aftermath of the Armada campaign, but early in the next century gave way to the cannon, which remained the main battery gun throughout the rest of the life of the sailing warship. The reasons were put by Richard Hawkins:

To reach far in fights at sea is to little effect; for he that purposeth to annoy his enemy must not shoot at random, nor at point blank . . . neither must he spend his shot nor powder but where a pot gun may reach his contrary; how much the nearer, so much the better.[20]

At such ranges inside 100 yards, the culverin-type had no advantage in accuracy, and its smaller shot and higher muzzle velocity were both disadvantages. Here is Richard Hawkins writing of his experiences in the *Dainty* against two larger Spanish vessels in 1594; he fought them for three days before submitting with all but 16 of his complement either dead or wounded:

. . . although their artillery were longer, weightier and many more than ours, and in truth did pierce with greater violence; yet ours being of greater bore and carrying weightier and greater shot, was of more importance and of greater effect for sinking and spoiling, for the smaller shot passeth through and maketh but his hole and harmeth that which lieth in his way; but the greater shaketh and shivereth all it meeteth, and with the splinters, or that which it encountreth, many times doth more hurt than with his proper circumference . . .[21]

Nevertheless at the time of the Armada the culverin was the preferred type in the Protestant navies – or it might be put that the lighter cast guns most suitable for use aboard ship were always made with long culverin-proportion barrels – apart, of course, from the Perier and mortar types for the upper decks. Howard's fleet carried by estimation, 130 culverin, 200 demi culverin and 220 sakers, against only 54 demi cannon, one whole cannon and 38 Periers. This seems to have been absolutely and relatively a larger proportion of the culverin-type than carried in Medina Sidonia's fleet.[22]

The majority of the English guns were iron, for England had a large and efficient iron gun-founding industry. Henry VIII had established it by importing experts from the Low Countries; the raw materials were found in Sussex and Kent – good quality ore deposits together with forests to provide the fuel for smelting. By Elizabeth's reign England was in the forefront of the iron armaments industry with eight foundries producing guns famous for their cheapness and reliability; at £10–£12 a ton, they were a fifth to a quarter the price of bronze, or 'brass' ordnance, and although they had to be cast thicker, thus heavier, because the iron was more brittle and liable to burst, this was more than offset by the price advantage – especially for a poor, interloping country such as England. Sir Walter Raleigh called English guns 'a jewel of great value'; indeed they were. Their manufacture and sale was hedged about with restrictions to try and ensure they did not go to foreigners; foundries were required to send in annual returns of production; private persons buying guns had to provide sureties they would not resell them abroad. Naturally the system leaked, by how much is not known, but there is evidence of substantial purchases by Spain.[23]

Besides round shot, which was cast at the same foundries and cost about £8 a ton, cross-bar shot to tear rigging and sails was regular naval issue; this was five times as expensive – to be expected from the considerable work involved: each cross-bar shot for a culverin cost five shillings, for a demi cannon six shillings and eight pence.[24] Privateers regularly carried 'langerill' shot for the same purpose; these were canisters filled with small, jagged pieces of iron and with sufficiently thin sides to burst open and allow the contents to spray out; they scythed down exposed men as effectively as they chopped up rigging. The naval equivalent seems to have been the 'dice shot' for the smaller pieces.

The tactics developed to bring broadside guns into action depended on first working to windward of the enemy – gaining the 'weather gage' – then sailing

Lionel Willis' representation of a galleon in the Spanish fleet, somewhat higher in bow and stern-castles than 'race-built' English warships and correspondingly clumsier to handle. The 'cut-away' section of the illustration shows the 'gun room', which is stepped down from the level of the orlope deck, with a smallish 'stern-chaser' mounted on a ship-board carriage. At the forward end of the tiller extending in from the rudder, a 'whipstaff' can be seen passing up through a 'whip-scuttle' in the upper deck – where it is pivoted – to the 'steerage' room or space where the helmsman or helmsmen stood, probably on a raised platform. The timber wainscotted 'bittacle' holding the compass can be seen just before the whipstaff, and above it an arched opening through which the helmsman could look through the half-deck gratings at the set of the upper sails; it is probable he relied more on the orders of the officer of the watch. Whether many Spanish vessels with their high after castles actually employed the whipstaff seems doubtful; the English and Dutch certainly did by this date, but probably the majority of Spanish

vessels relied for steering on tackles rove from the end of the tiller to the side frames with parties of men hauling or slacking to instructions.

Below the end of the tiller, the 'scuttle' can be seen giving access to the magazine which, to judge by the explosion in the *San Salvador* was aft in Spanish ships.

Immediately above the 'gun room' was the Captain's, or in a flagship, Admiral's cabin, no doubt splendidly furnished and decorated and fitted with a verandah or 'gallery' outside. Above the Captain's cabin and below the 'quarter deck' which ran from the mizen to the stern above the half deck, were the other officers' cabins.

Forward of the cut-away section the 'chain wales' for the shrouds can be seen extending out above the main battery gun ports, and above these the 'secondary battery' of breech-loaders can be seen projecting through half-deck ports.

The rigged version shown in the inset is illustrated again on page 115 where a description of the sails and rigging appears.

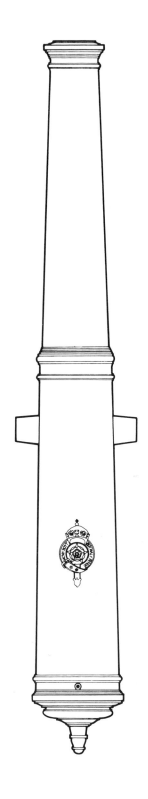

down on him in a rough line ahead or group until within effective range, when the leading ship 'luffed up' – turned towards the wind – firing its bow, then its broadside guns as they came on target. It then tacked while the following ship in the line opened its broadside on the same target ship, then tacked, and so on until the whole group had fired one side of guns; the leading ship then returned and gave the enemy its other broadside, again followed by the others in their turn, so, as Raleigh put it, 'keeping the enemy under a perpetual shot.' It was a method which used the manoeuvrability of the race-built ships to overcome the slowness of loading the cast guns of the battery. It was also a method of concentration fire, for all the attacking ships fired on one or two of the 'windermost' enemy which, as Raleigh put it in his 'Fighting Instructions':

. . . you shall either batter in pieces, or force him or them to bear up and so entangle them [with others] and drive them foul of one another to their utter confusion.[25]

These instructions are dated 1617, but there is every reason to believe they merely repeated or formalised tactics which had been developed by the northern sea rovers and which were employed by Howard's fleet in the Armada campaign. With such tactics a numerically smaller, but more nimble group of ships could prevail over a more unwieldy mass.

The only battle between fleets of sailing galleons before the Armada campaign occurred in 1582: the Huguenot Admiral Philip Strozzi in command of a mainly French force intending to capture the Azores on behalf of the Portuguese Pretender, Dom Antonio, was confronted off the island of St Michaels (Sao Miguel) by a Spanish fleet under the veteran Admiral, Santa Cruz. Strozzi had the weather gage on the first day of the battle and bore down on the Spanish fleet in three squadrons three times without – according to the Spanish version – making an attack; what was meant, perhaps, was that Strozzi did not close for a boarding contest in the Spanish manner but held off, firing his broadsides and tacking; the descriptions are too vague tactically to do more than guess. The next days were bedevilled by calms, but on the fourth day Strozzi bore down again and this time closed for a boarding and entering fight; he took the Spanish *Saint Matthew* but Santa Cruz came up in his flagship and turned the tables. Strozzi's second in command held his squadron out of the fight – it was said he had been corrupted by Philip – and when those who had followed their chief in to close quarters saw him yield to Santa Cruz they also disengaged and fled, leaving two of their number sinking; several others had more or less severe damage, especially to masts and spars. Thus Santa Cruz held the Azores for Spain.

Walter Raleigh commented in his *History of the World*:

. . . To clap ships together, without consideration, belongs rather to a madman than to a man of war; for by such an ignorant bravery was Peter Strozzi lost at the Azores . . .'[26]

There have been assertions that Spanish guns were liable to burst and Spanish iron shot to break up on contact; the damage done to Strozzi's ships off the Azores is proof that both were effective enough if the enemy gave them a chance to be used at close range. What the Spaniards could not do – nor any others – was hit the hull of an enemy at anything outside 300 to 500 yards.

According to Richard Hawkins, the Spanish did not have their own gunners, this being a trade looked down on by the Dons; the gunners in Medina Sidonia's fleet seem to have been Germans, Flemings or other foreigners. By contrast the English produced expert sea gunners who specialised in firing low into their opponents' hulls – as Medina Sidonia reported to Philip before he sailed. To judge by Elizabeth's Privy Council order for a register to be drawn up of all

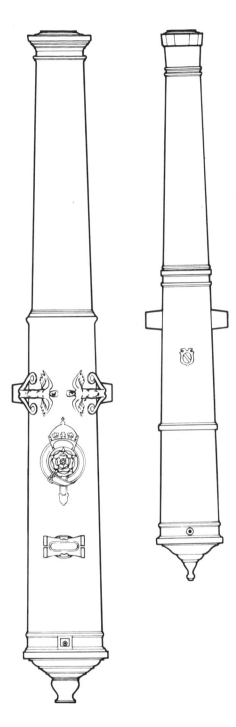

gunners serving in royal forts or ships or in the merchant service, gunners were as highly prized as guns; for the register was to be kept under annual review in order that 'none may leave the realm'.[27] They were not paid accordingly; at sea their wages were less than the other principal non-commissioned officers, the bo's'n, master carpenter and purser – in large royal ships less even than the bo's'n's mate, quartermasters, coxswain, trumpeter, cook or steward.

Like shipwrights, masters and pilots, gunners were not scientific men; theirs was a craft based like the others' on custom and lore handed down from one to another. Those who could read might have learned from a recently translated Italian treatise that a gunner should drink and eat a little meat before action; the fumes of the powder would 'otherwise be hurtful to his brains', but it was 'very unwholesome for him to shoot in any piece of ordnance while his stomach is full.'[28] His most important attribute was to be steady, reliable and conscientious, for he had charge of the most hazardous materials, and weapons which were as potentially dangerous to the men who served them as to the enemy. He was assisted in his careful duties by as many mates, quarter gunners – in charge of different sections of the decks – and quarter-gunners' mates as the size of the ship warranted. These were paid scarcely more than ordinary sailors.

What all this adds up to is that England, in terms of wealth a pygmy beside Spain, was ahead in financial and naval administration, warship building, gun-founding and not least shipboard gunnery technique and organisation. Spain's failure in these areas was due partly to exigencies of empire; more, probably, to the military origins and thought patterns of Castilian society. Even Spanish naval commanders had served their apprenticeship for the most part in the galley fleet, where campaigns were little more than soldiers' manoeuvres and occasional hand-to-hand fighting on the water; few seem to have been able to shake themselves free of this tradition and come to grips with the vastly different problems of naval warfare in broadside-gunned sailing ships; those who did found little support. So, for most Spaniards, ships remained an unpleasant necessity for communications within the empire and from a military point of view for transporting armies.

The English, on the other hand, courtiers, gentry and common people alike, viewed the sea as a highway to wealth by the trinity of trade, piracy and smuggling, and the English Royal navy was an integral and natural extension of this drive. The difference was fundamental; the other differences were all reflections of it; thus in the manning scales of the two fleets about to meet in the Channel, while Howard's great ships carried over 300 sailors and perhaps 200 soldiers, usually less, Medina Sidonia's carried over 300 soldiers and in most cases far fewer than 150 sailors; the positions of the two arms were completely reversed.

The difference extended to discipline aboard. Military officers commanded the Spanish Royal ships whether or not they had ever been to sea, and they brought rigid military habits of command to sailors, whose environment, beset by emergency, called for a more adaptable and individually responsive way of getting things done. They also brought actual disdain; in the Guipuzcoan squadron of the Armada, the seamen were turned out of their quarters and left without shelter to make room for the soldiers. This does not seem to have been an isolated incident. Richard Hawkins, who had ample opportunity to observe Spanish ships as a prisoner, wrote:

The mariners are but as slaves to the rest, to moil and toil day and night; and these but few and bad, and not suffered to sleep or harbour themselves under the decks. For in fair weather or foul, in storms, sun or rain, they must pass void of covert or succour.[29]

Cast brass guns recovered from the wreck of the *Mary Rose*, and now in the Rotunda Museum, Woolwich; (opposite) demi-cannon, (above) culverin bastard (shortened) and saker.

There can be little doubt that the Spanish galley service, employing slaves and convicts on the oars, had a brutalising influence. Galleys were hotbeds of potential mutiny, consequently their crews were kept under with extreme severity – and, of course, the other way about. The unpleasant effects on the character of jailers and oppressors in such situations has been too well documented in the present century to need stressing, and the system can hardly have failed to have had effects beyond the galleys, in society, especially in the sister sea service. Spanish sailors disliked the King's service, complaining they were treated like dogs by the military; so they were. They also received less pay than soldiers – when they were paid – far less than they could earn in merchants' ships. It is not surprising they did not volunteer and had to be impressed or simply taken over with the foreign ships Philip commandeered in port. Medina Sidonia's orders stated that they were to be quartered in the fore and after castles 'out of the way of the soldiers who might embarrass them.'[30]

English sailors also preferred merchants' ships, where they could earn more than in the Royal Navy, or privateers where the discipline was freer – in some cases it seems almost non-existent – and they too had to be impressed for the Queen's service; in the Armada year this was facilitated by the lists of seafaring men drawn up for just this eventuality a few years before. They were required to appear before the Queen's commissioners in their home port; there the necessary number were chosen and told to make their way to Deptford or Gillingham by a certain date, and given a sum of money for 'prest' – or advance – and 'conduct' to provide for the journey; as an example, that from the Suffolk port of Ipswich amounted to one shilling 'prest' and two shillings and sixpence 'conduct'. Arriving at the fleet base they had to present themselves to the officers of Her Majesty's ships to be placed as required, 'and not to fail as you and every of you will answer to the contrary at your uttermost perils.'[31]

Once aboard they were subject to traditional punishments for misdemeanours; these were read out to the ship's company from a parchment fixed to the main mast; a sailor drawing a weapon on the captain – presumably also on his lieutenant – to lose his right hand; a murderer to be lashed fast to the corpse of his victim and thrown overboard with it; a man found asleep on watch for the fourth time to be triced up under the bowsprit with a knife and a can of beer where he had the choice of dying slowly from exposure and starvation or cutting himself down and dropping into the sea for a quicker end – since probably few sailors could swim. A thief to be ducked two fathoms under, then towed ashore behind a boat and dismissed.[32] Blasphemers to be gagged hard with a marline spike tied behind their head and left for an hour 'till their mouths be very bloody'.[33] Flogging and keelhauling – or hauling a man on a rope from the yardarms from one side of the ship to the other beneath the keel, thus bumping him over the crustacean life attached to the ship's bottom – were other traditional punishments. How often any of these were used is impossible to say; as in later times it must have depended on individual captains.

Brutal deterrents were necessary, both because it was an unruly age and there were wild, belligerent elements among those attracted to the sea, and because slackness, indiscipline and insubordination could put a sailing man-of-war at risk, as indeed they seem to have done in the case of Henry VIII's *Mary Rose*. Nonetheless, in contrast to the Spanish service, the English sailor was treated as a man, if not exactly a free man since he was required to serve for the duration of the commission, still in the spirit of dealings between free men. This is apparent from the petitions in which seamen brought forward complaints – chiefly about their food – and abundantly clear from Hawkins' or Howard's correspondence:

'I know not which way to deal with the mariners to make them rest content with sour beer,' Howard wrote on one occasion 'for nothing doth displease them more.'[34]

In a privateer-led service, officered for the most part by men with much sea experience, and where all hands might gain by success, not only in the official share-out of prize money according to rank or rating, but in the frenzied looting which took place before an Admiralty official ever saw the prize, there was bound to be a freer discipline and greater mutual respect between officers and men than in ships ruled by the military as the Spanish were.

In many cases, however, 'freer discipline' gave way to anarchy, 'mutual respect' to mutiny. An authority for the period has suggested that the terrible mortality from disease in nearly every voyage induced much of this spirit of recklessness and insubordination. Another reason undoubtedly was the lure of plunder. One captain towards the end of the Spanish war told Burghley of how he had examined a merchantman and when it turned out to be French, not Spanish, his company had grown mutinous 'by reason I would not rob them.'[35] The difference in discipline between Royal naval ships and privateers is brought out by the contemporary naval officer, William Monson:

Nothing breeds disorders in our sailors but liberty and overmuch clemency. The one thing they have in their ordinary ships of war (privateers) where no discipline is used, nor authority obeyed; the other is escaping punishment when they justly deserve it . . . It is strange what misery such men will choose to endure in a small ship of reprisal though they be hopeless of gain, rather than serve Her Majesty, where their pay is certain, their diet plentiful and their labour not so great. Nothing breeds this but the liberty they find in one and the punishments they fear in the other.[36]

English sailors were berthed below decks; they slept probably on a straw mattress, although some were already slinging hammocks from the deckhead beams, a custom that was made the rule a few years later to improve cleanliness. They ate four to a mess, and if after a few days the food and water or sour beer were more apt to poison than nourish, this was not the fault of their officers, nor even the victualling officers; it was due to ignorance. The rations were generous by any standards: on four 'flesh days' a week, Sunday, Monday, Tuesday and Thursday, each man's allowance was a pound of beef each meal, thus for that day two pounds of beef, together with a pound of biscuit and a gallon of beer; this might be varied on Mondays with a pound of bacon and a pint of pease instead of the beef – which was, of course, always salted, casked beef at sea. On Wednesdays, Fridays and Saturdays, the three 'fish' days', the allowance was a whole stockfish, or half a ling to a mess, thus a quarter of a stockfish per man for one meal, ¾ lb of butter and ¾ lb of cheese per man for the other meal, together with the same allowance of biscuit and beer as on a 'flesh day'. When it was necessary to go on short rations six men were put to the mess, drawing the usual food for four, a simple method often adopted in 1588.

Spanish rations were similar, but slightly less plentiful and entirely lacking beef. They had only two 'flesh days', Sundays and Thursdays, when each man was allowed 6 ounces of bacon and 2 ounces of rice; on Mondays and Tuesdays it was 6 ounces of cheese and 3 ounces of beans or chick peas, and on the three 'fish days' 6 ounces of tunny or cod, 'or in default of these, 6 ounces of squid, or five sardines' together with 3 ounces of beans or chick peas, an ounce and a half of oil and a ¼ pint of vinegar. Each man was allotted 1½ pounds of biscuit each day and an allowance of approximately a bottle of wine.[37] From fish hooks and varieties of fish vertebrae found by divers in Spanish wrecks and in the English

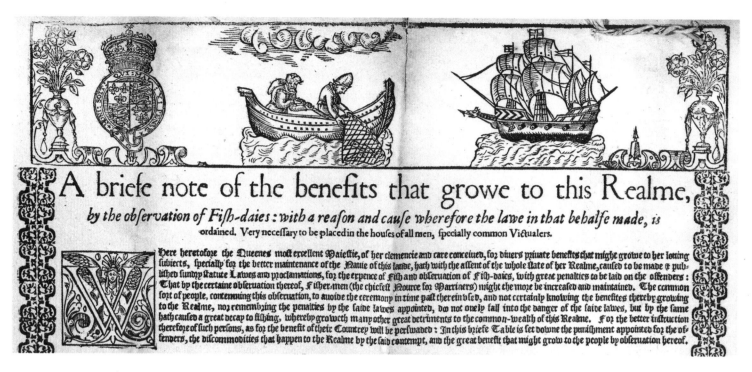

Part of a broadsheet urging
observance of Fish-days (1595) in
order to support the English fishing
industry, and thus ensure that
experienced seamen would be
available for the English navy.

Mary Rose it is evident that the official salted rations were supplemented by fresh
fish caught when occasion offered. Similarly traces of spices and herbal
seasonings among the personal belongings found in the *Mary Rose* suggest that
attempts were made to make the monotonous salt rations palatable. Remains of
several kinds of exotic fruit, nuts and bayleaves in the wreck of the *Trinidad
Valencera* are more likely to have come from the private stores of officers and
gentlemen adventurers than from the ordinary sailors or soldiers.[38]

One man from each mess collected the mess rations from the galley, together
with four individual plates and mugs – or in the case of the Spanish soldiers
aboard the seven or eight individual plates, bowls and mugs required for the
groups known as *camarada* who cooked and ate together. Medina Sidonia's
orders stipulated that only those appointed for this duty should collect the
rations and a sergeant or other company officer should be present at the
weighing and distribution to prevent disorder. Two distinct sizes of dish, one
size for the mess rations, one size for the individuals, have been found in both the
English *Mary Rose* and in the *Trinidad Valencera* and other Armada wrecks.[39] In
the *Mary Rose* mess kids and barrels containing fine wooden plates were found in
a storage area on the orlope deck immediately above the galley.[40] The majority
of the Spanish utensils found have been of Seville or Lisbon earthenware.[41] After
the rations had been brought up to the part of the berth deck where the mess
congregated, no doubt in a place established by habit on a hatch coaming, by the
mast, around a gun carriage, the food would be apportioned to the individual
plates or bowls and the men would set to with their fingers, aided by the
ordinary ballock daggers they used for their work about the decks. It was a far
cry from the officers' quarters aft, where the gentlemen sat at a cloth-covered
table attended by servants and perhaps musicians, eating from china dishes with
silver knives and forks, drinking from pewter or silver goblets or fine glass.
Robert Sténuit found the remains of no less than 48 forks on the site where the
galleass *Girona* and her complement had perished.[42]

There was no uniform dress for officers or men, nor were any coats or jackets
provided by the Crown as they had been once; some idea of the usual dress in the

Queen's service may be gleaned from a consignment of material sent to ships on the Irish station in 1580; this included canvas for breeches and doublets, cotton for linings and petticoats as well as shirts, stockings, shoes and caps.[43] The shoes are surprising since later generations of sailors found that bare feet gave a surer grip on wet decks and rigging and yards. Yet it is apparent from documentary evidence, as well as many examples found in the *Mary Rose*, that seamen did wear them at this time, and they were made either of leather or canvas; they also wore baggy knee breeches of worsted and worsted doublets, calico shirts, woollen or worsted hose, and probably simple sleeveless leather jerkins like those worn over 40 years before and found in the wreck of the *Mary Rose*.

As for the rest, the sailors of both sides had more in common with each other than allowed by the ideological propaganda they were subject to; they were an international community, for the most part very young, speaking in a strange jargon meaningless to landsmen, reciting strange chants, inured to long periods of wet and cold and discomfort, short hours of sleep between watches, sudden emergencies and perils demanding all their endurance, agony from toothache, the dulling, rousing grip of drink. In their brief spells of free time between duty or emergency – for the majority worked watch on, watch off – four hours on duty followed by four hours below – they might gamble with dice or cards or listen to the honed and seasoned, endlessly discursive yarns of an established storyteller; or if the weather were fine in the evening join in choruses of the sailors' folk-songs which passed down the generations and came to be known as 'fore-bitters' from the stand on the bitts by the foremast which the sailor minstrel mounted to render his ballad. The songs were usually long, but were memorised word-perfectly; the audience sitting around on the deck joined in the choruses or the final line of each verse. Probably then as in later ages those who could convey an element of sadness or wistfulness in their performances held the rapt attention of their audience.

> As I lay musing in my bed,
> full warm and well at ease,
> I thought upon the lodgings hard
> poor sailors had at seas.
>
> They bide it out with hunger and cold
> and many a bitter blast,
> and many times constrained are they
> for to cut down their mast . . .
>
> Our ship that was before so good,
> and eke so likewise trim,
> is now with raging seas grown leakt,
> and water fast comes in . . .[44]

And so it went – this one believed to have been adapted from a genuine sailor's folk-song of the time. Perhaps on other fine evenings the men danced to an extemporised band, lutes or tambourines, as sailors did in later centuries; remains of musical instruments have been found in both the *Mary Rose* and the Spanish wrecks.[45]

The details of their lives must be left to speculation and imagination. Each man had his tale; none has left a record. Each had seen the grandeur of the elements, the clean blue ridges of the sea and the stars striking through the rigging to remind him of worlds beyond the present. Each had known the fear of death, felt the exhilaration of a foreign dawn, and whether it was a Catholic or a Protestant God, each was in awe of Him because he had seen His works.

8

The Fighting Up-Channel

In the early morning of Friday, July 29th, a pirate named Thomas Flemyng, serving as one of Howard's scouts in command of a small barque, *Golden Hinde*, sighted a portion of the Armada 'hovering' off the Scilly Isles as if awaiting the rest of the fleet. The weather was hazy but he counted or estimated 50 sail and immediately bore away before the westerly wind to bring the news to Plymouth. What he had seen were 40 Andalusian and supply ships and a few small pataches which had become separated from the fleet in the gale two days before; they were waiting for Medina Sidonia at the appointed rendezvous position.[1]

Exactly when Flemyng reached Plymouth is not known; he probably had the best part of 80 miles to sail, perhaps more, depending on whether the Spaniards were to windward of the Scillies as Medina Sidonia's orders stipulated, or nearer the Lizard, where the Duke sent a patache to look for them that same day; in either case Flemyng could scarcely have got in before evening, probably late evening. Legend has it he found Drake playing bowls on Plymouth Hoe, the green overlooking the Sound. The story has been traced back to a pamphlet of 1624, thus, it is said, 'well within living memory of the event'. The pamphlet made no mention of his legendary response, 'Time to finish the game and beat the Spaniards after!' This flourish was added over a century after the pamphlet.[2] Since neither the game nor Drake's response were mentioned in any of the immediately contemporary accounts, nor in the account by William Monson, who took part in the campaign and was never loth to spice his descriptions with gossip or scandal, it is probably a patriotic myth.

For there was no time to finish the game – if there was a game that Friday evening – and Drake for all his natural cheek and swagger was the last person to have thought there might be: that Spring he had written to Elizabeth 'The advantage of time and place in all martial actions is half a victory.'[3] Now was the proof. Some of the English ships were anchored in the Sound, but the greater part probably were in the sleeve known as the Catwater with the wind blowing directly in; others were probably alongside quays, others on the mud for scraping and repairs. All had to be got ready for sea, and those in the Catwater and alongside had then to be 'warped' out laboriously by laying out anchors ahead and heaving round on the capstans or towing with boats. The business had to be started immediately; no one knew how close the Spaniards might be on Flemying's heels; the wind was in the west. And nothing, it might be supposed, would suit Medina Sidonia better than to come on the English fleet bottled up in a cul de sac. If he were to seize his opportunity that would be the end of the naval campaign and probably of Elizabeth, and England as a Protestant nation. There was no time to be lost.

Howard and his captains set to and the ships were warped out of the Catwater that night; in the early hours of Saturday morning the leading captains set sail to a

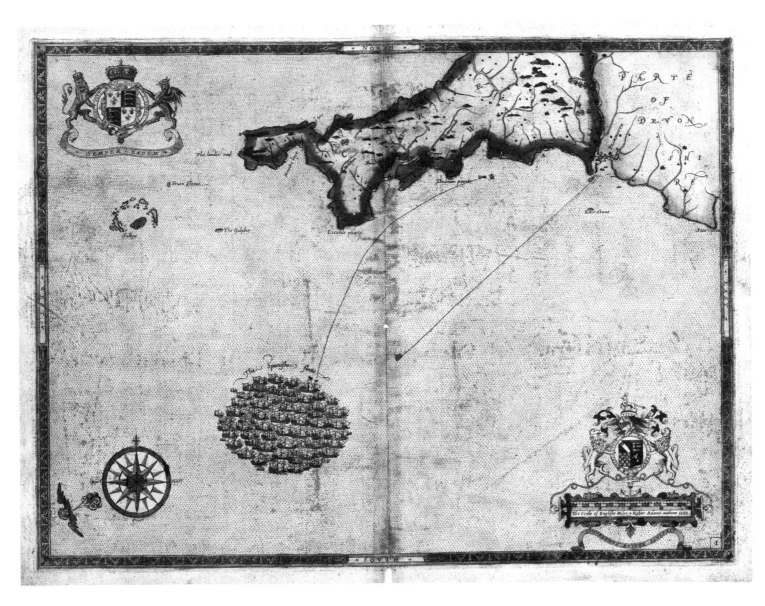

The first of a series of plans of the progress of the Armada up-Channel, and the engagement with the English fleet, engraved by Augustin Ryther in 1590 after drawings by Robert Adam to illustrate the narrative of the campaign by Petruccio Ubaldino. This shows the arrival of the Spanish fleet off the Lizard, the southernmost tip of the western extremity of England, and its discovery by Captain Thomas Flemyng, who brought the news to Plymouth.

light southwesterly and started to beat out of the Sound towards the open sea, as Howard wrote 'very hardly' and only 'through the great travail used by our men' for the wind was 'very scant' and the tide flooding.[4]

Meanwhile all England was alerted. A system of beacons on every rise along the coast and inland through the shires to London and northwards towards the Scottish border spread the news with the speed and urgency of fire. The Lords lieutenant of the counties, their muster masters, provost marshals, sheriffs, constables and all the panoply of authority prepared for the possibility of invasion since the first serious alarms two years before hastened into action. The clergy – reluctantly in many cases – pondered their duty to raise troops of light cavalry. Yeomen and farmers, servants and labourers of the home defence militia known as the trained bands who had been drilling in the evenings and on holidays with musket, arquebus, pike or bill, wrestling and taking part in races to improve their agility, shouldered their arms and made for assembly points in town squares and village greens, by all accounts in high spirits now the hour of trial had come at last. The whole country responded with a quickening of the pulse: 'Myself can remember,' one coastal inhabitant recalled later, 'when upon the firing of the beacons, the country people forthwith ran down to the seaside, some with clubs, some with picked staves and pitchforks, all unarmed, and they that were best appointed were but with a bill, a bow and a sheaf of arrows, no captain or commander appointed to direct, lead or order them.'[5]

Rumour blossomed. Dutch printers had fleshed out the bare numbers of 'Justices' in Medina Sidonia's Lisbon muster list with invented details of instruments of torture carried in the holds. Propaganda stories had been inspired about a 'shipload of halters' to hang Englishmen:

. . . and another shipload of scourges to whip women, with 3,000 or 4,000 wet nurses to suckle the infants (made orphans). It was said that all children between the ages of 7 and 12 would be branded in the face so that they might always be known. . .[6]

Leading English Catholics had been rounded up already. They were confined in Wisbech Castle, Norfolk, and in other fortresses and prisons on the pretext that for their own sake they ought not to be at large; in the event of a Spanish landing the populace might vent its fury on them. The hunt for spies and subversive agents of the Pope and Spain had been stepped up by offering informers half the property of those they helped bring to book. Tolerance was dead. With danger, primitive emotions were abroad.

The Armada was less than 50 miles from Plymouth on this Saturday morning as Howard's leading ships beat out of the Sound. The lookouts had sighted the Lizard the previous afternoon, but Medina Sidonia had taken in sail to wait for stragglers and allow repairs to ships battered by the storm, in particular the flagship of the galleasses, whose rudder had been shattered. Meanwhile he had called a council. The minutes have not been discovered, but it must be assumed the usual members were present, the veteran Vice Admiral of the fleet and commander of the Biscayan squadron, Juan Martinez de Recalde, the Commander-in-Chief of the Army, Don Francisco de Bovadillo, who was sailing in the fleet flagship, the Inspector General of the Fleet largely concerned with administration, Don Jorge Manrique, the commander of the Castilian squadron, Diego Flores de Valdés, sailing in the fleet flagship as the Duke's chief naval advisor, in modern terms his Chief of Staff, and the other squadronal commanders, Don Pedro de Valdés (Andalusian), Miguel de Oquendo (Guipuz-coan), Don Hugo de Moncada (Galleasses), Martin de Bertondona (Levant), together with the captain of the fleet flagship, Alonso Vanegas, and a young cavalry general, Don Alonso de Leyva, a dashing caballero whose spirit and charm had won even Philip's slow, old heart; he had been a serious contender for command of the Armada; as it was he had a secret commission signed by the King to take over should anything happen to the Duke. Until then he had no particular responsibility; he was sailing as a volunteer in his own ship, *La Rata Santa Maria Encoranada*, attached to the Levant squadron.

At the Council he suggested attacking Plymouth. Philip's instructions to Medina Sidonia, however, were quite clear; he was not to land or attempt anything on shore unless jointly with the Duke of Parma. His purpose was to join Parma, provide him with 6,000 soldiers and the siege train and munitions he carried, and command the Channel for the crossing to England; 'your sole function on your own account being – what is indeed the principal one – to fight at sea.'[7] In any case, from all that had been seen of the sluggish ships and in many cases the captains too, sailing into the narrows of the Sound against shore guns commanding the approaches meant risking disorder and separation of the supply hulks which it was their duty to escort safely to the other end of the Channel. According to the only reliable account of the Council, by the flag captain, Vanegas, the decision not to attempt Plymouth was unanimous.[8]

However a letter the Duke wrote to Philip the next day, Saturday, makes it

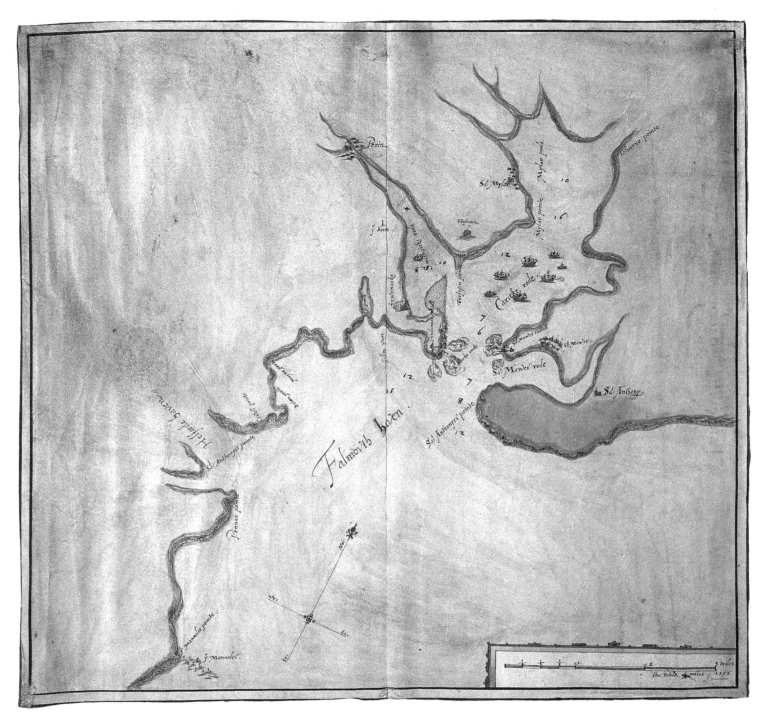

Map of Falmouth (1592) showing ships in the haven. Philip II planned to land troops here from an Armada he sent against England in 1597 under Don Martin de Padilla, a far more promising scheme than that with which Medina Sidonia's Armada was burdened. Padilla's fleet was so scattered and damaged by gales it never reached the Channel.

certain the Council did decide to go against instructions in another respect. So far nothing had been heard from Parma, nor had they been able to learn anything about the state of his preparations for putting out with his army to join them when they arrived. Medina Sidonia had sent a despatch vessel to Flanders four days previously to tell him their position and course and ask his views on where they should meet and how to combine their operations. Until they received a reply they were, as Medina Sidonia put it, 'groping in the dark'. It was consequently decided, strictly against Philip's instructions, to establish themselves in an anchorage off the Isle of Wight, and go no further until they had made contact with Parma and agreed a joint plan. The reasoning was impeccable; Medina Sidonia expressed it in his letter to Philip:

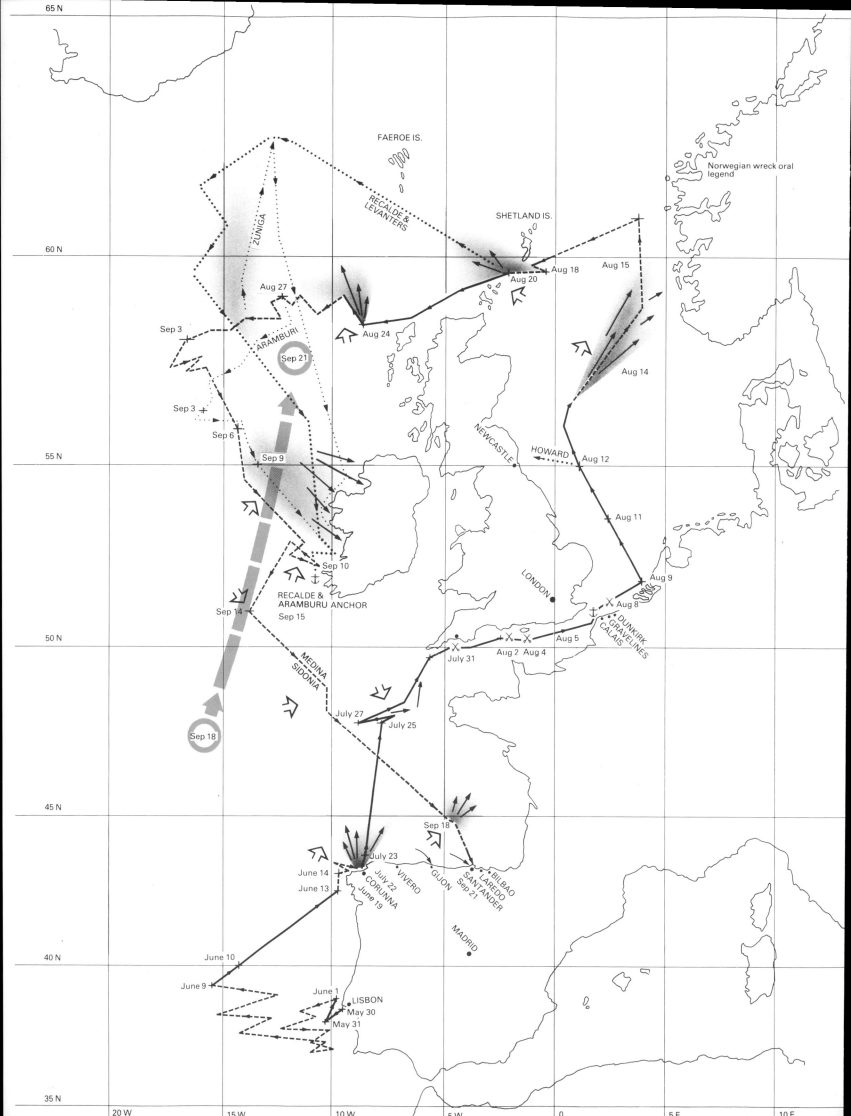

65 N

FAEROE IS.

Norwegian wreck oral
legend

SHETLAND IS.

60 N

ZUNIGA

RECALDE &
LEVANTERS

Aug 18   Aug 15

Aug 20

Aug 24

Aug 27

Aug 14

ARAMBURI

Sep 21

Sep 3

Sep 3

NEWCASTLE   HOWARD   Aug 12

55 N

Sep 6

Sep 9

Aug 11

LONDON

Sep 10

Aug 9

RECALDE &
ARAMBURU ANCHOR
Sep 15

Aug 8

DUNKIRK
GRAVELINES
CALAIS

Sep 14

50 N

MEDINA
SIDONIA

Aug 5

July 31   Aug 2 Aug 4

July 27

July 25

Sep 18

45 N

Sep 18

BILBAO
LAREDO
SANTANDER
Sep 21

GIJON

July 23

June 14   July 22 VIVERO

June 13   CORUNNA
                 June 19

MADRID

June 10

40 N

June 9   June 1
                LISBON
                May 30
                May 31

35 N

20 W   15 W   10 W   5 W   0   5 E   10 E

Map devised by the author and drawn by Lionel Willis showing the track of the Armada and the engagements; since there was no means of finding longitude at this date many parts of the track are highly conjectural, based on wind directions, weather conditions, reported latitudes and sightings of land. It is, however, correct in general outline.

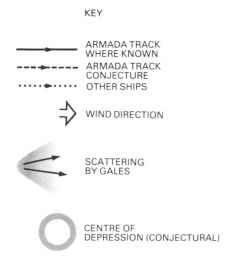

KEY

━━━━━▶ ARMADA TRACK
        WHERE KNOWN
-·-·-·-▶ ARMADA TRACK
        CONJECTURE
·····▶····· OTHER SHIPS

⇨ WIND DIRECTION

SCATTERING
BY GALES

◯ CENTRE OF
   DEPRESSION (CONJECTURAL)

As all along the coast of Flanders there is no harbour or shelter for our ships, if I were to go from the Isle of Wight thither with the Armada our vessels might be driven on to the shoals, where they would certainly be lost. In order to avoid so obvious a peril I have decided to stay off the Isle of Wight until I learn what the Duke is doing, as the plan is that at the moment of my arrival he should sally with the fleet, without causing me to wait a minute. The whole success of the undertaking depends on this . . .[9]

He was still waiting for repairs to be completed on Hugo de Moncada's galleass as he wrote this on the Saturday; the weather was thick, only the lightest breezes ruffling the surface of the swell moving in ponderously from the Atlantic. The ships were close enough to the shore to see the glow and smoke of the nearest beacons, and the country people gathered there could marvel at the tall hulls and masts stretching into the mist, but towards Plymouth where Drake was supposed to be with a small squadron, the view was obscured by banks of rain.

A weak tide and the westerly wind took them slowly along the coast during the morning and in the early afternoon Howard and the leading group of English ships, who had worked some seven miles out of the Sound until almost level with the Eddystone rocks, caught a glimpse of them through a break in the rain, stretching 'westwards as far as Fowey'.[10] It must have been a brief and hazy glimpse for according to Spanish accounts the English ships were not sighted until the evening; then, as Medina Sidonia recorded, 'many ships were seen, but by cause of mist and rain we were unable to count them.' By another Spanish account the English were steering 'towards the east, the wind being at south west.'[11] Evidently they were on the south-easterly leg of a beat to seaward to gain the windward position.

Repairs had been completed by this time and the Armada was under sail again; however, Medina Sidonia ordered sail taken in after the enemy ships were seen and sent a pinnace in charge of an English-speaking officer to reconnoitre Plymouth. When he returned he had four Falmouth fishermen with him who said that both Howard and Drake with the whole English fleet had sailed from Plymouth that afternoon. Medina Sidonia sent a boat through the squadrons with instructions to the commanders to take up battle formation next day. At about two in the morning he was roused with a report that the enemy was in sight; a half moon glinted through a break in the clouds and by its light groups of dark hulls and spectral sails could be made out to the south and sou-west. Howard had succeeded in taking the windward position – not difficult since the Spanish ships were lying to.

There has been much speculation about the 'crescent' shape of the Armada formed during its progress up Channel which the English first saw forming as the sun got up on that morning, Sunday, July 31st. There are several clues; the first lies in the Spanish naval tradition, bred in galley warfare. Military order and discipline were the watchwords. Medina Sidonia's senior Admiral, Recalde, had served as superintendent of the Royal Dockyards – for the galley fleet – and in the Indies Guard and at the battle for the Azores he had been second in command to the great Santa Cruz, who had learned his business in Mediterranean galley warfare. Oquendo had also served under Santa Cruz at the Azores, handling his ship 'like a horseman'. Hugo de Moncada was a veteran Venetian galley commander. Even those like Medina Sidonia's chief of staff, Flores de Valdés, who had experience of the 'stand-off' gunnery tactics of the Protestant interlopers through long service in the Castilian 'Indian guard', could not have thought that the sluggish and unwieldy mass of the Armada could have been handled in any other way than as an ordered body closed up in lines for mutual support. One of the standard Spanish treatises on naval warfare from the first half of the century expressed the concept: 'Ships at sea are as war horses on land, since admitting they are not very nimble at turning at any pace, nevertheless a regular formation increases their power.'[12] This work, by Alonso de Chaves, recommended ordering the fleet in squadrons, each disposed in line abreast when – having gained the weather gage – they bore down on the enemy.

> . . . placing always the greater ships in one body as a vanguard to grapple first and receive the first shock; the Captain General should be stationed in the centre squadron so that he may see those which go before and those which follow . . .[13]

This was taken straight from galley warfare, where fleets formed in three divisions, each in line abreast, the commander-in-chief in the centre of the centre division. Frequently the wing divisions were advanced in echelon to attempt the flank of the enemy, or retarded to counter an enemy flank attack, thus forming a crescent shape. The largest vessels were placed in the centre either side of the fleet flagship, and there was usually a second line behind which could be ordered to reinforce any part of the formation.

An order of battle for the Armada, which had been sent to the Grand Duke of Tuscany by his Ambassador in Lisbon as Medina Sidonia's ships were dropping down towards the mouth of the Tagus that May, corresponds exactly with the ideas expressed by Alonso de Chaves, and the time-honoured practice of galley warfare. It showed an arrangement in three divisions in line abreast. The centre division consisted of the main battle squadrons of Castile and Portugal, the port or left wing division consisted of the Levant and Guipuzcoan squadrons, the right wing, the Andalusian and Biscay squadrons; both wings were advanced in curving echelon so that a crescent shape was formed. In the middle of the crescent in advance of the centre of the main battle division were twelve ships arranged in three lines abreast; the leading line consisted of 'four ships of the vanguard' led by the gallant Don Alonso de Leyva in the *Rata*. Immediately astern of these four came the four galleasses under Don Hugo de Moncada, and immediately astern of them the flagships of the Biscay, Guipuzcoan and Castilian squadrons flanking the fleet flagship, *San Martin*, second from starboard in the line. This corresponded to the 'greater ships in one body as a vanguard to grapple first and receive the first shock' with the fleet commander 'in the centre squadron so that he may see those which go before and those which follow.' The small despatch vessels and scouts were shown in line abreast behind each of the three divisions and behind them the store hulks, also in three divisions, each in line abreast with more small craft behind them.

The interesting point about this battle order is that it shows Recalde at the extreme tip of the right wing, where he was as the Armada formed for battle on that first Sunday morning, and de Leyva in the vanguard, where he was stated to be that day. The picture is complicated by the fact that the left wing division was termed the vanguard in reports (the right wing division the rearguard) so that if the formation was as detailed above there were two places termed the van, the left wing *and* the advanced line of the centre division. Although no precise tactical picture can be drawn from the different accounts of the fighting that day they make more sense if it is assumed that there were indeed two 'vans' and it was the central 'van' that Howard attacked – as contemporary pictorial representations indicate.

The wind was west-sou-westerly as the day broke – discounting Medina Sidonia's report of a shift to the west-nor-west – and the English were plain in sight, most of them, perhaps 80 sail large and small, in the southwest; a few,

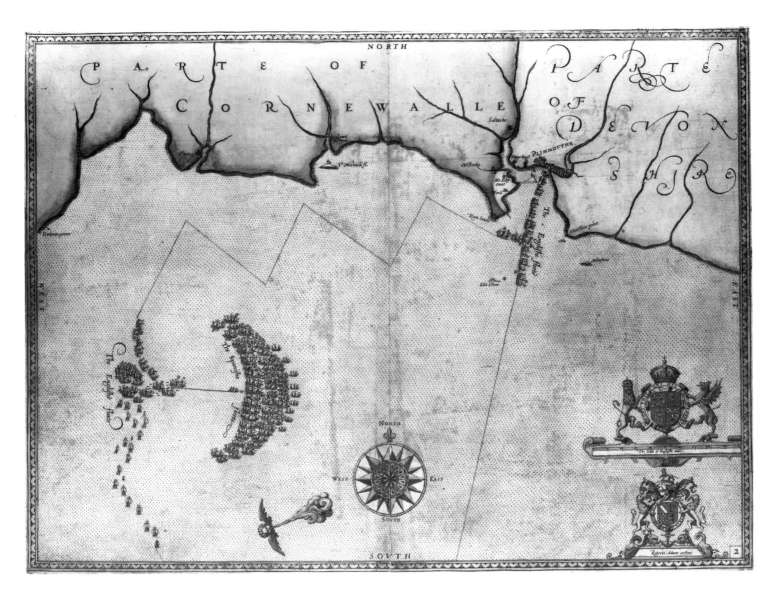

The second of Ryther's plans showing at the right the English fleet beating out of Plymouth, the main body steering southerly, another inshore squadron tacking westerly to gain the windward position. On the left the Spanish fleet off the coast between Fowey and Looe has formed its famous crescent order, and Howard in the *Ark Royal* has sent his pinnace *Disdain* to give Medina Sidonia his 'defiance'.

including three large galleons – probably Frobisher in the high-castled *Triumph*, and the other Royal ships which had not been cut down – were working up to windward inshore, thus to the north or nor-nor-west.

Aboard the Spanish ships preparations for the coming fight were well in hand: canvas waist-cloths were secured along the upper deck rails to conceal the gunners stationed there, similar canvas 'top armings' were rigged to hide the swivel-gunners and musketeers in the tops, and all their ammunition, stones, grenades, incendiary devices, stinkballs (*pildoras*) and other missiles for hurling down on the enemy decks were hoisted aloft; heavy netting to snare and hold up boarders was triced up between the castles over the waist; on the orlopes carpenters were taking down any cabins or temporary partitions which may have survived in defiance of an order by Medina Sidonia before departing Corunna; officers' beds, chests and other furnishings which impeded a clear run of the decks – also in defiance of the order – were swayed below; sponges, rammers, ladles and worming irons were placed ready for use by the great guns, and lengths of match fitted into the linstocks; the different weights of balls were distributed to their pieces, cartridge and chambers for the swivel guns prepared aft above the magazine; tubs and buckets of salt water and vinegar were placed between the guns, also half pipes of drinking water to quench the men's thirst in

Plan devised by the author and drawn by Lionel Willis showing the opening of the first engagement off Plymouth near the Eddystone rocks. The Spanish formation is largely conjectural, based on the English descriptions and diagrams, together with the battle plan sent to the Duke of Tuscany from Lisbon. The most conjectural aspect is the wedge of four ships and four galleasses, termed the 'van', to windward of Medina Sidonia's flagship; this is not indicated on English representations. However, if de Leyva was *not* somewhere in the centre, rather than with his own Levant squadron at the *southern* horn (also the 'van'), his later appearance in support of the *northern* wing (rearguard) is difficult to understand.

the heat of battle; old sails and wetted blankets were distributed through the different quarters for extinguishing fire. Officers donned gleaming steel corselets.

Meanwhile sailors tended the sheets and braces as the captains attempted to bring their vessels into close line with their squadron flagships; slowly, miraculously from the serpentine groupings of the night a cresent shape emerged, the wings or horns extending westerly, particularly the northern wing, or 'rearguard', where the Vice Admiral, Recalde, in the 1,000-ton Portuguese galleon, *San Juan*, hung as close to the wind as he could. Medina Sidonia also luffed up as close as possible in his flagship, *San Martin*, in the centre, probably heading south or sou-sou-easterly under easy sail as he awaited the English. Being to leeward, there was nothing he could do to bring on an action; the initiative lay entirely with Howard.

To the watching English the sheer mass of the Spanish ships and their good order inspired awe; the contemporary chronicler, Camden, was not over-fanciful when he wrote of the Spanish fleet 'with lofty, turret-like castles in front,' arranged 'like a half moon, the wings thereof spreading out about the length of seven miles, sailing very slowly with full sails, the wind being, as it were overrid with carrying them, and the ocean groaning under their weight.'[14]

It appeared a daunting prospect to tackle; the English captains took some time arranging themselves in groups, and it was not until about nine o'clock that Howard led down with the *Ark* towards the centre of the crescent, where he saw the Royal standard flying at the fore of the *San Martin*. He sent his pinnace, *Disdain* 'to give the Duke defiance';[15] she fired a small gun, no doubt with the customary shout, 'St George for England!' then filled away, and Howard came round into the wind after her to open his broadside at the enemy flagship, or what could be made out of her in the press of the four galleons and the galleasses which should have been to windward of her if the Lisbon battle order was being adhered to strictly. How close Howard approached is impossible to say – a considerable distance by all accounts – perhaps 500 yards, perhaps further. An English volunteer with Howard wrote, 'The majesty of the enemy's fleet, the good order they held, and the private consideration of our own wants did cause, in myne opinion, our first onset to be more coldly done than became the value of our nation and the credit of the English navy.'[16] After the *Ark*, the others of Howard's group luffed up and fired their broadsides at the *San Martin* or the great ships about him, one of which was de Leyva's *Rata*. Most of the balls fell harmlessly short or over, as did the Spanish shots in return; little if any damage was done on either side. Howard filled away and tacked to be in position to return with his other broadside when the range was clear again. To the Spanish it seemed as if the English extended themselves in line as they came down to the attack.

Meanwhile the few English ships of the separated inshore group had sailed down towards the main fleet and attached themselves to Drake in the *Revenge*. The vagueness of the accounts leaves it open whether Drake was leading this inshore group in the first place; the probability is that he was with Howard and the main body working around the seaward flank of the Spanish during the night. In any case he led a small detachment of perhaps eight ships including Frobisher's *Triumph* and John Hawkins' *Victory* against Recalde in the *San Juan* at the extreme northern and westernmost tip of the enemy crescent. Recalde kept his luff as the English ships bore down one after the other, discharged their broadsides and filled away; after the first fire of his own heavy pieces – no doubt at the *Revenge* – he could do little but stand and listen to the great shot whining

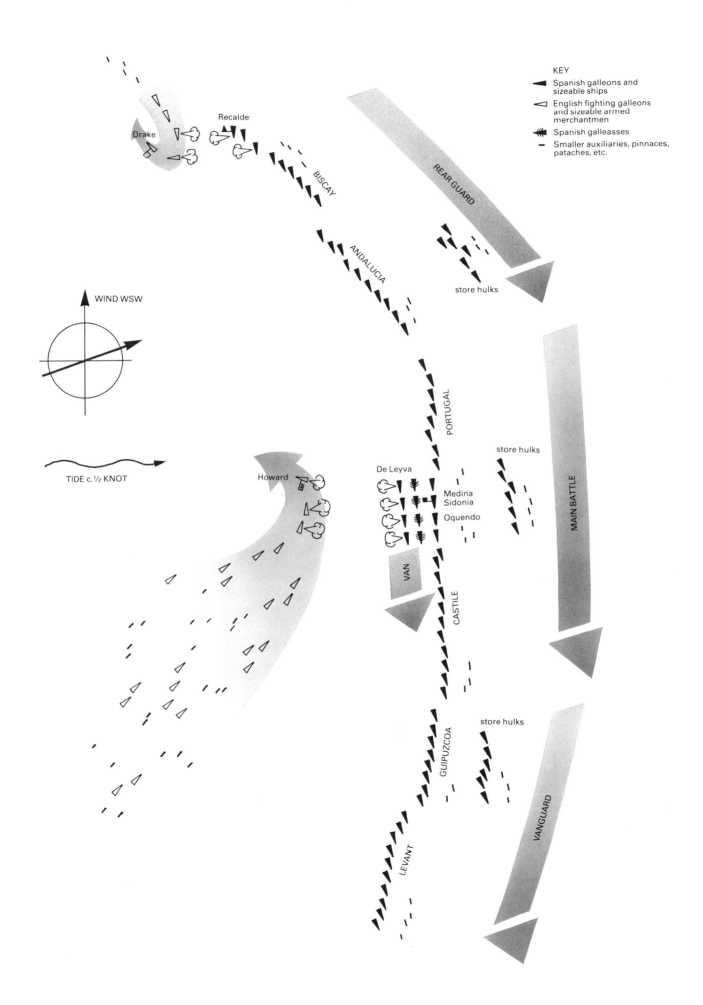

KEY
◀ Spanish galleons and sizeable ships
◁ English fighting galleons and sizeable armed merchantmen
✺ Spanish galleasses
– Smaller auxiliaries, pinnaces, pataches, etc.

WIND WSW

TIDE c. ½ KNOT

Recalde

Drake

BISCAY

ANDALUCIA

PORTUGAL

REAR GUARD

store hulks

store hulks

MAIN BATTLE

De Leyva

Medina Sidonia

Oquendo

Howard

VAN

CASTILE

store hulks

GUIPUZCOA

LEVANT

VANGUARD

Ten tapestries recording the Armada campaign were commissioned by Howard from Cornelis Vroom and Francis Spiring. They hung in the House of Lords from 1616 until they were destroyed in the great fire of 1834. Fortunately John Pine had made and published engravings based on the tapestries. Here are plates III and IV from the sequence; they show (top) the first engagement off Plymouth, followed by the Spanish fleet proceeding on its way, pursued by the English, and (bottom) the following morning Sir Francis Drake and adherents capturing Pedro de Valdés' galleon, *Rosario*; the Spanish fleet has re-formed in its defensive crescent awaiting attack.

through the rigging and the ineffective popping of his own swivel guns angled up for range. He was supported by the second-in-command of the squadron, Don Pedro de Mendoza in the *Gran Grin*, one of the largest vessels in the fleet.

It is impossible to interpret the subsequent course of the action; Medina Sidonia's account suggests that Recalde's other ships bore away towards the centre, leaving his flagship, *San Juan* and the *Gran Grin* exposed to the full weight of attack from Drake's squadron; certainly the *San Juan* suffered most damage that day, having her rigging torn, two shots in her foremast, her captain wounded and some fifteen men killed according to one of the Portuguese crew who was interrogated later.[17] It seems certain that the Duke ordered the fleet to go about, and went to Recalde's aid with his van and centre:[18] de Leyva, commanding the van in the *Rata*, seems to have mixed in the fighting at the rear, as did the *San Mateo*, of the centre division, perhaps one of the four advanced ships with de Leyva. According to one account de Leyva attempted to work towards Drake but Drake refused to close because the *San Mateo* would then have been in a position to get up with him. He turned his guns on her instead.[19] By another account the galleasses also took part in this fighting in the northern part of the crescent;[20] the contemporary engraving shows a galleass there.

Whatever the course of events which no single person could have witnessed, so vast was the canvas, Spanish reports stress the good gunnery of the English, and the speed and manoeuvrability of the English ships; as Medina Sidonia put it 'their ships being very nimble and of such good steerage, they did with them whatsoever they desired.'[21] Since neither Howard nor any of the English commanders had any intention of allowing themselves to fall far inside the northern horn of the crescent they tacked and filled and came in again with their broadsides at long range; thus the only seriously damaged ship seems to have been Recalde's *San Juan* at the very tip of the horn. By noon she was so crippled aloft that when Don Pedro de Valdés, commanding the Andalusian ships – adjacent to Recalde's Biscayan squadron in the rearguard – sent a pinnace to him during a lull in the firing, Recalde sent back word that he was so damaged he could not stand up to another attack and asked Don Pedro to relieve him. He attempted to do so, but in the press found his flagship, *Nuestra Senora del Rosario*, driving towards a Biscayan vessel; the wind was freshening now and the sea rising and he could not avoid falling aboard her, carrying away his bowsprit, spritsail and fore yard; unable to manoeuvre, he was blown down on to one of his own squadron, the *Santa Catalina* and suffered further damage.

Seeing this, Medina Sidonia took in his foresail and loosed his sheets as a signal to the fleet to lie to, allowing the *San Juan* and the *Nuestra Senora del Rosario* to sail down into the lee of the centre division to make repairs. Howard, frustrated by the splendid order the Spanish were keeping, could do nothing; as he put it in a hurried note to Walsyngham that day, 'we made some of them bear room (retire downwind) to stop their leaks notwithstanding we durst not adventure to put in among them, their fleet being so strong.'[22] Having seen his injured ships to safety, Medina Sidonia put about again, steering sou-sou-easterly, according to his own account, 'endeavouring to recover the wind of the enemy.' No doubt Howard conformed, keeping his distance up-wind.

The fight had started in the morning just to the west of Plymouth and outside the treacherous group of rocks called the Eddystone; it had drifted easterly, opening the Sound, and the Mayor and people of Plymouth, crowding the front and all vantage points, were able to witness the action, unprecedented in English annals; myriad sails stretched to the horizon; clouds of gunsmoke rose from separated groups lit by the summer sun; the sounds of gunfire reverberated

Published by John Pine, June 24, 1739, according to Act of Parliament.

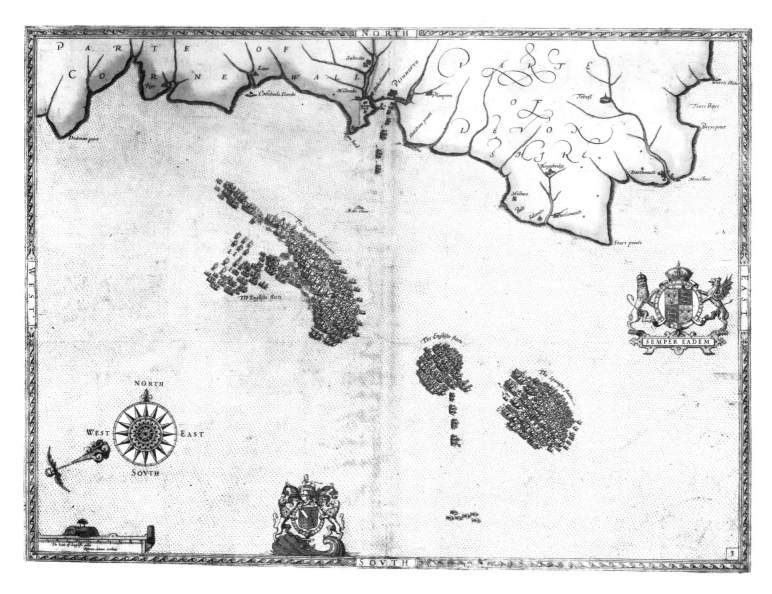

The third in the sequence of Ryther plans; this shows the first engagement off Plymouth, on the left Drake's squadron attacking Recalde at the northernmost (windward) horn of the Armada crescent, Howard and the main body of the English fleet crowding in closer on the Spanish centre than contemporary descriptions suggest. Note the galleass with Recalde and the two galleasses at the southern horn (van) of the Spanish crescent. On the right the Spanish are seen carrying on their course up-Channel 'in a roundel', pursued by the English.

across the intervening white-flecked sea like peals of distant thunder. And in the Sound and further out between the shore and the fleets a host of small craft, crowded with volunteers animated by danger and a sense of high events, headed out to join Howard and Drake, white sails and tan, cutters and luggers and barks leaning to the fresh wind, specks of bravery against the anonymous sails beyond.

Some time that afternoon after the guns had fallen silent, attentive watchers might have seen a cloud of dark smoke rise from somewhere in the Spanish fleet and after it have heard a roar louder than anything that had gone before, rattling the glass in the windows of the merchants' houses along the front. To those aboard the close-packed ships in the left wing or vanguard of the Armada, it must have sounded like the last trump. A powder barrel aft in the *San Salvador*, flagship of the second-in-command of Miguel de Oquendo's Guipuzcoan squadron, had ignited and the explosion had blown out the after end of the stern-castle, killed scores of the soldiers crowded there, horribly burned others, set off the loaded guns whose shot must have hummed about the nearest ships, wrecked the rudderhead and tiller and started fires about the decks. Many shocked survivors leaped overboard.

Presumably the powder barrel or barrels had been brought up from the magazine into the steerage in order to fill cartridges for the fight; 128 other powder barrels remained undamaged below; perhaps unused cartridges contributed to the force of the explosion. The story went round the Spanish ships that the gunner, apparently a German, had thrown a lighted match deliberately into the powder after being hotly berated – in one account struck – by the ship's captain for not shooting better. Dutch deserters from the Spanish ships gave this account to interrogators in Holland in August, and the purser, Pedro Calderon, who could not have known this but who had talked with the captain and survivors of the *San Salvador*, told a similar tale when he returned to Spain in September.[23]

Medina Sidonia had probably given up the vain attempt to work to windward of the English by this time, and was heading easterly up-Channel; seeing the crippled ship begin to fall out of line and wallow astern he fired a gun and went about as a signal for the fleet to do the same. The English, who had sensed the chance of an easy prize and were bearing down, rounded up and kept their distance as they saw the *San Salvador* supported.

Going about was too much for Don Pedro de Valdés' *Nuestra Senora del Rosario*; either new head stays had not been rigged yet, or they were not stout enough; the wounded foremast broke near the deck and fell aft on to the main yard, which it carried away. Medina Sidonia left a galleass to take the *San Salvador* in tow, and bore away with two other galleasses to Don Pedro's relief. According to his account they were unable to get a hawser aboard because the wind and sea had risen; certainly the *Rosario* must have been unmanageable without any headsails to counter-balance the vast area of the stern-castle, and towing her would have been a feat of seamanship at the best of times; with the English hanging just out of range, the wind rising, evening beginning to close in, and many of the other Spanish ships spreading downwind, Medina Sidonia took the counsel of his naval advisor, Diego Flores, who was concerned lest the fleet become separated during the night; he decided to take the men off and leave the crippled vessel for the English. Of course, if it were possible to take men off it must have been possible to put towing warps aboard, thus some doubt is cast on his narrative here. But Don Pedro refused to abandon ship, and finally Medina Sidonia fired a gun to collect the others who had stayed, and bore away up-Channel. It was sunset, the time for evening prayers. Above the sounds of the wind in the rigging and the plash and soughing of the waves along the side, the pure tones of boys' voices rose in the 'Ave Maria'.

Howard had called a council of war that afternoon. Drake, Hawkins and the other experienced commanders had converged on the *Ark* and congregated in the great cabin among heavy furnishings and curtains of tudor green trimmed with yellow mock velvet. What suggestions were put are not known. Really they had no options: to close such a fleet, keeping such good order and with so many soldiers aboard, was to play into the enemy's hands; however nimble the English ships, any of them might be crippled aloft by chance shots and fall away into the enemy mass; worse, those going to their support would become involved in a general close mêlée which would probably end in disaster. The only prudent strategy was to keep up to windward and follow, harrying to prevent them coming to an anchorage – and if they attempted a landing to use the many smaller vessels of the fleet to cut out the boats carrying the soldiers between ships and shore. Howard expressed the policy in a letter next day: 'We mean so to course the enemy as that they shall have no leisure to land.'[24] Finally, 'dismissing each man to go aboard his own ship, his Lordship appointed Sir Francis Drake to set the watch that night.'[25]

What Sir Francis actually did that night will never be known. Frobisher and

Vischer's engraving of the Armada off Portland. It is difficult to relate the course of the engagement depicted here to contemporary descriptions or plans; it may be that the two galleasses in the foreground are closing to support the fleet flagship assailed by the bow guns of the diminutive English squadron (centre), but the wind direction (NE'ly) does not fit contemporary descriptions of this stage of the action. The galleasses appear to have an outrigger construction for the oars and broadside gun-ports below, not a design to inspire confidence either in their speed under oars or their stand-off gunnery power. Hugo de Moncada seems to have rigged a pavilion on his poop – but where is the mizzen-mast? Note the Spanish soldiers drawn up for a boarding contest along the outrigger, and in the background to the picture the warning beacons burning along the shore.

Poortlant

The sails of a large English warship were, from forward: on the bowsprit the spritsail – which can be seen here furled on its yard poking out ahead of the 'bonnet' laced to the foot of the fore-sail – on the fore-mast the fore-course, on the fore-topmast the fore topsail and on the fore t'gallant mast the fore t'gallant sail; similarly on the main, the main course, main topsail and main t'gallantsail. The mizen set a lateen sail, and often a lateen mizen topsail on a mizen topmast, and finally the bonaventure mizen set a smaller lateen sail. The stays can be seen leading forward from the masts to the foot of the equivalent next mast forward or in the case of the foremast down to the bowsprit, the back stays and shrouds leading aft either side outboard to the chain-wales. The shrouds were crossed with ratlines to enable the sailors to climb up into the 'tops', used in battle as posts from which to fire or hurl down grenades and incendiary devices on the enemy decks. With the development of stand-off gunnery this post had become, at least for the English, less important. For clarity only one side of the running rigging has been shown. The 'braces' used to angle the yards can be seen running from the fore yards to a single purchase on the main t'gallant-, main topsail- and main-stays; those from the main upper yards led similarly to the mizen stay, from the main yard itself to the quarter deck.

While the upper part of the sails were set by bracing the yards to the required angle to the wind, the lower corners or 'clews' were held by tacks and sheets; on the weather 'clew' the tack was hauled forward and belayed to bits – hence a ship was said to be sailing on the port or starboard tack; the leeward clew was controlled by the sheet which led from a ring outboard aft to the clew, back to a block by the ring, thence inboard to be belayed under the shrouds. The leading edge or 'luff' of the sail was held up into the wind by a 'bowline' seen here on the leading edges of the main sails running to blocks on the main stays. The running rigging used for taking in sail is described on the facing page which illustrates a Spanish rigged ship.

English warship

There are no 'footropes' suspended below the yards on either the English warship, or the Spanish warship illustrated here; none are mentioned in contemporary descriptions, no doubt because sailors seldom had to go out along the yards, which were lowered to the deck, or in the case of the upper yards to the top when sail was furled. Before that the canvas would be gathered in by hauling on three sets of lines, the 'clew garnets' which pulled the lower corners or 'clews' up to the centre section of the yard, the 'buntlines', not shown here, which hauled the 'bunt' or central cloths up to the yard, and the 'martnets' shown here in a crow's-foot pattern to the after edges or 'leeches' of both fore and main courses.

The balance of canvas a ship carried had to be attended to carefully with changes in wind force and direction so that she almost steered herself; the spritsail, mizen and bonaventure were the principal balancing sails.

Spanish warship

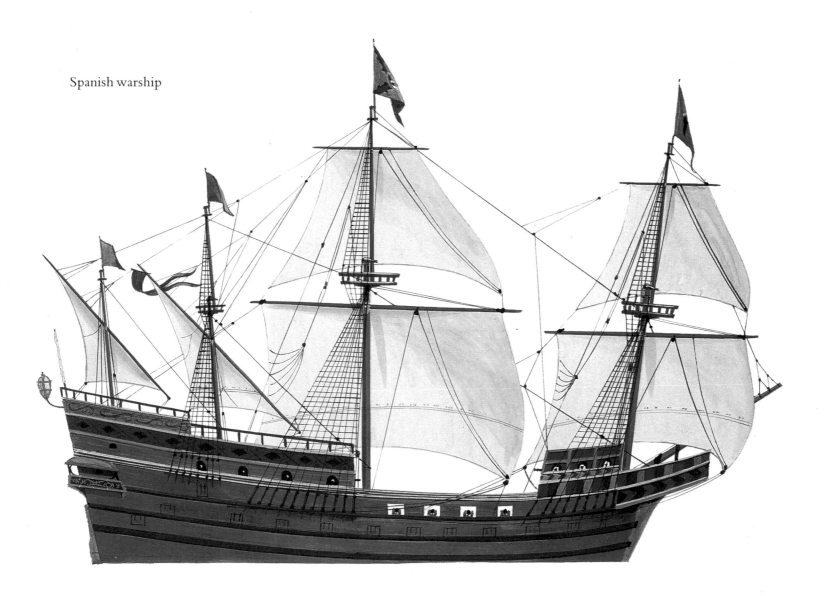

others suspected him of keeping the watch on Don Pedro's galleon as she was deserted by the rest of the Armada; certainly he extinguished his lights, and Howard, apparently mistaking Spanish lights for the *Revenge*'s, found himself dangerously close to the enemy next morning with most of his ships straggling far astern. Drake's own story was that he extinguished his lights in order to investigate ships he feared might be doubling back to gain the wind of them in the night. It is an unlikely tale since the *Nuestra Senora del Rosario* was seen falling astern of the rest by the whole English fleet that evening; as darkness fell the 200-ton merchantman, *Margaret and John*, approached her, but hesitated to lay her aboard because of the way she was rolling in the trough of the seas; instead they gave her a volley of muskets, some loaded with balls, some with arrows, into the high stern-castle, apparently to see if anyone was still aboard. For answer they received two round shot. They fired their own broadside in reply, then kept her company until about midnight when, 'fearing his Lordship's displeasure if we should stay behind the fleet',[26] they made all sail to catch up with Howard. So she was left; so Drake, accompanied by the 300-ton merchantman, *Roebuck*, owned by Sir Walter Raleigh, and one or two small craft, found her at first light.

Pedro de Valdés was alone without possibility of relief; he was beside himself with rage at Medina Sidonia for abandoning him and now, with no less a figure than *el Draque* in the *Revenge*, guns loaded and match alight, calling on him to yield, he sent emissaries across to seek terms. The best they could obtain were 'the safety of our lives and courteous entertainment'; he accepted without ado. Drake gave him his hand 'and word of a gentleman', which he kept, taking Don Pedro and his officers and gentlemen adventurers aboard his flagship and introducing him to Howard when he caught up with the fleet later that day. Howard received the Spaniard courteously and sympathised with him for the treatment he had received at Medina Sidonia's hands.[27] What Howard thought of Drake's proceedings is not recorded. Meanwhile the *Roebuck*, whose captain Drake had appointed to take the galleon to the nearest port, was heading downwind with her towards Weymouth, presumably after a jury foremast had been set up.

Another prize fell into English hands that day, Monday, August 1st. The *San Salvador* had been proving difficult to handle under tow during the night, and was obviously a liability until major repairs had been undertaken, and there was no time for that. Some of her injured men and some of the money she was carrying were taken out and on receiving a report at about 11 o'clock that she was making water, Medina Sidonia ordered the rest of the men brought off and the ship sunk. She was evidently trailing by then and the English were hanging to windward, also it was not easy to get the badly burned men down the side so, after as many as possible had been rescued by the pataches, she was simply cast off. Late in the afternoon John Hawkins' *Victory*, and the *Golden Lion* commanded by Howard's cousin, Lord Thomas Howard, glided up to her in light airs and the two commanders went aboard. They found her in a ghastly state:

. . . the deck of the ship had fallen down, the steerage broken, the stern blown out, and about 50 poor creatures burnt with powder in most miserable sort. The stink in the ship was so unsavoury, and the sight within board so ugly that the Lord Thomas Howard and Sir John Hawkyns shortly departed and came unto the Lord Admiral to inform his Lordship in what case she was found.[28]

Howard ordered Thomas Flemyng of the *Golden Hinde* to take her into the nearest port. It was Weymouth again.

No fighting took place that day, probably because Howard had spent most of the morning gathering up his scattered ships, and during the afternoon the wind fell away until both fleets lay becalmed.

Medina Sidonia, evidently dissatisfied both with the previous day's battle formation and the way some of the captains had behaved, drew up a new order of battle with only two divisions, a vanguard and a rearguard. Since Recalde's flagship was still making repairs, he appointed de Leyva overall commander of the rear, giving him '43 of the best ships of the Armada' including three galleasses and the galleons of the Portuguese squadron, *San Mateo*, *San Luis*, *Florencia* and *Santiago*. His task was 'to withstand the enemy and prevent him from standing in the way of our junction with Parma'.[29] He himself would take command of the van. Having appointed every ship in the fleet to a precise station, he had the new battle order copied out six times by his secretaries and despatched six pataches around the fleet, a sergeant major in each to ensure that every captain knew his station. They carried written instructions to be shown with the battle order that any captain whose ship left her assigned place was to be hanged; provost marshals and executioners accompanied them to lend grim weight to the warning. Whether this was Medina Sidonia's idea or that of Diego Flores, it was a nonsense typical of the military mind, as the next day's fighting in shifts and flukes of wind was to demonstrate. Perhaps it was simply intended as a warning not to retire from the enemy.

The same day he sent his English-speaking officer, Juan Gil, in a patache to Parma in Flanders; Gil took a letter the Duke had written after the previous day's action beseeching Parma to reply to the points he had put to him in his earlier letter, also asking for pilots for the Flanders coast; 'without them I am ignorant of the places where I can find shelter for ships so large as these, in case I should be overtaken by the slightest storm.' The English fleet had exchanged cannon fire with them, he wrote, and were following with the intention 'apparently of delaying and impeding our voyage. If their object had been to fight, they had a good opportunity of doing so today.' He added a note to say that the enemy continued to harass his rear, and signed it 'Off Portland, 20 Leagues from Plymouth.'[30]

By dawn next day, Tuesday, August 2nd, a light breeze had sprung up from north-easterly, giving Medina Sidonia the weather gage for the first time since Howard had taken it off Plymouth. Now in the early light of a fine day, he saw the English ships casting round to sail north-westerly, hauling taut on the lee braces and the weather bowlines and clawing into the wind to try and recover their advantage around his landward flank; he loosed his sails, fired a signal gun and had his flagship turned on to the same tack to head them off. What the order of the fleet was like after the calms of the night is impossible to know; from his own account it seems he led with the galleasses in company 'and the rest of the fleet followed.' Probably there was no set order as the captains did what they could to conform to his movements. It is equally impossible to know exactly where the fleets were. The previous day he had signed his note to Parma 'off Portland'; almost certainly that was in the morning since the letter he sent had been written the day before that, and he had been desperate to contact Flanders. The winds had been westerly then until they fell away in the afternoon. Probably he was well past Portland now; the tide had been running eastwards since before midnight.

In the brief diary of events which Howard sent Walsyngham a fortnight later, he recorded the action as beginning 'over against St Albans about five of the clock in the morning'.[31] In that case the Armada was even further up-Channel before the fleets started their north-westerly haul; they were probably past Durlston Head, opening the view into the bay which sweeps around to Bournemouth and the Hampshire coast leading into the Solent. Perhaps the dawn breeze was a land breeze with more north than east in it, and Howard, somewhere off St Albans Head and rather further offshore than the Spanish – since the wind had last been in the south-west and he had been keeping to windward – was heading towards Lulworth with the grey line of Portland Bill rising like an island over the rim of the horizon on his lee bow. Medina Sidonia put on all sail and steered rather more westerly to close. Now, he must have felt, was his opportunity. This hypothesis fits the Spanish purser Calderon's account: 'The Duke steered towards them with the intention of engaging them, but the enemy clapped on all sail and fled.'[32]

Howard soon realised he had no chance of working to windward inshore; since there is no question about the vastly superior sailing qualities of the English ships, this tends to confirm the suspicion that he started further from the shore than the Spanish. He therefore 'cast about to the eastwards' with the intention of trying to work for the wind around the seaward flank of the Armada – what Calderon described as fleeing. Medina Sidonia went about after him and steering large with the wind on his quarter again tried to close for a boarding contest. Up to this point there is no conflict between the accounts from both sides but now, by the Spanish account the English sheered off when they saw it was their intention to close, by the English account they 'stood fast and abode their coming.'[33]

It is evident the English ships did not 'stand fast' for long; had they done so Medina Sidonia could have brought on the close, grappling mêlée he longed for. What they probably did was to practise a variant of the tactics they had employed from the windward position, staying and firing a broadside at the leading Spanish vessel as it bore down, then filling and showing a nimble wake, leaving the next astern to fire her broadside and follow suit. Martin de Bertondona in the huge converted Venetian merchantman, *Regazona*, led the Spanish attack on Howard in the *Ark*; presumably he was following the Duke before they all went about; with him were the Portuguese galleons *San Marcos*, *San Luis*, *San Mateo*, *San Felipe*, *Santiago*, the splendid new galleon, *Florencia*, of the Duke of Tuscany, de Leyva in the *Rata*, the *San Juan de Sicilia*, and huge *Trinidad Valancera* of the Levant squadron, and the flagship of the Guipuzcoan squadron, Don Miguel de Oquendo's *Santa Ana* – several of the best and biggest of the Spanish first line which the Duke had designated for the 'rearguard' under de Leyva the previous day.

Howard, no doubt, 'stood fast' as Bertondona bore down hugely on the *Ark*, gave him his broadside, then put his helm up and stood away; Medina Sidonia wrote, 'as he (Bertondona) came near her (the *Ark*) she bare room (bore away) and stood out to sea.'[34] The other English Royal ships with Howard, John Hawkins' *Victory*, Robert Southwell's *Elizabeth Jonas*, Thomas Fenner's *Nonpareil* 'and divers others' gave their broadsides in turn and followed their Commander-in-Chief. The English 'Relation' virtually concedes that something like this happened: 'the enemy, seeing us to abide them, and divers of our ships to stay for them . . . were content to fall astern of the *Nonpareil*, which was the sternmost ship.'[35] In other words the English showed them their heels in something like a group line.

Meanwhile a small group around Frobisher in the *Triumph* had become separated from the main body of the fleet with Howard. One of these was a sizeable merchantman called the *Merchant Royal*, the four others were smaller merchantmen, including the *Margaret and John*, which had challenged Don Pedro's crippled *Rosario* after the first day's action. Probably they had started some distance from Howard and it is certain the high and cumbersome *Triumph* would not have been able to point as close to the wind as the *Ark* during the run towards the land; now the group was some considerable way to leeward and the galleasses with Medina Sidonia, according to the English account, 'took courage' and bore down to attack them. The Duke sent a patache to order them to use sails and oars to close and board the enemy, and turned his flagship in the same direction.

What happened after this is impossible to disentangle from the reports. The wind either dropped away – perhaps the reason for the Duke's order to the galleasses to use oars as well as sails – then sprang up again from seawards, or light breezes veered round steadily through south-east into the south. Calderon gives the time of the wind shift to the south at 10 o'clock. By then the fleets must have been near Portland Bill. The tide had been setting west since six o'clock[36] and although not strong at that period of the moon, it would have carried the ships some five miles; the original north-westerly courses, the leeway the ships made and the continual bearing away of the English as they evaded Spanish attempts to close must have accounted for much of the other 14 miles distance between St Alban's Head and Portland Bill. The contemporary engravings done to Howard's direction show Frobisher's separated group just to the west of the Bill, and there has been speculation that he was, perhaps, trying to lure the enemy over the dreaded Portland Race. In the engraving the galleasses are shown precisely where the race would be on a westerly run of the tide. No contemporary made any mention of such a scheme, and there is no evidence of any kind to support the idea. The race would not have been at its worst during this period of neap tides and would have been slackening from about nine until scarcely noticeable by half past 10. Another theory that he was trying to entice them on to the Shambles rocks to the east of the Point is flawed by the fact that the tide was running all morning south-westerly *away* from the Shambles into the race beyond the Point. Howard thought Frobisher was 'in distress'; this is the only evidence about his position. It probably sums it up.

The galleasses approached close enough to Frobisher's little group to provoke an artillery duel; in the engraving they are shown using oars but this is probably a convention to differentiate them. Frobisher's ships are depicted in what looks like a typical stand-off manoeuvre – three pointing towards the enemy, firing bow pieces, one broadside to the enemy while firing, one heading away firing her stern pieces.

With the shift of wind to the south, veering into the sou-sou-west, Howard recovered the weather gage, but Frobisher's separated group on the northern wing was in danger of being completely cut off if the Spanish interposed between them. Howard gathered his ships and bore away northwards to Frobisher's relief, instructing the captains – presumably by sending a pinnace round – to follow him 'and to go within musket-shot of the enemy before they should discharge any one piece of ordnance'.[37] This is a historic order, the first example of what was to become standard in English Fighting Instructions and the basis of English naval supremacy in the heyday of fighting sail – to bear down with guns silent until so close the broadside could not miss its target.

Medina Sidonia recorded this foray as the enemy returning 'with tide and wind in their favour'; the tide turned about noon, so it was perhaps some time after noon that Howard bore down on what Medina Sidonia called his 'rear' – presumably the southern end of whatever formation the fleet was in by this time.

OVERLEAF
Plate V of John Pine's sequence, showing the fleets off Portland, gives a different impression to the Visscher engraving and the Ryther plan described in the text. Perhaps the right-hand skirmish shows the opening engagement with the wind in the east and the Spaniards bearing down on the English, who stand close-hauled to receive them; note the extreme angle at which the English yards are braced into the wind. The left and centre must show the position after the wind had gone round to the south and west in the English favour, and the Spaniards – re-formed in their perfect crescent – had resumed their course up-Channel, followed by the English. There is no record of a ship having lost her foremast as depicted centre-left. Note the galleass (centre) which does not differ materially from Visscher's apart from a line of presumably light guns along what appears to be the oar outrigger, and the lack of an after-castle.

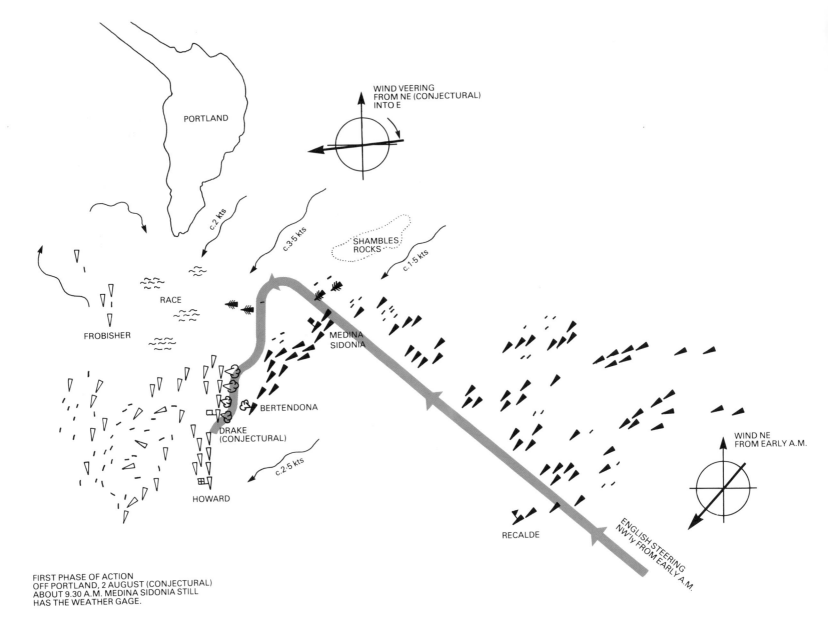

WIND VEERING
FROM NE (CONJECTURAL)
INTO E

PORTLAND

SHAMBLES
ROCKS

c.2 kts

c.3.5 kts

c.1.5 kts

RACE

FROBISHER

MEDINA
SIDONIA

BERTENDONA

DRAKE
(CONJECTURAL)

WIND NE
FROM EARLY A.M.

c.2.5 kts

HOWARD

RECALDE

ENGLISH STEERING
NW'ly FROM EARLY A.M.

FIRST PHASE OF ACTION
OFF PORTLAND, 2 AUGUST (CONJECTURAL)
ABOUT 9.30 A.M. MEDINA SIDONIA STILL
HAS THE WEATHER GAGE.

Plan devised by the author and drawn by Lionel Willis of the first phase of the action off Portland, on 2 August. It is largely conjectural; Medina Sidonia still has the advantage of the wind and is attempting to close with Howard who has no intention of allowing it. Martin Frobisher has sagged well to leeward and is off Portland with accompanying armed merchantmen. Far from plotting to ensnare the Dons in the race, he is in danger of being cut off himself, and two galleasses are already heading in his direction.

Here Juan Martinez de Recalde in his refitted flagship, *San Juan*, was holding the extreme windward position as in the first encounter off Plymouth, and it was against him that the English launched their first attack. The contemporary engraving shows Drake and a small group attacking the southern wing of the Spanish formation, and a Spanish soldier in a ship near Recalde reported that two shots from his vessel struck Drake's flagship, so it is probable that, as on the first day, the English bore down in two groups, the main fleet with Howard, a few adherents following Drake. Alonso de Leyva worked up to Recalde's support, and Medina Sidonia sent a message to the ships about him to do the same. He was following in the *San Martin*, when, according to his account the English left Recalde and bore down towards him instead. Since it was Howard leading and the southern group must have been shrouded in gun smoke, it is probable that the Duke mistook the situation and this was simply the main prong of a dual English attack. In any case, he fired a gun and went about to meet this challenge, then lowered his topsails in an invitation to Howard to close for what he regarded as a fight; instead 'the enemy's admiral and all the fleet passed her, each ship firing at our flagship as it passed.'[38]

She was unsupported during this enemy promenade, taking the full force of the broadsides of the chief English ships one by one but returning the fire with spirit, presumably with her lighter breech-loaders since it would not have been possible to reload the heavier pieces for some time after their first fire into the *Ark*. By one Spanish soldier's account she 'played with her cannon almost with the whole (English) army in such sort that in more than one hour we could not see her for smoke.' Calderon stated that the Duke engaged the enemy fleet alone for one and a half hours before any ships could work up to her support and fired 80 shots from one side, while the enemy fired at least 500 'some of which struck his (the Duke's) hull and others his rigging, carrying away his flagstaff and the stays of his mainmast.'[39] Another eyewitness from the Spanish side wrote:

The galleon, *San Martin*, being to windward of the Armada and near the enemy's ships, the latter attacked her with the whole of their cannon, she returning the fire with so much gallantry that on one side alone she fired off a hundred shots and the enemy did not care to come to close quarters with her although she was alone and her consorts were unable to aid her for one and a half hours.[40]

In the Duke's own diary of events his flagship 'fired her ordnance very well and fast, so as half the enemy's fleet did not approach, but shot at her from afar.' Gradually Recalde and the ships which had been supporting him, Oquendo in the *Santa Ana*, Alonso de Leyva in the *Rata*, the Marquis of Penafiel in the *San Marcos*, and others worked up to his support. By that time 'the hottest fury was past' and the enemy put about to seaward.[41]

The picture as described in the English 'Relation' looks rather different. The order of the English line was Howard leading in the *Ark*, and after him Sir Robert Southwell in the *Elizabeth Jonas*, George Fenner in the *Galleon Leicester*, Lord Thomas Howard in the *Golden Lion*, John Hawkins in the *Victory*, Edward Fenton in the *Mary Rose*, George Beeston in the *Dreadnought* and Hawkins' son, Richard, in the rather smaller *Swallow*. Against them Medina Sidonia 'came out with 16 of his best galleons to impeach his Lordship and to stop him from assisting of the *Triumph*. At which assault, after wonderful conflict, the Spaniards were forced to give way and flock together like sheep.'[42]

The English 'Relation' described the range of the action as half musket shot – perhaps 100 yards – 'yet could they not be discerned nor heard for that the great ordnance came so thick that a man would have judged it to be a hot skirmish of small shot.'[43]

All accounts agree that the English gunners were more expert and fired three times to the Spanish once. Despite this and the close range of at least a part of the action, damage and casualties seem to have been extraordinarily light. The *San Martin* which withstood the English first line for over an hour emerged with only her main stays and flag halyards parted, an unspecified number of holes in her hull and a few casualties, no doubt caused chiefly by the splinters of wood sent flying like darts across the deck as the round shot burst through the side. All the Spanish ships together lost only 50 killed – the English probably a good deal less although their casualties are not known. Spanish accounts and prisoners' depositions agree that little damage was done to the Spanish ships. The English Master Gunner, William Thomas, could only think that the English were being punished by the Almighty for their unworthiness; 'What can be said but our sins was the cause that so much powder and shot spent, and so long time in fight, and in comparison thereof, so little harm?'[44]

Since Medina Sidonia's account of the main action when Howard sailed to the relief of Frobisher is supported by so many independent witnesses it carries more credibility than the English account written afterwards in honour of the Lord Admiral. Nevertheless Howard did succeed in removing the threat to Frobisher. There were skirmishes later in the afternoon, but by evening the guns were silent, the ships gathering together, sailors in those ships which had been closely engaged repairing rigging and swabbing blood from the decks, carpenters' gangs making the rounds of the orlope and below to find and plug shot holes. All must have been tired to exhaustion, none more than the rival Commanders-in-Chief both of whom had been in the thick of the smoke and din of battle from the first exchanges in the early morning, and had had the severer strain of command. For try as hard as they could, and both had been the inspiration of their fleet, neither had found the key to unlock the opposing tactical necessities of their opponent and bring about a decision.

Howard, for all the skill with which his ships had evaded the Spanish attempts to close and board, for all the shot they had loosed in concentrated attacks on the chief enemy flagships had not succeeded in seriously damaging, let alone crippling or sinking a single vessel; both the prizes' injuries had been self-inflicted. Nor had he managed to break the order with which the Armada was proceeding or deflect it from its stately course up-Channel. More serious, his first line ships were running dangerously short of powder and shot. He sent urgent messages for further supplies, and ordered the ammunition to be taken from both prizes and sent out to the fleet 'with all possible expedition for that the state of the realm dependeth upon the present supply of such wants.'[45]

Medina Sidonia had quite as many problems as Howard. He knew now that even with the advantage of the wind he would never be allowed to close; 'it was all useless', he wrote in his account of the action, 'for when the enemy saw that our intention was to come to hand-stroke with him, he bore away, his great advantage being in the swiftness of his ships.'[46] The galleasses especially disappointed him; in the light and shifting winds of the day and holding the weather gage in the earlier stages, they should have been able to use their extra mobility under oars to bring a decisive concentration to bear on a part of the enemy. 'A fine day this has been!' he wrote tersely to the galleass commander, Moncada, 'If the galleasses had come up as I expected the enemy would have had . . .' What? He continued:

The important thing for us is to proceed on our voyage, for these people (the English) do not mean fighting, but only to delay our progress. In order to prevent this, and enable the Armada to keep on its way with safety, it is advisable that it should sail in two squadrons, vanguard and rearguard. The rearguard shall be reinforced by the best ships in the fleet, one half under the command of Juan Martinez (de Recalde), and the other half under Don Alonso de Leyva.[47]

With Recalde's flagship back in fighting order, the Duke had returned virtually to the original arrangement of three divisions, but in a different disposition. Now the chief fighting strength was concentrated in what were virtually two rearguard divisions under Recalde and de Leyva, and he instructed Moncada to attach his flag galleass and two others to Recalde: 'You will keep the three galleasses well together and ready to proceed without further orders to any point where they might be needed.' He took the fourth galleass with him in the van.

How these new divisions were disposed is not apparent; the English described no difference in the overall formation, which remained a crescent; the engravings show Medina Sidonia's flagship in the concavity of the rear rank at the centre, Recalde's Vice-flagship at the tip of the northern wing – thus both roughly where they had been in the first day's action. From the accounts of the fighting over the next two days it is apparent that de Leyva stationed himself close to Recalde and the galleasses with the Vice Admiral; it seems, therefore, that the '43 best ships of the Armada' which had been distributed to the rearguard two days before were in the northern wing with their two divisional commanders and the galleasses at the extreme northern tip of the wing. The twenty other fighting ships left for the 'van' must, therefore, have formed the southern wing of the crescent with Medina Sidonia commanding from *their* northern end – not quite in the centre of the line but about two-thirds of the way from Recalde. Why, when the prevailing winds were *south*westerly – and had been so during most of the passage up-Channel – the strongest ships should be placed on the *northern* wing is a mystery. Was the crescent perhaps inclined so that the northern wing or 'rearguard' trailed more than the van? If both rearguard and vanguard were sailing in quarter line (diagonally) on their respective commanders, the rear having twice as many ships would have stretched further back – twice as far back as the van. But this is pure speculation and there are doubtless other ways of interpreting the scanty evidence.

The formation itself, either a curving line abreast as in the English depictions, or quarter lines from the divisional commanders, cannot be doubted because it was the obvious and essential tactical formation – a point which has been widely misunderstood. 'Line abreast' with a following wind – as this was – immediately became 'line ahead' as the ships turned into the wind to meet an enemy attack, and close-hauled 'line ahead', as the formation then became, was the only rational formation for broadside-armed sailing ships. It not only allowed unimpeded use of the main battery, but enabled ships to come up in support of consorts. Running before the wind in line or lines ahead would have been disastrous, exposing the rear ships to defeat in detail, the ships ahead of them unable to work up to their support, or mixing in total confusion if they tried to do so.

The wording of the Duke's note to Hugo de Moncada, 'The important thing for us is to proceed on our voyage', suggests that he had dropped his intention of making a stay at the Isle of Wight, despite still not having heard from Parma. Of course he realised by now that the English intended sitting on his tail, and he must have been advised of the difficulties at the best of times of bringing his unwieldy mass of ships into the shoals and fast tides of Spithead, the actual dangers of running into the Solent; to do so under fire and to attempt a landing in the face of the myriad small craft which had attached themselves to the English fleet must have looked the more dangerous of his options. And if he were to succeed, with the English fleet parading outside, he would be bottled up like a rat in a sack with no hope of getting replenishments of powder and shot or men from Parma. It is probable he had abandoned the idea of the Isle of Wight. Alternatively, he may have left the decision open; perhaps he intended allowing God to give him indications with wind and weather. There is no evidence of his thoughts.

By dawn next day, Wednesday, August 3rd, he was up with the Isle of Wight but well to the south as prudence dictated; he was sailing before a westerly breeze with his fleet in good order, and from his poop he could see the English sails, as ever stretching across the windward horizon, showing perhaps hints of red reflected from the eastern sky, the nearest of them probably five to six miles away. To the northwards one of the largest of the enemy galleons with smaller escorts was closing the gap to Recalde and the galleasses at the rear. She fired. Puffs of smoke rose about her foc's'le, thinning before the head sails as the reports carried, thudding across the intervening sea. The galleasses replied with their stern pieces, and Recalde and de Leyva and the others at the rear joined in without deviating from their course. Intermittent reports crashed out, then a shot from one of the galleasses carried away the Englishman's main yard, and she began to fall back; the firing ceased.

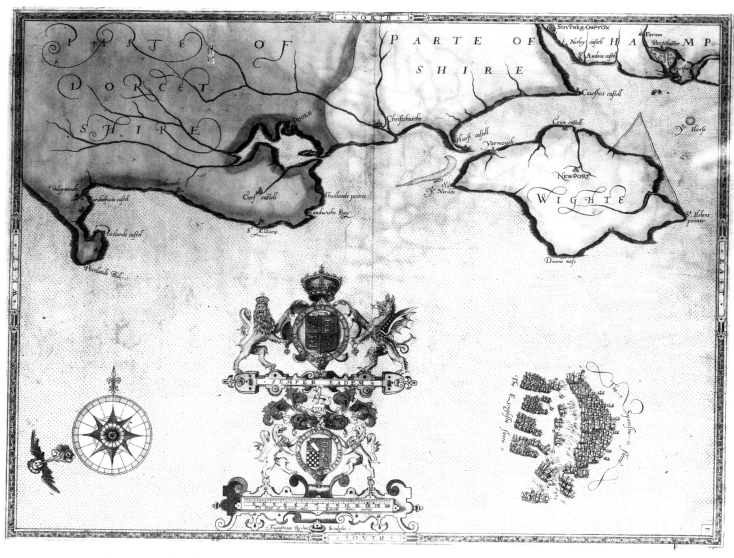

The seventh in the sequence of Ryther plans showing the opening phase of the action south of the Isle of Wight. A total of eight ships from the four distinct English squadrons have been towed ahead by boats and are engaging the Spaniards arranged in an immaculate defensive crescent, except at the southernmost tip where there appear to be two stragglers.

The English account makes no mention of this skirmish. Probably the large galleon was Frobisher's *Triumph* for he seems to have been on the northern flank in all the fighting; it was not Howard, or the Spanish accounts would have referred to the fleet flagship.

Presently the wind fell away and the two fleets lay becalmed with some five miles of flat, gently heaving sea between them. Howard spread his flag for a council; there is no record of the discussion, but it was decided to formalise the group tactics that had been pursued naturally up to then; the fleet was divided into four squadrons commanded by Howard, Drake, Hawkins and Frobisher respectively. Probably Howard repeated his exhortation of the day before to waste no powder and shot 'at random' but to close to musket-shot or less before opening fire. And to keep the enemy on edge and 'waking' that night, he ordered each squadron commander to choose six merchant ships from his group to 'set upon the Spanish fleet in sundry places.' An attack on the Isle of Wight was feared.

The trained bands on the Island were encamped under the command of the Governor, Sir George Carey, watching the cloud of sails along the horizon with anxious eyes and wondering if tomorrow they would be in action. The sky showed no signs of a change in the weather.

The ships drifted to the tide, their sails hanging lifeless for the rest of the day and through the night so the groups of merchantmen could not be sent out to tease the enemy's nerves. But by first light on Thursday morning, August 4th, light airs were stirring, riffling catspaws over the surface. The fleets were south of the southernmost point of the Isle of Wight by now and still some distance to seawards, perhaps 10 to 15 miles. Two of the Spanish rear had fallen astern of station and one, a great converted merchant hulk of the Andalusian squadron named the *Duqesa Santa Ana*, was by one Spanish account close to the enemy.

The English fleet is shown in the engravings formed neatly into the four squadrons which had been arranged the previous day. Frobisher's was the northernmost, Hawkins next on his right – both by inference from the subsequent course of events – next Howard's, the *Ark* depicted with the Royal Standard at the fore, the cross of St George at the main, and Drake's – again by inference – the southernmost. How they formed themselves in the calms of the previous day is not clear; no doubt they had been in roughly these positions before.

John Hawkins was nearest to the straying *Santa Ana*, and he immediately put down his longboats and had the *Victory* towed towards her; as they approached, the boat's crews were met by volleys of musketry from the Spaniard's castles. By this time both the *Ark* and Lord Thomas Howard's *Golden Lion* were under tow in support of Hawkins and from the Spanish rear Moncada's galleasses were towing Recalde's flagship and de Leyva's *Rata* to the support of their ship. No doubt Frobisher was also towing into action towards the Spanish rear, and it is difficult to believe that Drake was not doing the same from his southern station; in the engravings eight English ships are shown under tow. The approach of the galleasses and the galleons of Recalde and de Leyva prevented the English from closing with the *Santa Ana*, and a hot artillery duel ensued in which, according to the English 'Relation', the *Ark* and the *Golden Lion* damaged the galleasses and forced them to retire, one of them listing. According to Spanish accounts the galleasses succeeded in towing the stragglers back into the main body of the fleet.

Meanwhile a breeze sprang up from the southward which allowed Medina Sidonia to bring his flagship and the galleass with him, the *Patrona*, under captain Peruchio, towards the action. Seeing these two coming up without support Howard collected his ships and led an attack on the *San Martin*; by the Duke's account 'they came closer than the first day, firing their heaviest pieces from the lower deck and cut the flagship's main-stay, and killed some of our soldiers.'[48] This suggests that in the previous days' fighting the seas had been too high for the English to risk opening their lower tier of gunports; alternatively the Duke may simply have meant that the two heaviest pieces aft where the gun deck stepped down had not been used before. He was rescued from what appeared to be another lone defence against odds by Oquendo's *Santa Ana* and other ships from the rear, who sailed up close-hauled and covered him, receiving the full force of the next English attack, which was close and heavy.

As the last of the English line bore away to recharge and regroup, Medina Sidonia saw Frobisher's great ship, *Triumph*, to leeward and led down to cut her off. Frobisher had evidently been in close action with the northern wing and now the breeze had sprung up he was in the same precarious situation he had been in off Portland. His heavy ship was sluggish in light airs, and seeing the danger he was in as the *San Martin*, Recalde's *San Juan*, *San Juan de Sicilia*, *San Cristobal* – flagship of the Castilian squadron – *Gran Grin* and others bore down towards him, he lowered his flag and fired guns to call for assistance, and had his boats' crews tow him away; nearby ships sent their boats to assist until he had 11 straining to move him clear. Still the Spanish group coming down with the wind filling the sails blazoned with crosses gained on him. Medina Sidonia felt that his moment had come. Other English ships to windward, Lord Sheffield's *White Bear* and Robert Southwell's *Elizabeth Jonas* among them, were coming round to go to her assistance, and once his own ships managed to grapple the *Triumph*, as it seemed they must quite soon, the English would be bound to close to try and rescue her. 'We made sure that at last we should be able to board them, which was our only way of gaining the victory', he wrote afterwards.[49] The chance was snatched from him. 'At this moment the wind freshened in favour of the enemy's flagship (*Triumph*) and we saw that she was getting away from us and had no further use of the boats.' With this stronger breeze even the *Triumph* could outsail the fleetest of the Spanish. The purser, Calderon wrote, 'she got out so swiftly that the galleon *San Juan* and another fast ship – the speediest vessels in the Armada – seemed in comparison with her to be standing still.'[50]

It was about 11 o'clock by now. Medina Sidonia, seeing he could do nothing more to bring the English to close action, fired a gun to gather his fleet and bore away easterly on his course, the ships re-forming about him in their tight crescent. Howard and his squadronal commanders gathered their groups and followed.

Sir George Carey, watching from the Isle of Wight, saw the sails disappear over the horizon in the south-east; by three o'clock they were out of sight; he had sent Howard several pinnaces with reinforcements, and one returned bringing him the news that 'thanks be to God, there hath not been two of our men hurt.'[51] If so, the Spanish gunnery was extraordinarily ineffective; since there are other indications of the very few English casualties, it probably was.

That afternoon Medina Sidonia sent off yet another message to Parma, which he entrusted to a captain of soldiery, Pedro de Leon. Since his last advice, he wrote, he had only made slow progress because of calms and the enemy's harassment:

. . . but the enemy has resolutely avoided coming to close quarters with our ships although I have tried my hardest to make him do so. I have given him so many opportunities that sometimes some of our vessels have been in the very midst of the enemy's fleet to induce one of his ships to grapple and begin the fight; but all to no purpose as his ships are light, and mine very heavy, and he has plenty of men and stores. My stores are running short with these constant skirmishes; and if the weather do not improve, and the enemy continues his tactics, as he certainly will, it will be advisable for your Excellency to load speedily a couple of ships with powder and ball of the sizes noted in the enclosed memorandum, and to despatch them to me without the least delay. It will also be advisable for your Excellency to make ready to put out at once to meet me, because, by God's grace, if the wind serves, I expect to be on the Flemish coast very soon . . .[52]

Although he assumed that the small craft he had seen joining Howard from practically every port they had passed on the way up-Channel were bringing replenishments of ammunition, after three battles and several skirmishes, the English had practically expended their powder and shot and Howard had decided he could not attempt anything more until he had been joined by Lord Henry Seymour's fresh ships from Dover, and had received further supplies from the shore. All he could do was shadow the Armada as it proceeded east-nor-easterly for the Straits.

Despite this failure to affect the Spanish progress, he seems to have been well pleased with his commanders; perhaps he felt that the constant harrying had prevented the Spanish from attempting a landing from the various anchorages and havens they had passed, and the last day's action had prevented Medina

Plate VIII of John Pine's sequence showing the Armada being 'harried' up-Channel by the English fleet formed in four squadrons and on the right Lord Henry Seymour's squadron sailing out from the Downs to join Howard off Calais.

Sidonia taking the Isle of Wight, always the most exposed threat in English eyes. Perhaps it had. At any rate, as the light breeze dropped away again on the next morning, Friday, August 5th, and the two fleets lay becalmed a few miles from each other with the gentle undulations of the Sussex Downs lined above the northern horizon, he called his squadronal commanders and other captains who had distinguished themselves to his flagship and knighted them on the quarterdeck. Drake had already been knighted by Elizabeth; if fleet rank counted, John Hawkins should have been dubbed first but hereditary rank counted more and it is probable it was done in the order in which the names are listed in the 'Relation' of events – his kinsman, Lord Thomas Howard, commanding the *Golden Lion* which had always supported the *Ark* in the thick of the fighting, Lord Sheffield, commanding the great *White Bear*, who had hazarded himself in going to Frobisher's support off the Isle of Wight, Sir Roger Townshend, whose special service is not now known, Martin Frobisher, who had fought his way out of dangerous scrapes off Portland and the Isle of Wight, John Hawkins, whose initiative had precipitated the last action and George Beeston commanding the *Dreadnought*; each knelt before him in the swinging shadows of the rigging and furled canvas to receive the touch of his sword on their shoulder. Undoubtedly they deserved this battlefield honour; undoubtedly it was also effective theatre; the news must have spread rapidly through every ship in the fleet, heightening morale.

Medina Sidonia, increasingly desperate about the lack of any reply from Parma, sent yet another patache off with a message for him; again he asked for powder and shot, also for 40 flyboats light and swift enough to catch the enemy ships and force them to fight, and he reiterated his plea for the Army to be ready to come out directly the Armada arrived in sight of Dunkirk.

That evening the wind got up again from the south-west, and he bore away for the Straits; the English fleet followed his crescent in its four squadrons under Sir Martin Frobisher, Sir John Hawkins, Lord Howard and Sir Francis Drake. During the night the wind freshened and Saturday blew in with a heavy overcast and rain squalls reducing visibility. Through the grey light the coast of the Pas de Calais was sighted at about 10 o'clock and course altered northerly to round Cape Gris Nez; the tide was running northwards, reaching more than two knots by noon, helping them along at a fair speed over the ground and by early afternoon they had rounded the Cape and were sailing easterly towards Calais. As the tide turned the Duke discussed with his staff whether to anchor or carry on to Dunkirk. His diary records a difference of opinion, 'the majority' – probably his chief of staff and the other naval and military officers – 'being in favour of sailing on.' His pilots however told him that if he did so the tides would carry him into the North Sea and make it difficult to return to the Straits.[53] He took their advice, deciding to go no further, but have Parma join him here. A signal gun was fired; the flagship turned for the shore, and with men in the chains crying decreasing soundings and the tide picking up ever more strength against the lee bow, she dropped anchor just short of Calais roads. Howard did the same, coming to anchor about two miles astern of his rear ships, 'within culverin shot'.

Lord Henry Seymour had been lying at anchor with his small squadron in the Downs that morning; he had instructions to sail to Dunkirk to prevent Parma coming out, an order he disagreed with since, as he explained to the Privy Council, while the wind held in the west-sou-west the enemy could not come across; moreover the merchant ships with him would not be able to maintain a blockade if the wind changed and blew off the land. He had sent a pinnace to Flushing on the second of the month immediately he learnt that the Armada was in the Channel, to ask for the promised Beggars' ships to join him but, like Medina Sidonia, had had no reply, and no ships had come. He suspected they were more interested in guarding their own coast than helping him.

He was flying his flag in the *Rainbow*, one of the Queen's smaller fighting galleons; his chief naval advisor, the veteran Sir William Wynter, commanded the *Vanguard*, and Sir Henry Palmer the *Antelope*, both Royal ships similar to the *Rainbow*; otherwise, he only had two 150-ton Royal ships whose largest gun was a Saker, a galley, *Bonaventure*, of doubtful use in anything but smooth water, and for the rest mainly small coasters of little fighting value from the cinque ports and East Anglian rivers; their poor sailing qualities were likely to make them more of a handicap than a source of strength.

In the early afternoon one of his scouts brought the thrilling news that both Medina Sidonia and Howard were approaching the Straits. He had been itching to join the earlier actions; now, disregarding his instructions from the council, he ordered his squadron to prepare for sea, and as the tide turned and set southwards through the anchorage he beat out around the south Goodwin sand, then trimmed his sheets for the French coast. In his later letters to the Queen he was at great pains to point out he had 'both message and letter from my Lord Admiral to repair unto him with all my forces, which I did incontinent.'[54] Perhaps that is how it happened; with his shortage of ammunition Howard needed all the force he could muster. The galley *Bonaventure* followed the squadron out of the Downs, but could not contend with the wind and seas, and returned to the anchorage on the change of tide. Seymour and the rest of the squadron joined Howard at anchor at eight that evening.

The Spaniards watched them come; with the reinforcements the English had had all the way up-Channel, they numbered 150 sail or more by now; the impression was more of a vast flotilla of mainly small vessels than a powerful fleet; only 18 or 20 looked sizeable galleons;[55] only 18 or 20 were. Yet for Medina Sidonia all the signs were ominous; he was over 20 miles short of Dunkirk, he had not heard from Parma, he was beginning to doubt if he was there; he had no pilot with detailed knowledge of the shoals which flanked the run of the Flanders coast and did not know of any harbours where his fleet could lie safely; beyond Flanders were the islands of Zealand and the Scheldt which the Sea Beggars commanded; where he was, he was in the utmost peril if a storm should blow up; meanwhile the English, who were undoubtedly receiving fresh stores of powder and shot, could creep up on wind and tide and bombard him at leisure and he had no means of replying effectively; he needed to husband the little ammunition he had left until Parma sent him replenishments. He despatched one of his secretaries in a boat up the coast with yet another message for Parma; in it he allowed some of his extreme anxiety to show:[56]

I have constantly written to your Excellency, giving you information as to my whereabouts with the Armada, and not only have I received no reply to my letters, but no acknowledgement of their receipt has reached me. I am extremely anxious at this, as your Excellency may imagine; and to free myself of the doubt as to whether any of my messengers have reached you safely, I am now despatching this flyboat with the intelligence that I am at anchor here, two leagues from Calais, with all the Armada, the enemy's fleet on my flank, and able to bombard me, whilst I am not in a position to do him much harm. I feel obliged to inform your Excellency of this, and to beseech you, if you cannot at once bring out all your fleet, to send me the 40 or 50 flyboats I asked for yesterday as, with this aid, I shall be able to resist the enemy's fleet until your Excellency can come out with the rest, and we can go together and take some port where this Armada may enter in safety . . .

9

The Battle of Gravelines

Parma was at his headquarters in Bruges, somewhat further to the east of Dunkirk than the Armada was to the west of the port, when he received Medina Sidonia's latest, anxious message next day, Sunday, August 7th. He had received the first of the series of messages detailing the progress of the Armada since sailing from Corunna five days before and had replied the following day, August 3rd. It is not known what he said, nor why it took the bearer, Captain Don Rodrigo Tello, so long to reach Medina Sidonia; the Duke did not receive it until this same Sunday morning off Calais. Meanwhile Parma, according to his own account, prepared his boats and troops for embarkation.[1] He did not leave his headquarters to take personal charge of the arrangements, however, and officers who landed from the Armada and saw the state of the boats were horrified; one found 'the vessels still unfinished, not a pound of cannon on board, and nothing to eat,'[2] and an intelligence report dated 11th August stated 'There has been very bad management with the Flemish ships, which cannot be ready for another fortnight . . .'[3]

Why Parma was unprepared despite all the news of the Armada's progress he had received from Philip and lately from Medina Sidonia emerges from his correspondence, but the parallel mystery of why Medina Sidonia expected him to furnish the Armada with flyboats able to tackle the English ships when it was his task to protect the Flanders boats has never been resolved satisfactorily and possibly never will be. Neither man was a fool, neither was idle. Parma was one of the most able, energetic and successful commanders to lead a Spanish Army; Medina Sidonia was equally energetic and determined, and enjoyed the advice of the most experienced naval commanders. It used to be the fashion to blame him for obtuseness; more recently Philip has been blamed for not telling him of Parma's weakness at sea, not only in relation to the English but to the Sea Beggars of Zealand and Holland.

Philip and his council had ample reports of the strength of the Sea Beggars' fleet; the Spanish Ambassador in Paris, Bernadino de Mendoza, who had a wide and efficient net of informers, had reported at the end of 1587 during Santa Cruz's preparations that the rebel states had '80 armed ships in the river at Antwerp and other places to prevent the sailing of the Duke of Parma's vessels', and had promised all these and a further 20 to Elizabeth should the Armada attack England.[4] He had added, however, that the Queen did not rely on them; she could not trust the rebel states.

The significance of this report did not strike Philip or his council; the instructions given to Santa Cruz in January 1588 made no mention of the Sea Beggars; the 'enemy' was merely the English fleet which, it was expected, would be divided into two separate forces under Drake and Howard; now came the crux of the mistake on which the whole Armada campaign was founded, the military habit of thought which estimated the strength of the opposing forces, as

Map of Flushing (1585), headquarters of the Dutch rebel fleet; from here the 'Sea Beggars' blocked all sea trade and communications with Antwerp, capital of the Spanish Netherlands, and controlled the coast of Flanders. This map allegedly shows the Earl of Leicester's fleet arriving to take possession of the town in aid of the rebel Dutch.

with armies on land, by numbers of men. And yet even in land campaigns, the nature of the ground and fortifications, weapons, discipline and morale all counted as much as numbers; for Philip and his advisors the advantage of training, discipline and experience lay with their own forces, and the possibility of the enemy making better use of the ground – in this case the sea and winds – did not enter their calculations. Thus:

as the most favourable statements with regard to the English fleets admit that they can hardly muster 3,000 seamen, and as many soldiers in each of their two fleets; so that even when they are united they will be inferior to ours, both as to quantity and quality . . . the Marquis (of Santa Cruz) may give the enemy battle, hoping that our Lord may give us the victory.[5]

This was the central mistake from which most others flowed.

Meanwhile Parma in Flanders had become alarmed both at the loss of secrecy, which had been an essential point in his original strategy, and at Philip's over-estimation of the ability of his 'fleet' in Flanders to cross the Channel in the presence of hostile forces. At the end of January he wrote to Philip to warn him of the little reliance that could be placed on his small craft, which were:

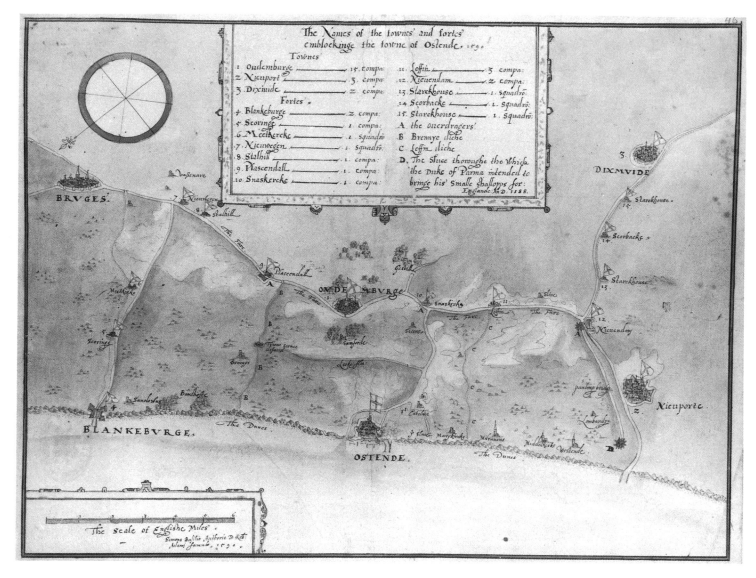

Map of the Netherlands coast near
Ostend (1590), showing the canals by
means of which Parma concentrated
his invasion flotilla.

not fit for anything but the passage itself, as they are too small for fighting, and so low
that four of the *esquifes* of the fleet could send to the bottom as many as they might meet.
They could hardly live through a freshet, much less a tempest, so that they can only be
used in settled weather . . .[6]

Despite this, he wrote, he could have taken the Army across the previous
Autumn had the Armada arrived then, since neither the English, Dutch nor
Zealanders had been prepared. Now, Holland and Zealand had armed their
fleets, had blockaded his few fighting ships in Antwerp, and the English had
made energetic preparations for defence. He asked Philip to instruct Santa Cruz
to come 'in great force . . . in case the English and the rebels form a junction.'

On February 22nd he wrote to Philip again, saying that his preparations were
complete, the transport boats collected at Sluys and Dunkirk, the munitions
aboard and the men concentrated nearby; again he reminded Philip that Santa
Cruz must come in sufficient force since 'the English and the rebels are now
strong and fully prepared with their fleets.'[7]

A month later, March 20th, he wrote to say that Elizabeth's peace commissioners had landed in Flanders. He was now completely pessimistic about the
chances of a successful invasion of England; this appears clearly from between
the lines as he advised the King to conclude peace with Elizabeth:

by this means we should end the misery and calamity of these afflicted States, the Catholic religion would be established in them, and your ancient dominion restored; besides which, we would not jeopardise the Armada which your Majesty has prepared, and we should escape the danger of some disaster, causing you to fail to conquer England, whilst losing your hold here . . .[8]

He repeated later in the same letter that 'the conclusion of a good and honourable peace' would 'avoid the risk of the disasters that may happen'. So far as strategy was concerned, he favoured making the island of Walcheren at the mouth of the Scheldt the first target; there at Flushing, headquarters of the Zealand fleet, was the strategically vital base for commanding the whole trade and communications on which the rebels depended. Afterwards, he assured Philip, with 'the island of Walcheren in your hands you may with perfect safety carry out your intention (with regard to England) without any possibility of interference.'

Two days later Parma wrote to Medina Sidonia, sending the letter with a Captain Moresin, who arrived on board the *San Martin* as it was dropping down the Tagus from Lisbon to Belem on May 11th. Medina Sidonia informed Philip that Moresin had been sent to find out the state of the Armada and to let him know about Parma's preparations in Flanders:

He has less troops than I expected, as this man tells me that they will not exceed 17,000 all told, with 1,000 light horse, and 300 small vessels, but none with oars or topmasts.[9]

Here, from his own pen, is proof that Medina Sidonia knew that Parma's 'fleet' consisted of small craft; it would be surprising indeed if Moresin had not told him that most were simply canal barges, and the larger fighting ships were blockaded in the Scheldt by the Sea Beggars. Nevertheless, not all were barges; some 30 or 40 were shallow-draft sailing craft, armed with guns, and Medina Sidonia might have formed the impression they had fighting value. Moresin was an Army captain, probably unversed in naval matters. There was ample scope for misunderstanding.

Parma, on the same day he addressed his message to Medina Sidonia, March 22nd, had written to Mendoza, Spanish Ambassador in Paris, about a planned Scottish intrigue, namely a force which was to be gathered by the Catholic Lords there and brought to the English border 'to make a diversion as soon as they should hear that the Queen is being pricked elsewhere' for 'if orders were sent to me to attempt anything, the help of these Catholics would be important, and would save expense, besides which, if they supported us, we could effectually assist them afterwards.'[10] Either he was convinced, despite his doubts about the outcome, that Philip intended to carry out an invasion of England and he meant this Scottish army to make common cause with the northern English Catholics, so forcing Elizabeth to divide her troops, or he still hoped he would be able to proceed against the rebels and their English allies with the aim of taking Walcheren – in which case the Scottish force would be a threat to prevent Elizabeth sending reinforcements across the Channel. There was also the possibility of the Armada being used against Ireland. No doubt he was insuring against all possibilities.

Philip appears not to have taken his advice about making a good peace; instead he instructed him to string the English commissioners along for as long as he could:

To you only, I declare my intention is that these negotiations shall never lead to any result, whatever conditions the English may offer. On the contrary, the only object is to deceive them, and to cool them in their preparations for defence . . .[11]

George Clifford, 3rd Earl of Cumberland. Miniature by Nicholas Hilliard, *c.* 1590. Cumberland was a favourite of Elizabeth, and commanded her ship *Elizabeth Bonaventure* against the Armada. This miniature probably commemorates Cumberland's appointment as Queen's Champion in 1590.

He completely misjudged Elizabeth and those about her. In any case, his instructions to Medina Sidonia, dated April 1st, like the earlier instructions to Santa Cruz, ignored the Sea Beggars entirely. Even more surprising in view of what Parma had told him about the rebel fleet, he seemed to think it possible the Flanders Army might get across the Channel without opposition; he added a rider to his instructions about fighting the enemy fleet or fleets under Howard and Drake, that these only held good if Parma's passage could not be effected in other ways:

. . . it being possible to secure the passage for the Duke without fighting, by diverting the enemy or by any other means, it will be good to achieve this while conserving the whole force.[12]

In addition to the general instructions, Philip sent Medina Sidonia secret instructions which directed him, in the event of failure in managing Parma's crossing, or failure in joining with him, to:

consider whether you cannot seize the Isle of Wight, which is apparently not so strong as to be able to resist . . . This will provide you with a safe port for shelter, and will enable you to carry out such operations as may be rendered possible by the importance of the position . . . If you obtain possession of the Isle of Wight, you will from there come to an understanding with my nephew, the Duke, and endeavour mutually to assist each other . . .[13]

On no account, however, was he to attempt the Isle of Wight on his way up-Channel, or before making every attempt to carry out the main plan.

With the secret instructions, Philip sent him a sealed despatch to be delivered to Parma when 'he has either landed in Britain, or exhibits uncertainty of being able to do so.' These instructions which neither Medina Sidonia nor Parma ever read, were in case the outcome appeared neither 'so favourable that (the affair) could be settled by force of arms, nor so unfavourable that there was cause for concern in face of the enemy', but things were so 'counterbalanced' that there were prospects for a favourable peace. Then Parma was to avail himself of the '*reputacion*', or prestige, of the Armada and open negotiations, fixing his sights on three principles: the first and most important to Philip was freedom for Catholics in England to practise their faith, and for Catholic exiles to return; the second was the return of the fortresses in the Netherlands held by the English, especially Flushing; the third was an indemnity for all the injuries the English had visited on Philip and his subjects. However, this last was more for use 'as a lever to obtain the other two.'[14]

Here Philip shows himself as having been closer to Parma's pessimism about the likely outcome of the invasion than is revealed by his open instructions to either commander, and quite as aware of the vital strategic importance of Flushing. When these sealed instructions to open peace negotiations with Elizabeth after the arrival of the Armada – either in the Thames or, failing a successful invasion of the mainland, off the Isle of Wight – are compared with his instructions about the current negotiations with Elizabeth's peace commissioners, which 'should never lead to any result', the purpose of the Armada seems clearer. It was a big stick to be waved in front of Elizabeth's nose in order to force terms, which could not be obtained under existing conditions; it was a means to negotiate from strength; it was also a visible proof to all the world and the bankers of the power and reach of the Spanish Crown.

Viewed in this light the Armada preparations and the orders issued to Medina Sidonia and Parma were a gigantic diversion. Professor Thompson has pointed out that Philip 'certainly did not want England for himself and knew he could

not possibly govern it personally . . . any attempt to annex England was
obviously foolhardy. Militarily it was likely to open for Spain another ulcer like
the one in the Netherlands; diplomatically no French King could ever accept
it.'[15] Philip's real purpose therefore was to neutralise England, and the cheapest,
most effective way was to support the Catholic party and provoke a civil war.
Hence, probably, the first and most important of the three principles Parma was
to strive for in negotiations, hence Philip's support for Parma's intrigue with the
Scottish Catholics.

This was possibly why Philip appears to have taken so little notice of the Sea
Beggars; perhaps the real tasks of the Armada were to maul Elizabeth's navy,
and flaunt itself at England's maritime gateway, when Parma would be able to
force the withdrawal of the English army from the Netherlands. In these
circumstances he would not need to hazard his troops in the barges at sea, but
could use them – and the barges – to complete the conquest of Zealand and
Holland. In short Philip was at one with Parma, but in order to conceal his real
intentions from the enemy felt it necessary to mislead his Commanders-in-
Chief.

The alternative is that the sealed orders amounted to no more than a reserve
position and the Armada was what it appeared to be, a force to overwhelm
English naval resistance to invasion. In that case his neglect of Parma's warnings
about the Sea Beggars must have stemmed from nautical and geographical
ignorance. That he *was* ignorant in these respects is shown in yet another
document delivered to Medina Sidonia with his instructions in April; this was a
copy of a letter dated September 14th, 1587, to the Cardinal Archduke in Lisbon,
containing instructions for Santa Cruz. He was directed to sail up the English
Channel and, having advised Parma of his approach, to anchor in the Downs –
'off Margate Cape' – whereupon Parma:

> as soon as he should see his crossing made secure by the presence of the Armada at
> Margate, or in the vicinity of the Thames Estuary, if the weather should have freshened,
> would then proceed to pass across his whole camp in small vessels . . .[16]

The words 'if the weather should have freshened' reveal ignorance of the
nature of Parma's barges and of the Flemish coast; weather strong enough to
drive the Armada from the Downs would have made it impossible for the barges
to emerge from their ports, let alone live in the seas outside. This also applies to
the galleys intended for the Armada, the only craft which might have been able
to protect the barges in the shallows off the Flanders coast. And the idea that the
crossing could be secured 'by the presence of the Armada at Margate' or in the
Thames reveals similar ignorance of naval realities, especially the superior
manoeuvrability of English warships, and of local conditions.

It is difficult to decide, therefore, whether Philip's unrealistic instructions to
Medina Sidonia, very similar to his earlier instructions to Santa Cruz, were due
in the main to ignorance or to unconcern – that is to say, if Parma were to get
across all well and good but that was not the essential purpose: the main thing
was to convince the English they were in imminent danger of invasion.

In any case the immediate effect was to convince Parma of the hazard of the
enterprise. His alarm was heightened when Captain Moresin returned with a
letter from Medina Sidonia on June 22nd; the letter had been written on the 10th,
before the Duke put in to Corunna and his fleet was scattered by the gale; it
informed him that the Armada was on the way but the Duke intended remaining
on the English coast until he had established contact with him (Parma);[17] and
from Moresin Parma learned that there were doubts about giving him the 6,000

Spanish troops he had been promised from the Armada. He wrote to Philip immediately, stressing the necessity for these men because the enemy was fully prepared and waiting; it would add greatly to the prospects of success if he could have an even larger number.

He was equally concerned that Medina Sidonia seemed to have convinced himself that he (Parma) could go out and meet him with his fleet of small boats:

These things cannot be, and in the interests of Your Majesty's service I should be very anxious if I thought the Duke (of Medina Sidonia) were depending upon them . . . with these little, low, flat boats, built for these rivers and not for the sea, I cannot diverge from the short, direct passage across which has been agreed upon . . . if I were to attempt . . . going out to meet the Duke and we came across any of the armed English or rebel ships, they could destroy us with the greatest of ease. This must be obvious, and neither the valour of our men nor any other human effort could save us. This was one of the principal reasons which moved Your Majesty to lay down the precise and prudent orders you did, that your Spanish fleet should assure us the passage across, as it was perfectly clear that these boats could not contend against big ships, much less stand the sea, for they will not weather the slightest storm . . .[18]

Before he received this, Philip had heard from Medina Sidonia how part of the Armada had been scattered after he had put in to Corunna. He had also received his subsequently pessimistic letter advising 'making some honourable terms with the enemy' (see p. 51) rather than continuing with the enterprise. Despite having all Parma's letters about the extreme fragility of his 'fleet' of small craft and his concern about the Sea Beggars' squadrons Philip made no mention of either in his detailed reply to Medina Sidonia. He gave instructions about restoring the men's health, preventing desertion and concentrating the fleet at Corunna, but added no single word to his general instructions about the strategic conduct of the campaign. When Medina Sidonia sailed from Corunna on July 22nd he was unaware of Parma's anxieties, and still believed that the Flanders Army would be able to put out to meet him in small boats. His ideas were exactly in line with his instructions. Recalde described them in a letter to Philip after a long discussion about the expedition with the Duke:

. . . the object of the Armada is to meet and vanquish the enemy by main force, which I hope to God we shall do if he will fight us, as doubtless he will. In the contrary case we have to proceed to the Downs, and there join hands with the Duke of Parma's force in Dunkirk, whose passage across we are to protect to the most convenient point which may be agreed upon. This point should be the nearest possible one on either side of the Thames. This will take some little time, as in the case of there being a cavalry force, as I understand there will be, it cannot be carried over in one passage, and we shall be fortunate if it can be done in two.[19]

With this clear statement of strategy to set against Parma's equally clear statement of despair about the possibility of going out to meet the Duke with 'these little, low, flat boats built for these rivers and not for the sea', Philip and his council could scarcely have been in doubt about the possibilities for misunderstanding. Yet his next letters to Medina Sidonia – which were in any case too late to reach him before the campaign had been decided – merely contained recommendations that since the season was so advanced, he should find a secure anchorage where the fleet could refit, and stressed 'how important it would be for you to enter and make yourself safe in the Thames itself.' This would compel the English to maintain two armies, one on each side of the river, and prevent them from receiving aid – the implied reference to the Hollanders and Zealanders is the only hint of the Sea Beggars' forces to be found in his correspondence –

'whilst keeping clear the passage from Flanders for sending the necessary reinforcements and supplies.'[20]

It seems as if Philip wilfully disregarded Parma's repeated, and finally despairing warnings about his own impotence in face of the Sea Beggars' fleet; 'These things cannot be,' he had put in his letter of June 22nd, 'I should be very anxious if I thought the Duke were depending upon them (his own boats)' – against which Philip had scrawled, 'God grant that no embarrassment may come from this.'[21]

To try and understand Philip's obduracy, it is necessary to recall that he did not know what we know and what Medina Sidonia had just discovered about the performance of the English fleet as that letter was penned. Philip was conducting the campaign in terms of traditional Mediterranean galley warfare where sizes of fleets and numbers of men counted, and where fleets and armies and seaside fortresses were mutually dependent, one on the other. Philip possessed no seaside fortresses in the Channel, and the Flanders coast was untenable for large ships, therefore it was necessary to take the Isle of Wight or the Thames Estuary. The most recent and only great battle between sailing galleons, when Santa Cruz had defeated and dispersed the French Protestant fleet off the Azores must have confirmed him in his ideas. For Strozzi, as related, had allowed himself to be drawn into a traditional boarding and entering contest.

In light of the known English tactics of stand-off artillery action and firing low to pierce the hull timbers, it would have been useful for Philip to have studied the Portuguese campaign in the Indian Ocean at the beginning of the century. Faced with the numerically hugely superior combined fleet of Egypt and Calicut, Vasco da Gama had instructed his captains 'by no means to board, but fight with the artillery,' and, sailing in two squadrons his ships close-hauled 'one astern of the other in a line', had shattered the enemy with gunfire; the wind had completed the destruction without the need for a single soldier to enter an enemy vessel.[22]

It would be absurd to expect that Philip, with all his vast responsibilities, could have studied and drawn lessons from naval history: that inferior fleets always had and presumably would devise tactics to avoid being overwhelmed by superior numbers. Yet he had been told of the English ships and their artillery tactics. The puzzle is to discern from his correspondence whether he and his close counsellors were simply obtuse about Parma's repeated warnings, and Medina Sidonia's doubt about his own ships and captains, discounting them because they did not fit the designed scheme, or whether he did not really expect Parma to go across, and held to the plan and intentionally misled both Commanders-in-Chief because that was the best way of convincing the enemy of the seriousness of the threat. Philip was not as bright as Elizabeth, but he was shrewd and experienced, devious and mistrustful, and it is easier to think that the Armada, as it finally sailed, was intended to overawe Elizabeth, not to mount a serious invasion, and that the true purpose was identical with Parma's: to subdue the rebel states and gain the island of Walcheren – after which, if England had not already dissolved in civil war, it would be time to settle matters finally with Elizabeth.

On the other hand, his illness and age and long exercise of supreme and unchallenged authority may have worked their usual decay; he may have been impervious to argument, rigid and obstinate, desperate, ill-advised and determined to strike this blow for the faith in the short time he expected might remain to him in this world. It is not impossible that shut up in his close chambers by the chapel at San Lorenzo, he also heard voices and saw visions.

And Parma? The greatest soldier of his day, who combined energy and organising ability with a cool, analytical brain, and sufficient experience in the Netherlands to be able to calculate the chances of any undertaking precisely, obviously he had ceased to believe in the enterprise of England long since. Had he ever believed in it? His letters cannot be taken at face value. It is possible that he, too, had seen the invasion of England as a brilliant artifice to throw dust in his opponents' eyes, and the canals dug with enormous labour, and the barges converted for carrying men and horses had all along been intended for Walcheren or some other coastal or river outpost of the rebels. Lord Henry Seymour, whose duty it was to prevent his crossing, believed Walcheren was Parma's real target: he wrote to Walsyngham that July:

The Duke (of Parma) levelleth at many marks, yet shooteth but at one, I mean Zeeland; which, once obtained, his attempts for England will be far easier. [23]

Seymour's chief advisor in the Dover squadron, William Wynter, who had a great deal of experience of amphibious operations, was quite certain Parma would never dare to cross the Channel; he had written to Walsyngham in June that if Parma knew that Holland and Zealand warships were ready to intercept him, 'I should live until I were young again ere the Prince would venture to set his ships forth.' [24]

The English peace commissioners parleying with Parma in Flanders were of the same opinion with regard to the Dover squadron; one reported that it was only necessary for Seymour to 'have a vigilant eye to scatter them at their coming out of this coast, which is very easy to do by God's grace (if they steal not out privily), by reason that they are not sufficiently furnished with ships.' He reported Parma had 'but 37 ships with tops and such as common port ships are, not able to stand against her Majesty's . . . Yet they do rig with all diligence possible.' [25] Evidently Parma was putting on a show of action for their benefit. His own agents kept him fully informed of the Sea Beggars' readiness for action; he knew they were keeping away from the Flanders coast deliberately to entice him out. He had no intention of coming.

Yet, of course, he had to keep up a pretence for his King. When Medina Sidonia's latest emissaries came with the news that the Armada had arrived in Calais roads, he wrote to Philip:

God be praised for this! I cannot refrain from repeating once more what I have said so often already. I, for my part, will exert every possible effort to fulfil my obligation, and will duly co-operate with the Duke and assist him to the full extent of my power. But it appears that he still wishes me to go out and join them with these boats of ours and for us, together, to attack the enemy's fleet. But it is obviously impossible to hope to put to sea in our boats without incurring great danger of losing our army. If the Duke were fully informed on the matter, he would be of the same opinion and would busy himself in carrying out your Majesty's orders, at once, without allowing himself to be diverted into another course. [26]

He meant that the fleet should sail up to Dunkirk and Nieuport to protect his small craft. And to pre-empt the criticisms he knew would be brought against his own preparations, he continued:

The men who have come hither from the Duke, not seeing the boats armed or with any artillery on board, and the men not shipped, have been trying to make out we are not ready. They are in error. The boats are and have been for months in a proper condition for the task . . . it is impossible to keep the troops on board of them for long. There is no room to turn around, and they would certainly fall ill, rot and die. The putting of men on board these low, small boats is done in a very short time, and I am confident that in this respect there will be no shortcomings in Your Majesty's service . . .

Despite all his protestations, the facts remain that he had known of the imminent arrival of the Armada for several days, but had not gone to the embarkation ports to bring his authority and energy to bear on preparations, the invasion flotilla was far from ready, the embarkation of stores and men had not been begun.[27] The reasons are obvious; he had stated them frequently to Philip; neither he nor any of his officers wished to deliver the army in its flotilla of 'wherries or cockboats', as Seymour called them, to the rebels on their own element, the sea. Even if he had ever thought there was a chance since secrecy had been lost – and it should be remembered when considering Philip's real aims that secrecy had not only been lost but inflated lists of the Armada had been published deliberately – his intelligence reports from Flushing and more recently all Medina Sidonia's reports showing the English fleet intact, undamaged, and following remorselessly reinforced his conviction that to obey Philip's instructions would be to sacrifice the army and imperil the whole Spanish position in the Netherlands.

Medina Sidonia's attitude shows as clearly from his various messages. At first he had intended following Philip's instructions to proceed up the Channel, forcing his way through the two divisions of the English fleet when they tried to prevent him, as he expected they would, and come to anchor in the Downs; from there he would establish contact with Parma and command his passage across from Flanders to the Thames. By August 1st, after he had entered the Channel and experienced Howard's long-range shoot-and-run tactics, he had decided to stay instead at the Isle of Wight until he could agree a joint rendezvous with Parma – this for the excellent reason that there was no shelter for his great ships on the Flanders coast.

The plan, as he made clear in his letter to Philip, was 'that at the moment of my arrival he should sally with his fleet, without causing me to wait a minute.' He believed 'the whole success of the undertaking depends on this.'[28] And from his letter to Parma of the same date it is clear he expected him, as the man on the spot with local knowledge and local pilots, to arrange the most suitable rendezvous; he expected to receive 'from Your Excellency (Parma) instructions as to what I am to do and where I am to wait for you to join me.' This was entirely correct. He did not know how Parma had arranged his forces in the separated Flanders ports, nor how long he expected to take to come out, nor where the Armada could lie to protect them. If he had any inkling of the threat from the Sea Beggars, he no doubt expected that Parma could deal with it with the armed ships which Moresin must have told him about.

Nothing Medina Sidonia wrote makes it clear why he abandoned the idea of stopping at the Isle of Wight until he had agreed a plan and rendezvous position with Parma. His note to Moncada after the Portland fight suggests he may have decided by then, having realised that the English did not intend to stand and fight, merely to harass and delay; probably he considered it too dangerous to try and work the whole of his diverse fleet into the shoals of Spithead and anchor and attempt to establish a position ashore with the English fleet at his heels and in a position to cut him off from communications with Flanders. Alternatively he may have made the final decision not to attempt the Isle of Wight after the fight south of the Island when, despite having the weather gage, he still failed to bring the English to close action.

It was not because the wind and tide were unfavourable that he did not try to enter Spithead; they were – at least in the late morning and early afternoon. But he set course for the Straits and informed Parma he expected to be on the Flemish coast very soon, and asked him to be ready to put out at once. Presumably the same considerations which ruled out a stop at the Isle of Wight caused him to abandon his original intention – conforming with Philip's orders – to anchor in the Downs. Thus it was Howard's strategy of 'coursing' him, together with the inability of any of his ships to force a decisive battle on the English, that drove him towards the exposed and dangerous anchorage off Calais.

Before arriving he sent off a request to Parma for '40 flyboats to join with this armada',[29] assuming their speed and manoeuvrability would match that of the English ships and perhaps enable him to bring on the desired close action. Yet, as the English peace commissioners had noted, Parma's vessels were simple merchant coasting vessels 'not able to stand against Her Majesty's ships'.[30] Since the only detailed information the Duke had received about Parma's 'fleet' had been from Captain Moresin, it must be assumed that the misunderstanding about the fighting value of these craft arose in these conversations.

Arriving off Calais, he proceeded no further, partly because of the turn of the tide against him, chiefly probably because of his pilots' advice that if he went on there was grave danger of being forced off the coast by the Dunkirk shoals and up into the North Sea. It was not an easy decision, nonetheless, and he could not have taken it had he realised that the threat of the Sea Beggars' fleet would keep Parma in port. Then, worried by the ease with which the English, to windward, could drop down and bombard him while he lay at anchor, he repeated his desperate plea for '40 or 50 flyboats, as with this aid I shall be able to resist the enemy's fleet until Your Excellency can come out with the rest, and we can go together and take some port where the Armada may enter in safety.'[31] Nothing demonstrates better his total misunderstanding of the real value of Parma's 'flyboats' and his failure to recognise the danger from Zealand; had he any inkling that the Sea Beggars were lurking ready to pounce on the Flanders boats directly they put to sea, he could not have expected Parma to come, let alone send him the armed vessels that were his only defence.

Was this a failure of imagination on his own part? He knew the rebels had a fleet, and it was evident that their bases were not 40 miles up the coast beyond Nieuport. Did he discount them, or believe they would not interfere in their mortal enemy's designs on England? If so it was a bad miscalculation, induced perhaps by fatigue from his days of anxiety and the constant ill-feeling he had at sea. Was Philip more culpable in his failure to inform him of Parma's anxieties about his small boats and the Beggars' fleet? It appears a glaring and almost inexplicable oversight; yet Philip could hardly have guessed that his two commanders would not liaise before the Armada arrived off Flanders, indeed he had expressly instructed Medina Sidonia to make sure they did:

It is important that you and the Duke (of Parma) should be mutually informed of each other's movements, and it will therefore be advisable that before you arrive thither you should continue to communicate with him as best you can, either by secretly landing a trustworthy person at night on the coast of Normandy or Boulogne, or by sending intelligence by sea to Gravelines, Dunkirk or Nieuport . . .[32]

Medina Sidonia had, of course, complied with this to the letter; Parma had not replied to him. He had, however, set out his doubts and explained his position vis-à-vis the Sea Beggars to Philip. Then the Armada had put into Corunna and, like most other informed men, he must have been sceptical about its prospects of ever reaching the Channel. Finally, on August 2nd, he had received Medina Sidonia's first message after putting out from Corunna, sent nine days before when the Armada was almost up with the latitude of Ushant in the western approaches to the Channel. He had replied the next day, but the message had not reached Medina Sidonia. It is hard to fault Parma on this count. How much blame Philip should bear depends largely upon his real intentions, which are unlikely ever to be known. In any case the fault was not so much in his orders as in his under-estimate of the English fleet and even more of the natural hazards of tide, shoal and weather which his own ships would be exposed to. The whole campaign was devised from a soldier's, not a sailor's viewpoint, this was the crux of the mistake. Both Medina Sidonia and Parma had a better estimate of the real dangers than it seems Philip had.

Yet it was the English strategy of 'coursing' the Armada up-Channel, not allowing Medina Sidonia the opportunity of a 'fight' nor allowing him even a day's breathing space to seize a secure anchorage that forced the fatal error of sailing to Calais. Had Medina Sidonia gone on a few miles more to Dunkirk or Nieuport he would have been in graver danger from the shoals. Finally it was a quick English decision to use the favourable situation they had created without wasting a moment that sealed the Armada's fate. Drake had summed it up a few months before: 'The advantage of time and place in all martial actions is half a victory.'[33] It is doubtful if the English could have been defeated in the position that had been reached, but the prompt action they now took may have made the difference for Medina Sidonia between failure and virtual annihilation.

The idea of sending burning vessels down on an enemy fleet in harbour or at anchor was not original; it was a recognised stratagem. By the time Medina Sidonia arrived off Calais Elizabeth's council had ordered combustible materials for fireships to be sent to Dover – no doubt in case Howard failed to prevent the Armada sailing round into the Thames Estuary. Seymour's vice admiral, Sir William Wynter, who was invited aboard the *Ark* directly the Dover squadron joined the fleet on that Saturday evening, claimed that he suggested the idea to Howard then: 'Having viewed myself the great and hugeness of the Spanish army, and did consider that it was not possible to remove them but by a device of firing the ships, which would make them to lose (leese) the only road that was apt and meetest for their purpose' – of joining with Parma's forces.[34]

Howard called a council next morning – while about two miles downwind Medina Sidonia learned from Captain Don Rodrigo Tello that Parma had not even begun to embark men or stores – and it was decided to prepare fireships and, since the wind was still in the west, to send them down under cover of darkness after the tide had turned to flow easterly that night. Sir Henry Palmer was sent in a pinnace to Dover to bring back the combustibles gathered there, chiefly bundles of brushwood and barrels of pitch. It was also resolved that this attack should be followed up next morning with an assault on the enemy in three waves, or 'charges', the first to be led by Howard, the second by Drake, the third by Seymour.

At some point during the day it was realised that Palmer would not be back in time – and in fact he did not leave Dover until about midnight – so eight vessels were chosen from among the smaller craft with the fleet; they ranged from the 200-tonners, *Bark Talbot* and *Thomas Drake*, the latter belonging to Sir Francis and valued with her fittings at £1,000 in the subsequent claim for compensation, and the 150-ton *Bark Bond*, probably belonging to John Hawkins, down to the 90-ton *Elizabeth* of Lowestoft. These were filled with whatever combustible materials were at hand, probably old hemp, barrels of tar and pitch, fuel for the galley fires, and their guns were charged so that they would go off as the heat or flames reached the breech.

Saturday had been full moon; the tides were running at their fastest, almost three knots off Calais, the wind had freshened and that day the Spanish ships were each ordered to drop a second anchor. No doubt the veteran admirals, Recalde, Moncada, Oquendo and the Duke's adviser, Diego Flores de Valdés, recognised the conditions were ripe for an attack by fireships or even an explosive vessel such as the Sea Beggars had launched against Parma during his siege of Antwerp three years before. The Italian designer of that infernal machine which had been laden with gunpowder and had spread a huge arc of death and devastation, was said to be working for Queen Elizabeth – as he was, in London. It would be surprising indeed if the Duke were not warned that the English might hatch some devilment that night after the tide turned at about 10. In any case, according to his own account, he suspected something of the kind when he saw nine ships join the English fleet at sunset, and at the same time a squadron of 26 vessels shifted their berth closer inshore. He ordered the captain of the flagship's forecastle, a trusted officer named Antonio Serrano, to take a pinnace carrying a heavy anchor and cable out to windward ready to tow a fireship ashore in case the enemy should send one down. Why only one? Nine vessels had joined the enemy; a squadron of 26 had moved. Perhaps he or his advisors really had the 'mine machine' of Antwerp on their minds and doubted if the English would have the time or powder to construct more than one. At the same time he ordered each ship to have boats manned and alert to tow fireships away.

At midnight or soon after – by some accounts it was as late as two o'clock – the eight prepared vessels emerged from the English fleet; did the moon light their sails? No one has left a record. Each had main- and foresail set, and one man aboard to start the fire then lash the tiller when near the enemy; they were closely spaced in line abreast, yardarms almost touching, or so they started; it is difficult to believe that with their differing sizes and shapes and the fresh wind filling their sails, they remained in good order for very long; with a tide of anything from 2¾ knots (midnight) to 1½ knots (2.00 a.m.) helping them, they must have made anything from about 4½ knots to over 6 knots over the ground and they could have covered the distance to the nearest Spanish vessels in 15 minutes if the fleets were as close as one and half miles; probably they were further apart and it would have taken 25 minutes or more.

It is impossible to know how long it was before the fires were started and the flames began to show; undoubtedly they were alight some time before they reached the foremost Spanish vessels – not surprising since the firelighters had to get off into rowing boats and pull back against tide and wind and they would not have wanted to leave it too late. Perhaps there is a clue in the account by a soldier – probably in the Portuguese galleon *San Marcos* – who saw them 'coming all afire eight ships of the English in very good order towards us, with the flood, which was very swift.'[35] If they were in 'very good order' it might suggest they were nearer the beginning than the end of their short passage; that is probably reading far too much into three words. The English gallant, Robert Carey, watching from the *Elizabeth Bonaventure*, remembered 'they brought them very near the Spanish fleet so they could not miss to come among the midst of them; then they set fire on them and came off.'[36] An anonymous intelligence report sent to Philip stated that 'whilst they were yet between the two fleets one of them flared up with such fierceness and great noise as were frightful'.[37] This could have been from a Spanish survivor's account, there were plenty in Calais next day; it may have been embroidered hearsay. Calderon saw 'eight ships with artificial machines on board, which came towards us all in flames, burning furiously in the bows.'[38]

Antonio Serrano in his pinnace could not deal with them all; in any case Medina Sidonia shared Calderon's belief there were devilish devices aboard.

Launch of the English fireships off Calais in the night of 7/8 August, the turning point of the campaign.

Captain Marolin de Juan stated, 'they burnt with such fierceness it was believed they were "artificial machines" and as the Armada was in close order, the Duke, fearing the damage that might be caused by them, gave orders for the cables to be cut, and the whole of our ships spread their sails'.[39]

Tillers were hauled over to incline bows to the port tack, anchor cables were hacked through with axes or simply let fly to the bitter end, sailors raced out along the yards to loose sails, others hauled on lifts and halyards, tended sheets and braces as canvas flogged, then filled, weather rigging tautened, masts shuddered and the great ships, free of their restraining cables and moving already with the tide towards the banks off Calais, leant to the wind. Some must have been under way before others, some must have fallen down towards their close consorts before they could gather steerage way; the shouting and confusion as the anchored order dissolved into a free-for-all of manoeuvre in the darkness must have been great; yet only one serious mishap was recorded. This occurred at the windward end of the fleet, nearest the English and the line of blazing fireships. The flag galleass, *San Lorenzo*, lying close to the *San Martin*, tried to avoid collision with another galleass *Girona* and de Leyva's *Rata* and in doing so fell across the anchor cable of the Levanter, *San Juan de Sicilia*; as the flag galleass was driven round by the tide her rudder was torn off. All others got away without serious damage and sailed northwards away from the shoals as the fireships, swathed in smoke lit by flames up the masts and out along the yards, roaring and spitting like furnaces, their guns discharging at intervals, bore down over the field of anchors left behind.

When they had passed, still burning fiercely, the Duke tacked and sailed back and anchored again, somewhat further out and somewhat downwind from his former position, but with the intention of recovering it in the morning and picking up his anchors, which had been buoyed. A few others had stayed with

Engraving by John Pine, showing in the left-hand panel the launch of the English fireships on tide and wind, and on the right the Spanish formation broken at last.

him, but most of the fleet had spread out miles downwind and tide far beyond Calais.

He saw the extent of this dispersion in the early light of that Monday morning, August 8th, and saw Howard weigh and set sail towards him. According to his own account the wind had gone round to the north-west and was blowing onshore; according to Howard's account it was west and south-west; John Hawkins recorded it as westerly, 'a fresh gale' – meaning it had strengthened. Undoubtedly it was somewhere in the west, and watchers from the shore saw both fleets steering northerly, seawards, that morning; the probability is that Medina Sidonia fired a gun to gather his fleet and steered north-easterly to make it easier for the rest to beat up towards him; the tide was now running strongly to the west in their favour, nevertheless the unwieldy Levanters and hulks would have taken a long time to work up towards him had he simply waited for them. By his own account he weighed 'to go and collect the Armada and bring it back to its previous position.'[40]

Howard was diverted from his intention of leading the first charge against him by the sight of the rudderless flag galleass, *San Lorenzo*, close inshore and creeping towards the mouth of Calais harbour under oars assisted by foresail. She went aground on a bank close up with the entrance and was soon heeling with her seaward side of guns pointing uselessly skywards. Howard sailed in as close as he could, then stayed to support his smaller vessels and pinnaces which closed to attack on the harmless side of the galleass; Howard sent his lieutenant, Amyas Preston, with gentlemen volunteers and soldiers off in his longboat to assist and stake his claim.

Soon there were some 25 of the smaller English craft around the stricken vessel, exchanging a hot fire with swivels and muskets against musketry from her castles. A number of her crew had leaped into the sea at the first onset and

be treated with suspicion; it continues at some length about incidents when shots pierced the after quarters of the *Revenge*, leaving the impression that the author protested too much, probably inspired by Drake to do so. One reason, apart from Drake's natural bent for self-advertisement, may have been Frobisher's aspersions in front of John Hawkins and others that 'He (Drake) came bragging up at first, indeed, and gave them his prow and his broadside; and then kept his luff (i.e. held up to windward) and was glad that he was gone like a cowardly knave or traitor – I rest doubtful, but the one I will swear.'[64] Even taken at face value the fact that this narrative describes no casualties or serious damage reinforces the considerable testimony to the very slight damage the English ships suffered.

After Howard's fleet returned home, one of Mendoza's informants in London reported that the English were stating 'their loss does not exceed 300'.[65] Although he claimed to know that it was really over 1,500 he gave no source for this information and since he also claimed to know Howard had lost 12 ships – when he had not lost one – this figure can be discounted. Whatever the actual casualties, which will never be known, there is no doubt they were a tiny fraction of those suffered by the Spanish.

A mile or so downwind of Howard, divers and carpenters were using the respite to attempt to stop leaks in the riddled hulls of those ships which had borne the brunt of the English assaults, soldiers working the pumps in shifts and sailors splicing torn rigging or reeving new lines, sending down tattered canvas and bending on fresh. Medina Sidonia's flagship had been struck on the starboard side by 200 balls alow and aloft, by Calderon's estimate; many of the holes were low and the sea had risen with a freshening wind, making the divers' work more difficult. Aboard the *San Mateo* the pumps could not cope with the inflow of water, while the *San Felipe* without pumps was visibly settling; by early evening it was evident there was no hope for her and Don Francisco de Toledo fired a gun for assistance. The *Doncella*, a converted hulk in the Guipuzcoan squadron, approached and took her surviving complement off, but when a rumour started that she, too, was sinking Don Francisco decided he would rather go down with his own ship and went back aboard with a few others.

With the wind in the west and the shoals between Dunkirk and Ostend to the south, Medina Sidonia could do nothing but gather up his force and continue north-easterly under easy sail; according to his report to Philip, he still hoped to be able to put back to join Parma; it is difficult to believe he thought there was any hope of this, or that if he were to manage it, there was any hope of prevailing against the English fleet he had been unable to weaken by as much as a single ship, and which still hung taunting him a mile or so to windward, following as it had since he had entered the Channel. Moreover the ammunition in his first line ships was practically expended, his food was rotting, his drinking water dangerously low and foul, and it was certain the English would not allow him peace to replenish the great amounts of provisions he required even if he were to find an anchorage. His thoughts that evening must have been dark; undoubtedly he prayed for strength.

The *San Felipe* parted during the night; the wind must have veered to the north of west; the tide when it turned in the early morning set south-westerly and the combination took the wallowing and almost deserted galleon southwards into the shoal water off Nieuport. There the Zealand Admiral, Justinus de Nassau, who had sailed with his fleet from Flushing in response to Seymour's earlier request to join him, found her stranded and abandoned next day; Don Francisco and some half dozen with him had succeeded in getting away in a boat, and

An engagement between the English and Spanish fleets. English school, *c.*1590. This is thought to be a design for a tapestry. Although the treatment is heraldic, it gives a good idea of the appearance of Armada warships and the confused skirmishes that characterised the campaign.

finding their way to Parma. The Sea Beggars went aboard, pillaged, and started to patch her up sufficiently to take her the 30-odd miles to Flushing.

Meanwhile the *San Mateo* had also parted; Medina Sidonia had lent her a diver to help with her leaks, but with the high seas and gathering darkness nothing much could have been done over the side. Probably, like the *San Felipe*, she parted that night after the battle since the English, following closely, made no mention of seeing her go or chasing her. She, too, ended up on a shoal off the Flemish coast – off Blankenberg, some 15 miles east of the *Felipe* – she too was found by the Sea Beggars. Her commander, Don Diego Pimentel, and surviving soldiers put up a stout resistance to the small craft assailing her from every quarter, but eventually they had no option but to yield to terms. By this time, according to one Spanish prisoner she had been 'shot through 350 times'; no doubt a large proportion of the holes had been made in the fleet action. The Beggars towed her off on the flood and brought her the short distance to Flushing, but both she and the *San Felipe* were so riddled and strained that both sank before they could be berthed. Pimentel and the gentlemen adventurers with him were put up for ransom in the customary way.

There are specific reports of another large vessel or vessels sinking; according

Succeeding generations of English historians and artists re-interpreted and re-embellished the Armada legend for their own time. These two pictures by O. W. Brierly (1818–94), *The Revenge off Gravelines* (top), and *The Attack of the Vanguard*, tell us more about nineteenth-century British naval triumphalism than sixteenth-century realities.

to Calderon the *Maria Juan* of the Levant squadron had lost her rudder and mizen mast in the battle and about sunset that evening signalled for assistance as she was going down. Pataches went to her but could only rescue one boatload of men before she sank. Howard, in his first report of the action, stated that the next day, Tuesday, August 9th, Captain Robert Crosse of the *Hope* came up with 'one of the enemy's great ships . . . in great distress' – and obviously she must have been straggling – and called on her to yield. While they were still discussing terms she sank 'before their eyes.'[66] Calderon's account is confusing about times, and it is possible he was actually referring to sunset on Tuesday, not the Monday of the battle, in which case the ship that Robert Crosse saw go down may have been the *Maria Juan*. On the other hand the Spanish probably lost two great ships as well as the important first line fighting galleons *San Felipe* and *San Mateo*, and the flag galleass *San Lorenzo*.

Despite this, and despite the highly dangerous situation Medina Sidonia was now in without a safe haven to put into, with little ammunition, food or water, with many of his best ships holed and strained, and now with a north-westerly wind driving him towards the shoals off Zealand – for it is impossible to account for the unmanageable *San Felipe* drifting down to Nieuport without assuming a north-westerly – despite all this neither Howard, nor any of the other English commanders seem to have had any inkling they had just won the decisive battle of the campaign. Howard, writing in haste on the evening of the battle to ask for powder, shot and victuals to be sent with all possible speed in case they had to continue the pursuit, reported they had 'distressed them (the enemy) very much; but their fleet consisteth of mighty ships and great strength'; he added in a postscript:

I will not write unto Her Majesty before more be done. Their force is wonderful great and strong; and yet we pluck their feathers by little and little. I pray to God that the forces on the land (in England) be strong enough to answer so present a force.[67]

Drake, writing the same evening, assured Walsyngham that 'this day's service hath much appalled the enemy, and no doubt but encouraged our army', but added in a postscript, 'There must be great care taken to send us munition and victual whithersoever the enemy goeth.'[68] And two days later Hawkins wrote to Walsyngham stressing there should be:

an infinite quantity of powder and shot provided and continually sent abroad, without the which great hazard may grow to our country; for this is the greatest and strongest combination, to my understanding, that ever was gathered in Christendom; therefore I wish it, of all hands, to be mightily and diligently looked unto and cared for.[69]

Like Howard and Drake, he was confident they could 'weary them out of the sea' provided they were supplied with powder and shot, but he believed Medina Sidonia still had '50 forcible and invincible ships'.

If the commanders at sea remained anxious, not realising they had achieved the deliverance of their country and religion, it is not surprising if Elizabeth, her council and army leaders were extremely worried; they knew only that the Armada had proceeded up-Channel without serious delay or loss, had reached the coast of Flanders, and was no doubt in touch with Parma. Their alarm is betrayed in orders sent to Seymour after he had sailed to join Howard; they ended with an instruction to attack the enemy fleet before it could make the junction with Parma: 'upon conference between the Lord Admiral and you, you shall see no just cause to stay or delay the fight'.[70] Anxiety is even more clearly betrayed by a long questionnaire sent to Howard asking him among other things 'What losses of men and ships hath been on the Spanish side? And where were the

losses? and where are the prisoners?', and most revealingly 'What causes are there why the Spanish navy hath not been boarded by the Queen's ships?'

In the same document Howard was warned that some Spaniards had stated the purpose of the Armada was to 'draw along the English navy from the coast of Flanders; that the sea being clear, the Duke of Parma might come out with his forces to invade the realm, and namely to come to London.'[71]

Thus when Elizabeth travelled down to the camp at Tilbury, where the Earl of Leicester commanded the main English army for the defence of London, and delivered her most famous speech of defiance to Philip, while it might appear with hindsight that the danger was already past, that was far from the impression at the time; the threat was imminent and great.

She went down the Thames on August 8th, the day of the battle off Gravelines; her oared barge, flying the Royal standard, was accompanied by a flotilla of river craft carrying her Yeoman of the Guard, trumpeters, drummers, her tall gentlemen pensioners, courtiers and their entourage. Next day, after sleeping at a house some three miles from Leicester's camp, she donned martial outfit to inspect her troops; over a white velvet dress filled out enormously below the waist with a farthingale, she wore a burnished steel corselet and on her head over the red hair of her wig a white-plumed helmet. Mounting a great, white charger and grasping a silver marshal's baton, she rode out with her escort. None of the men who threw themselves to their knees as they saw her approaching and called on God to preserve her could ever have forgotten the sight. 'Lord bless you all! Lord bless you all!' she responded.

A mock battle had been arranged for her to watch. Afterwards the men were drawn up on rising ground near Tilbury church. She rode through their lines, preceded by Leicester and Lord Grey, gorgeously arrayed with their feathered hats in their hands, followed by a page carrying her helmet, liveried footmen, ladies in waiting and a troop of guardsmen, then halted in their midst to make her speech, a fabulous figure 'like some Amazonian empress', the red of her wig and rouged cheeks and the dark, imperious eyes in the high oval of her face the focus for some 10,000 men. She must have raised her voice mightily to make herself audible to even the nearest fraction straining to hear. No doubt the periods were well-rehearsed. As a call to arms it was as stirring as those Shakespeare was to put into the mouths of kings.

My loving people, we have been persuaded by some that are careful of our safety, to take heed how we commit ourselves to armed multitudes, for fear of treachery. But I assure you, I do not desire to live to distrust my faithful and loving people. Let tyrants fear –

One can imagine the pause as cheers and shouts rose from those nearest.

I have always so behaved myself that, under God, I have placed my chiefest strength and safeguard in the loyal hearts and goodwill of my subjects; and therefore I am come amongst you, as you see, at this time, not for my recreation and disport, but being resolved, in the midst and heat of the battle, to live or die amongst you all, to lay down for my God, and for my kingdom, and for my people, my honour and my blood, even in the dust.

I know I have the body of a weak and feeble woman, but I have the heart and stomach of a king, and of a King of England too, and think foul scorn that Parma or Spain, or any prince of Europe should dare to invade the borders of my realm; to which, rather than any dishonour shall grow by me, I myself will take up arms, I myself will be your general, judge, and rewarder of every one of your virtues in the field. I know, already for your forwardness you have deserved rewards and crowns; and we do assure you, in the word of a prince, they shall be duly paid you. For the meantime, my lieutenant general shall be in my stead, than whom never a Prince commanded a more noble or worthy

Philip James de Louterbourg (1740–1812) was of Polish origin and did not come to England until 1771. He was soon caught up in the British affair with the sea and celebrated Lord Howe's, Jervis' and Nelson's victories in glowing light and shade. His *Defeat of the Spanish Armada*, shown here, might more properly have been titled 'Come cheer up my lads, 'tis to glory we steer . . .'

subject; not doubting but by your obedience to my general, by your concord in the camp, and your valour in the field, we shall shortly have a famous victory over these enemies of my God, of my Kingdoms and of my people.[72]

She did not know, nor did any of those close to her who expected soon to be fighting the invader, that a hundred miles to the east the famous victory had already been won; now, somewhere off Walcheren and not knowing precisely where, the enemy fleet was clawing up into a north-westerly wind to prevent being driven down to the banks running out from Zealand. The English were following a mile and a half to windward.

Earlier it had seemed to Medina Sidonia that they had been bearing down for another attack and he had lain to with Recalde, de Leyva, the faithful Marquis de Peñafiel, Don Diego Enriquez in the Castilian galleon, *San Juan*, and the three galleasses to await them. They had not closed to attack. Now he had a more pressing concern; his pilots told him that with the wind as it stood no single ship of the fleet would escape the shoals to leeward. The sounding line seemed to confirm it; the depth was down to six and a half fathoms; the sandy brown-green of the disturbed water must have confirmed it too, and perhaps there were long rips of foam off to starboard where waves broke on shelving ground hidden

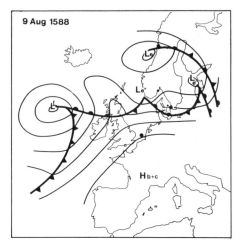

'The miraculous change of wind' reported by Medina Sidonia and Calderon marked the passage eastwards of a ridge of high pressure in front of an advancing low to the north-west of Ireland. These are the conclusions of the Climatic Research Unit at the University of East Anglia, based both on English and Spanish accounts and on daily weather observations recorded by the astronomer Tycho Brahe in the Danish Sound. On the afternoon of 9 August he recorded 'clear with a west wind' and that night a 'strong storm'.

beneath the white-flecked surface. The *San Martin* had an anchor hanging down lower than the keel and a man watching the trend of the cable so that it could be let go to bring the ship up before she went aground, or could be used to haul her off on the flood afterwards. This slowed her and increased the leeward drift; she was sagging astern of the rearguard.

Not realising the English shortage of ammunition, the Duke thought they were holding off from the attack because they knew his ships would soon be aground; then Drake and Howard and Juan Acles, as he called Hawkins, would have ample opportunity to surround his helpless vessels and reduce them in detail. The strange thing is that if this occurred to any Englishman, none mentioned it; nor is there any hint in any English account that there was danger from the banks. Did they have better pilots? Were they less conscious of danger because, with more weatherly ships, less damaged aloft, they did not have to worry? Surely, if any of the English commanders had believed Medina Sidonia was as close to disaster as he apparently feared, they must have suggested attacking – whether they had much powder and shot or not – in order to try and drive at least a few of these 'forcible and invincible ships' aground, in particular the fleet flagship apparently straggling astern. It would have been undoubtedly their best chance of removing the threat they still feared. There is no mention of any such thoughts; Howard and Drake, Hawkins and Frobisher, Fenner and Wynter were content to hold their distance to windward. The conclusion must be, either the Duke's pilots were raising imaginary bogeys or all these experienced English sea-dogs were incompetent and failed to seize the moment as the Armada was delivered into their hands; it is difficult to believe this of them, let alone of the supreme opportunist, Drake.

Confirmation that the English apprehended no danger comes from a letter written by an experienced sailor, the lieutenant of the London merchantman, *Margaret and John*; writing that day, Tuesday, August 9th, he stated his position as 12 leagues – 36 miles – off Walcheren. If this is correct both fleets were miles away from the banks; and it is clear from Captain Alonzo Vanegas' account of the debate aboard the *San Martin*, that the pilots, one of whom was English, one Flemish and the rest Spanish, Basque or Portuguese believed, correctly, that the Zealand shoals extended only three leagues out to sea.[73] The letter continued:

the wind hanging westerly, we drive our enemies apace to the eastward, much marvelling, if the wind continue, in what port they will direct themselves. Some imagine the river of Hamburg . . . others suppose . . . they will about Scotland, and so for Spain . . .[74]

These are not the conjectures of men who believed their enemy was about to be driven aground in shoal water.

It is possible that the danger the pilots warned Medina Sidonia about was not as present as it was represented in the Duke's and Calderon's – and most subsequent – accounts, and what they were really concerned about was the danger of continuing on the present course, when the Armada must either ground on the banks extending from Walcheren, Schouwen, Goeree and the Brill, or if it were to clear these, run ashore somewhere on the northerly trend of the coastline upwards from the Hook. In that case a shouted discussion or argument which by several accounts took place between Medina Sidonia and Oquendo, each in his own ship, may have been about whether to continue the present north-easterly course or go about and beat back south-westerly. The whole question, and especially the disparity between English and Spanish accounts, is puzzling and probably insoluble.

'He blew and they were scattered...'
The intervention of Providence is
recorded on these Dutch com-
memorative medallions of 1588–89.

Plan devised by the author and drawn by Lionel Willis showing the track of the fleets from their anchorage off Calais to Medina Sidonia's flight northwards, 9/10 August, still pursued by Howard. It is based on the assumption that the lieutenant of the *Margaret and John* was more or less correct in his estimate of passing '12 leagues off Walcheren' on 9 August.

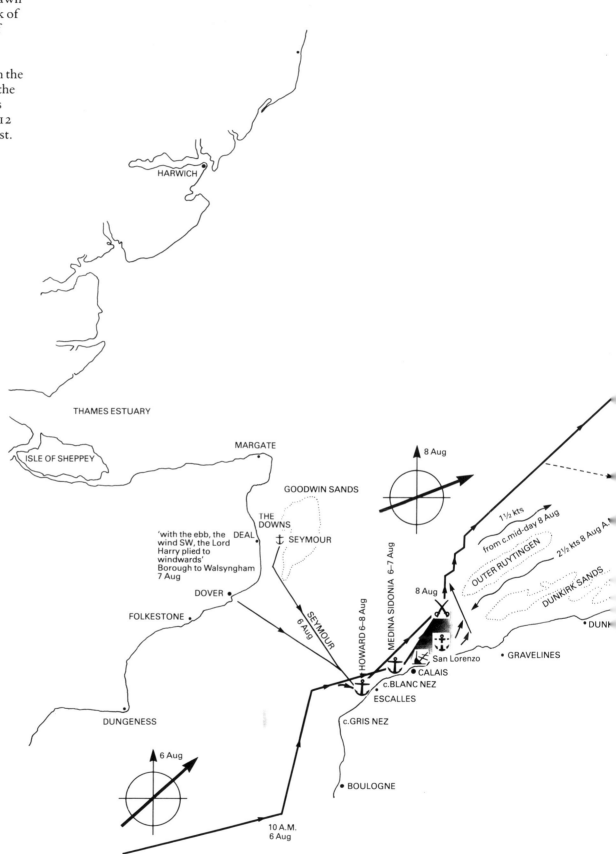

HARWICH

THAMES ESTUARY

MARGATE

ISLE OF SHEPPEY

GOODWIN SANDS

8 Aug

THE DOWNS

DEAL

'with the ebb, the wind SW, the Lord Harry plied to windwards' Borough to Walsyngham 7 Aug

⚓ SEYMOUR

1½ kts

from c.mid-day 8 Aug

2½ kts 8 Aug A.

OUTER RUYTINGEN

DUNKIRK SANDS

DOVER

SEYMOUR 6 Aug

8 Aug

FOLKESTONE

HOWARD 6–8 Aug

MEDINA SIDONIA 6–7 Aug

San Lorenzo

GRAVELINES

DUNK

CALAIS

c.BLANC NEZ

ESCALLES

DUNGENESS

c.GRIS NEZ

6 Aug

BOULOGNE

10 A.M. 6 Aug

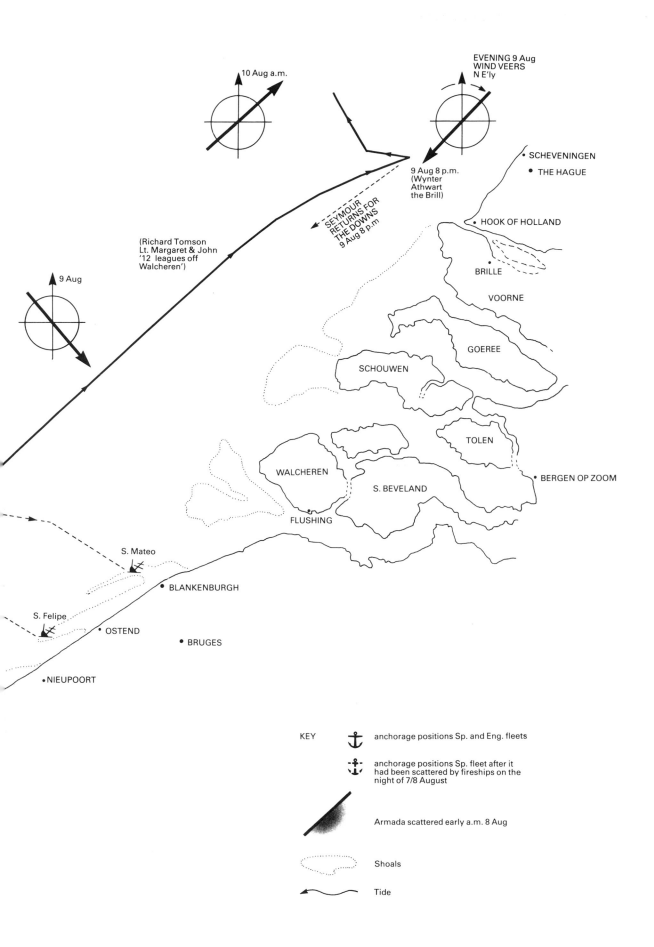

10 Aug a.m.

EVENING 9 Aug
WIND VEERS
N E'ly

9 Aug 8 p.m.
(Wynter
Athwart
the Brill)

• SCHEVENINGEN

• THE HAGUE

• HOOK OF HOLLAND

SEYMOUR
RETURNS FOR
THE DOWNS
9 Aug 8 p.m

(Richard Tomson
Lt. Margaret & John
'12 leagues off
Walcheren')

BRILLE

VOORNE

9 Aug

GOEREE

SCHOUWEN

TOLEN

WALCHEREN

S. BEVELAND

• BERGEN OP ZOOM

FLUSHING

S. Mateo

• BLANKENBURGH

S. Felipe

• OSTEND

• BRUGES

• NIEUPOORT

KEY   ⚓   anchorage positions Sp. and Eng. fleets

⚓   anchorage positions Sp. fleet after it
had been scattered by fireships on the
night of 7/8 August

Armada scattered early a.m. 8 Aug

Shoals

Tide

The Duke held on and, as he and Calderon remarked, 'God was pleased to change the wind' – to west-south-west by his account, 'in our favour' by Calderon's account. According to William Wynter, the wind was still at west-*north*-west at about three or four that afternoon, when Howard fired a signal gun and hoisted the flag for council aboard the *Ark*. There it was decided that Seymour's squadron – much to Seymour's chagrin – should stand back to guard the Thames in case Parma put out – thus anticipating the Privy Council's fears. So that the enemy should not realise they were going, they were not to leave until after sunset. By Seymour's account they were athwart the Brill when they put back; by Wynter's account the wind had died away by then, about eight o'clock, and veered into the north-east. This sounds authentic since it was when he and Seymour and Palmer and the rest of the squadron took their leave of Howard and stood back for the coast of England, and it is unlikely he would have mistaken the change in the wind that allowed them to do so.[75]

From another English account, it appears that it was calm in the Thames estuary that evening, and the following morning, August 10th, came in with such a strong blow from the south east that the writer was unable to beat down to the North Foreland – the extreme eastern point of the Kent coast.[76]

Seymour and his squadron, on their way back towards the Thames, could not make the North Foreland either, which they would have been able to do easily with a south-easterly; Wynter stated the wind was south-south-*west* that day, and they had to anchor off Badsey cliffs – Bawdsey – just north of Harwich. The conclusion must be that a frontal system was passing and the wind veered during the morning from south-east to south-south-west, heading the ships in the Thames estuary and forcing Seymour and Wynter up to the Suffolk coast.

Wynter's account fits in best with Medina Sidonia's actions; for on the evening of their peril, that is Tuesday August 9th, he called a council aboard the *San Martin*, and having explained the state of the ships and the lack of ammunition, put the question 'whether it would be best to turn back to the English Channel or to return to Spain by the North Sea; seeing that the Duke of Parma had not sent word that he would be presently able to come out.'[77] This question suits Wynter's account of a light north-easterly wind rather better than his own account of a change of wind to the west-south-west, which would have made it quite impossible to return to the English Channel – at least until it changed. It would have been a dead beat to windward, which none of the Spanish ships was capable of. According to the Duke's account, the council was unanimous that they should go back to the Channel if the weather permitted, otherwise they should return to Spain northabout around Scotland. According to Calderon, who attended, Diego Flores de Valdés suggested putting back to Calais 'but it was resolved that they should set course for Spain.'[78] In view of their condition and needs and the demoralising effects of their impotence to harm the English fleet in any way, Calderon's sounds the more probable version, Medina Sidonia's a gloss for Philip.

The following day the wind veered round, settling finally about south-south-west; the decision was made for them. They spread all sail and steered north-westerly, as it seemed to the English commanders making for Scotland; Howard reported to Walsyngham, 'notwithstanding that our powder and shot was well near all spent, we set on a brag countenance and gave them chase, as though we had wanted nothing . . .'[79] Hawkins wrote:

The Spaniards take their course for Scotland; my Lord (Howard) doth follow them. I doubt not, with God's favour, but we shall impeach their landing. There must be order for victual and money, powder and shot, to be sent after us.[80]

A spirit of the utmost confidence breathes through all the English accounts – not surprisingly in view of the results of the last battle – confidence mixed with frustration that they lacked the ammunition to finish the task. The master of one of the vessels expended as fire-ships, now aboard the *Mary Rose*, wrote that if they had had powder and shot to have attacked them twice more 'we had utterly distressed them', and regretted the 'parsimony at home, (which) hath bereaved us of the famousest victory that ever our navy might have had at sea. Our desire of victory is so great that we staid not to take the spoil of any of these ships we lamed'.[81] The lieutenant of the *Margaret and John* thought there was little more to fear from the Armada:

Their power being, by battle, mortality and other accidents, so decayed and those that are left alive so weak and hurtless that they could be well content to lose all charges to be at home, both rich and poor. There is want of powder, shot and victual amongst us which causeth that we cannot so daily assault them as we would.[82]

And Drake wrote to Walsyngham on this day, August 10th:

There was never anything pleased me better than the seeing of the enemy flying with a southerly wind to the northwards. God grant you have a good eye to the Duke of Parma; for with the grace of God, if we live, I doubt it not but ere it be long so to handle the matter with the Duke of Sidonia as he shall wish himself at St Mary Port among his orange trees.[83]

These impressions of the low mood of the enemy gleaned from prisoners picked out of the water and from observation during the close action, actually exaggerated the fighting spirit remaining by crediting Medina Sidonia with the intention of landing troops in Scotland. He had no such thoughts, nor could he have had with all his shortages; his one idea was to bring as much of his battered fleet and as many of his men home as he could. This involved a long and potentially perilous voyage around the north of Scotland and out into the North Atlantic to the west of Ireland, and it was possibly because of the need for fleet discipline if the ships were to be held together that he now caused or permitted the use of the terrible sanction he had threatened earlier in the Channel. The immediate cause seems to have been an incident in the evening of August 10th; the wind eased somewhat, and some of the rearguard with Recalde lagged astern; seeing the enemy closing them, Medina Sidonia 'struck his topsails and lay to, waiting for the rear, and shot off three pieces so as our fleet should also lie to, and wait for the rearguard and the fleet flagship.'[84]

Some of the fleet did not lie to; in particular one of the store hulks, *Santa Barbara*, commanded by Don Christobal de Avila, and a Castilian fighting galleon, *San Pedro*, commanded by Francisco de Cuellar, continued under full sail until some miles ahead of the fleet flagship. Medina Sidonia sent pataches to fetch their captains, then retired, leaving the captains' fate to the Army commander, Don Francisco de Bovadillo. Whether at the same time he told Bovadillo to deal with commanders of ships who had quit their stations during the previous fighting is not clear, but this was done and it must be assumed he had èither ordered or at least agreed to it. Nor, of course, is it clear why this was necessary. English accounts agree on the excellent order the Armada kept throughout, according to Wynter even during the terrible battering they received off Gravelines, and to keep such disparate vessels with such primitive steering apparatus sailing in close order during over a week of battles seems from this distance a remarkable and extraordinary feat of seamanship. On the other hand some of the vessels, on account of sluggishness or damage aloft, must have found it impossible to keep in their assigned places at all times; this was always the case during the massed fleet actions of the Anglo-Dutch wars in the following century; Dutch captains and even flag officers were constantly accusing each other of cowardice – especially after unsuccessful actions. That is how it must have looked to Medina Sidonia and Bovadillo from the fleet flagship. Whether they now proceeded to exact penalties to promote discipline by fear in the coming actions with the English and in the stormy waters of the North Atlantic, or whether it had more to do with the human need for scapegoats after all their humiliations, or more probably whether the motives were mixed, will never be known. It is remarkable, however, that while the captains and officers who had erred in battle were condemned to the galleys or reduced to the ranks, Cuellar and Avila were both condemned to a shameful death.

There were no judicial proceedings; according to Cuellar before he even arrived at the fleet flagship he heard that he was to be hanged.[85] He made an impassioned outburst against the injustice, reminding Bovadillo of the part the *San Pedro* had played in all the fighting and the damage and casualties received and told him to enquire of his men 'and if any one should lay blame on me, they should cut me in four quarters.' Bovadillo sent him across to the Judge Advocate, Martin de Aranda, probably in the *Lavia* of the Levant squadron; Cuellar repeated his plea: he had been taking a rest at the time in question, 'for I had not slept or taken time to attend to the necessities of life for ten days, when my scoundrel of a mate, without saying anything to me, hoisted sail and put out in front of the flagship a matter of two miles, in order to go on with our repairs, just as other ships had done.'[86] Aranda took his part, according to de Cuellar, after he had taken secret soundings among the *San Pedro*'s men, and wrote to Medina Sidonia, who then reduced his sentence to removal from his ship.

Don Christobal de Avila was not so fortunate. Aboard a patache the next day, August 11th, a rope was fastened around his neck, and he was hoisted to the yardarm, after which the patache sailed through the fleet exhibiting the hanging corpse.

Cuellar's account is interesting for the impression it gives of Medina Sidonia as a depressed and weak man who left the conduct of the fleet to Bovadillo and Diego Flores de Valdés. While aboard the flagship, he was not allowed to see the Duke since, he was told, he was very unhappy and did not want anybody to speak to him; besides the lack of success in the campaign he was particularly grieved about the loss of the *San Mateo* and *San Felipe* and all the nobility aboard them:

For this reason the Duke kept himself in his cabin and his councillors did acts of injustice right and left in order to correct his neglect, disregarding the lives and honour of those that were not to blame, and that is so public that everybody knows it.[87]

Criticism of the supreme leadership is natural in a defeated fleet, and by the time he wrote his account some months after the events Cuellar had witnessed the complete disintegration of the Armada, and had himself undergone barely credible hardships. By his own words, he had not seen or spoken to the Duke, he was retailing hearsay and while this seems to agree with Medina Sidonia's introspective nature and readiness to acknowledge lack of experience, it does not accord with other accounts of his steadfastness, energy and real concern for others. Perhaps he was suffering a brief collapse into exhaustion after the extraordinarily testing time he had been through. He had spent practically the whole time on deck for the past 12 days; perhaps he was quite properly

The 'Armada Portrait' of Queen Elizabeth I by George Gower. The Queen sits between two pictures, on the left English warships flying the red cross of St George, their sails full of wind, on the right the Spanish galleons with more of the winds of God than they can cope with.

delegating authority. Stern measures were especially necessary in a demoralised fleet, while summary execution was by no means uncommon then or indeed in later centuries.

The Armada continued north-westerly before a strong wind all that day, and the English continued to follow; towards sunset they closed as they had the previous evening and Medina Sidonia fired a gun and lay to to await them in battle order; once again they held off.

Howard called a council; it was attended by Drake, Hawkins, Fenner, Lord Thomas Howard, the Earl of Cumberland, Lord Sheffield and Howard's secretary, Edward Hoby; by this time, in the latitude of the Yorkshire coast, they had gained the impression from the course and press of sail kept by the Spanish ships that they were in full flight around Scotland rather than intent on a landing, and after discussing the acute shortages of provisions in their own ships, it was decided they would continue following until they had cleared the English coast and reached the latitude of the Firth of Forth, then turn back to re-victual and guard the coast at home 'with further protestation that if our want of victuals and munition were supplied, we would pursue them to the furthest that they durst have gone.'[88]

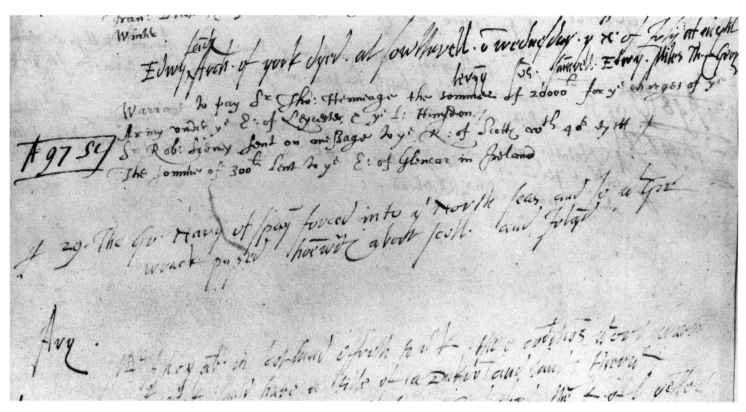

Entry from Lord Burghley's jottings book for 29 August:

'The Great Navy of spayne forced into ye North seas and so with Great wrack passed homewards about Scotland and Irland'.

Cumberland's friend Robert Carey wrote in his memoirs that the Council also decided to give the enemy a final charge next morning before leaving them.

However, early the following morning – August 12th – another council was called; by Howard's account they were as far north as Newcastle-on-Tyne, the enemy still shaping course for the Isles of Scotland rather than a landing in the Forth, and it was decided to make for the Forth themselves to replenish and warn the King of Scotland to take precautions. According to Carey the discovery that the fleet lacked powder and shot for 'even half a battle' caused them to give up the idea of a parting attack. At noon they bore away westerly, leaving only two pinnaces to shadow the Spanish; gradually the fleets which had been in company since the first morning off Plymouth drew apart and the sails each had been watching so closely shrank until they disappeared below the horizon.

Aboard the *Nonpareil*, Edward Fenner reflected:

If the wind by change suffer them, I verily believe they will pass about Scotland and Ireland to draw themselves home; wherein the season of the year considered, with the long course they have to run and their sundry distresses, and – of necessity – the spending of time by watering, winter will so come on as it will be to their great ruin.[89]

Two days later, after the wind had changed into the west forcing the English to steer south for England, then blown up into a regular south-westerly gale, he wrote to Walsyngham that in his opinion the great seas must affect the Spanish ships which were so high and crank 'as in fair weather would hardly bear their topsails', and the cold weather must affect the men, and was likely to do so more and more.[90]

Mine opinion is they are by this time so distressed, being so far thrust off [to the eastwards], as many of them will never see Spain again; which is the only work of God, to chastise their malicious practices, and to make them know that neither the strengths of men, nor their idolatrous gods can prevail when the mighty God of Israel stretcheth out but his finger against them.

10

Wreck and Massacre

The final scenes of the campaign were of unrelieved tragedy. On both sides many times more men were extinguished than in all the actions put together. The long-drawn moan of the famished and diseased was interrupted only by sharp tremors of death and the fear of death from tempest, rock, sword, axe, bullet, lance and the hangman's noose. On the Spanish side those who wasted away from hunger or disease were more fortunate than thousands of their fellows.

The first cries went up from the animals who had been shipped in the transports to draw the siege train and ammunition and commissariat carts; whether a few were slaughtered for meat is not recorded, but a merchant ship passing in the wake of the Armada soon after Howard turned back reported the uncanny sight of horses and mules breasting the empty sea. They had been cast overboard to save drinking water, which was already short and foul before the ships reached Calais. At the same time to preserve remaining provisions for the long voyage ahead Medina Sidonia ordered rations reduced to eight ounces of bread, half a pint of wine and a pint of water per man per day without exception. The salt meat and salt fish were either too rotten to be eaten, or would induce thirst when water was so limited; judging by the salt food on Drake's early prize, *Nuestra Senora del Rosario*, it was the former. At the beginning of September it was reported that little was left aboard her to sustain the Spanish prisoners; 'their fish savours, so that it is not to be eaten, and their bread (biscuit) full of worms.'[1]

After consulting a French pilot and offering him 2,000 ducats if he could bring them to a Spanish port, the Duke issued a navigational order to the fleet; they were to steer nor-nor-east until they reached the latitude of 61½ degrees, then 'parting from those islands and doubling the Cape in 61 degrees and a half, you shall run west-sou-west until you be found under 58 degrees' – the latitude of Lewis, northernmost of the Hebrides which lie off the north-west corner of Scotland – 'and from thence to the south-west to the height of 53 degrees' – roughly two-thirds of the way down Ireland – 'and then to the sou-sou-west, making to the Cape Finisterre'. No longitudes were given since, of course, it was impossible to find longitude with any exactness. 'The Cape' to be doubled at 61½° North was perhaps the northernmost point of the Shetland Islands, although there are several possible interpretations of these vague directions. However, Medina Sidonia did stress the need 'to take great heed lest you fall upon the island of Ireland, for fear of the harm that may happen unto you upon that coast.'[2] This probably refers to the dangerous rock-bound promontories and on-shore winds rather than the English troops who garrisoned the island.

The morning these orders were issued, August 13th, the wind went round to the north west, heading both Howard on his course towards the Forth and Medina Sidonia on his way around Scotland. Howard turned south for the Thames; Medina Sidonia must have been forced to steer north-easterly. The following day a south-westerly storm blew up, and to judge by both English and Spanish accounts of its severity it is doubtful if the 'crank' and damaged Spanish ships could have done anything but run before it under minimum canvas; Calderon records the next few days as 'squalls, rain and fogs with heavy seas, and it was impossible to distinguish one ship from another. It was therefore necessary to divide the fleet into separate groups.'[3] Obviously they were driven way to the east of their projected course, how far is impossible to say; the galleass *Zuniga* reported sighting the coast of Norway 'on our right' on August 13th,[4] thus *before* the storm. This does not seem credible: assuming Howard's estimated position for leaving the Armada in the morning of the 12th more or less correct – 55°13′N, '30 leagues from Newcastle', thus about 1°00′E – it was almost 300 miles to the nearest point of Norway; to see the land the next day would have meant making over 10 knots, clearly impossible. However, there is no other land that could have been seen 'on the right' with a northerly or north-easterly course, so it is possible that Norway was sighted from the *Zuniga*, but not on the 13th, perhaps on the 15th; this would be perfectly compatible with her reported sighting of 'the island called Shetland' four days later on the 19th. Medina Sidonia merely mentioned continuing northwards 'until we went out of the channel of the Sea of Norway without it being possible to return to the English Channel though we desired it.'[5] Then with the wind at north-east, he passed the Shetland Isles on the 20th/21st. Even this bare statement means he was blown far to the eastward since the direct route from the latitude of Newcastle to the Shetlands is scarcely 300 miles; even if the fleet's speed with a fair wind was no more than three knots, he should have made it, given the wind from a southerly quarter, in four days. As it was it took him more than eight.

That at least one ship came to grief on the Norwegian coast is suggested by an oral tradition from the island of Runde, just north of Alesund. An Armada vessel went aground near there, so the story runs, and bodies were washed ashore, among them women with lovely clothes and jewellery; the bodies were stripped of their clothes and valuables and some were then decapitated and the heads placed on stakes.[6] According to another legend seven monks from the Armada were buried at Jøttane on Runde. The small islets of Skorpa, close by Runde, Veiholmen off Smola and Sula off Froya just north of Trondheim are also connected by oral tradition with an Armada wreck. The ship was said to be called the *Invincible Castle* (*Uovervinnelige Borg*) and since the only 'Castle' name in the Armada fleet list is the 750-ton store 'hulk', *Castillo Negro*, recent tradition has substituted this name.[7] The *Castillo Negro* is known to have separated from the main body of the fleet after passing to the west of the Shetland Islands, and is assumed to have foundered in the Atlantic. It is not impossible that she did not founder, but was driven easterly by head winds until she fetched up on a Norwegian offshore islet. Alternatively 'invincible castle' may have been a description of a lofty vessel. In either case oral tradition should not be discounted. Colin Martin, investigating an Armada wreck on Fair Isle, found the facts about the stranding related to him by the islanders were borne out by his subsequent findings.

The unusual thing about one version of the Norwegian legend is, of course, that bodies of women were washed up. Camp followers were a normal feature of every campaign in those days, and it is interesting to speculate on whether one of the store hulks was perhaps adapted for this purpose. Medina Sidonia had ordered all women to be put ashore before sailing from Lisbon but it is not impossible that officers' and gentlemen adventurers' favourites were secretly embarked or tacitly condoned by the high command. Yet, if so, it is strange that it has not come to light in any accounts or prisoners' interrogations. Perhaps there is a clue in one chronicle of the campaign from the Low Countries which states that 'the women (camp followers) hired certain ships, wherein they sailed after the Navy; some of the which being driven by tempest upon the coast of France'.[8] Possibly one of these not wrecked in France continued the vain chase up the North Sea to fetch up on the rocks off Norway. It is a poignant thought. At least one woman, a German, is known to have sailed with the fleet, since she is listed in the English account of survivors from the *San Salvador*, which blew up after the first day's fighting off Plymouth.

Whether or not any ships ran for shelter or were driven ashore off Norway, the separated groups collected together again on the 19th; according to Calderon he noticed the *San Juan de Sicilia* was missing – and no doubt others too – and feared she might be lost: 'She had been so much damaged that not a span of her sails was serviceable'.[9] That night his own ship became separated once again in heavy weather, and he sailed on alone for the next few days.

Meanwhile a fishing vessel reported that on the 18th, while some 36 miles south-east of the Shetland Isles, 'they descried a very great fleet of monstrous great ships, to their seeming being about 100 in number, lying just West with both sheets aftward, whereby their course was to run betwixt Orkneys and Fair Isle.'[10] It is probable that the main body of the fleet sailed between the Shetlands and Fair Isle; to judge from the fishermen's report they had the wind right astern. Afterwards, according to the same report, the wind shifted into the south-east for the next week.

This is also suggested by Calderon's account; his ship found the fleet again on the 22nd, and two days later he went aboard the *San Martin* and talked to the Duke. By this time they were by his own reckoning and that of the pilots aboard the fleet flagship in 58½ degrees north. This is the latitude of the Butt of Lewis, the northernmost point of the Hebrides at the north-western corner of Scotland; that they were close to the Hebrides – or perhaps Cape Wrath, the northernmost point of the Scottish mainland in roughly the same latitude – is confirmed by a report from the galleass *Zuniga*, that the 'extreme point of Ireland' was sighted on the 21st. This could only have been Cape Wrath or the Butt of Lewis. The Duke asked Calderon whether he had seen or heard anything of Don Alonso de Luzon in the great Venetian, *Trinidad Valencera*, as he had not seen him for 13 days. Calderon replied that he had seen neither the *Valencera* nor for the last two days the *San Marcos* and a dozen other ships in a group with Recalde; 'He therefore suspected that he (Recalde) had allowed himself to drift towards Iceland or the Faroe Isles . . . Iceland being in 65° North, and Faroe in 62° North.'[11]

This suggests south-easterly winds which had allowed the main body with the Duke to make good the west-sou-westerly course stipulated in the instructions, while more damaged ships like Recalde's or worse sailers like the great Levanters and the hulks had been forced further north.

Calderon advised keeping well clear of Ireland, and was backed up by the Duke's French pilot; they were opposed by Diego Flores de Valdés. The only reason that suggests itself is that he hoped to seize an undefended anchorage where they might replenish their water; that is speculation. The Duke took the pilot's advice, but by this time, according to the account from the galleass *Zuniga*, the wind had veered into the south and freshened, driving them northwards. Calderon wrote, 'From the 24th to the 4th September we sailed without knowing whither, through constant storms, fogs and squalls,' and once again his ship became separated from the main body. Medina Sidonia, writing to

Examples (also on pages 174, 175) of Armada playing cards, produced in c.1675–1700. This pack illustrates people and events in the Armada Campaign, and has a distinct late seventeenth-century anti-Catholic tone.

Philip on September 3rd, said that since his last letter, despatched by pinnace from the Shetlands on the 21st, they had had 'on four separate nights heavy gales with strong head winds, thick fogs and rain. This has caused 17 vessels to separate from the Armada . . .'[12]

One of these was Calderon's *San Salvador*, Vice flagship of the squadron of hulks, another was Alonso de Luzon's *Trinidad Valencera*, which had joined three other hulks somewhere off the Shetlands – the squadron flagship, *Gran Grifon*, the *Castillo Negro* and the *Barca de Amburg*; the *Amburg* foundered on September 1st after her crew had been taken aboard the *Valencera* and *Gran Grifon*. Another of the missing vessels was the galleass *Zuniga*, whose rudder was smashed on September 2nd; she could only drive before the wind; five days later in 63 degrees north by her account, she came up with a group of 13 vessels under Recalde. These probably included the Marquis de Penafiel's *San Marcos*, and most of the great ships of the Levant squadron, including de Leyva's *Rata Encoranada*.

Conditions aboard the storm-blown ships can be better imagined than described. Even before the English had left them, Drake had learned from prisoners, 'that generally throughout the whole fleet, there was no ship free of sick people.'[13] In his letter of the 21st Medina Sidonia had reported 'over 3,000 sick, without counting the wounded, who are numerous.' In his September 3rd letter, he wrote:

I pray God in His mercy will grant us fine weather so that the Armada may soon enter port; for we are so short of provisions that if for our sins we be long delayed, all will be irretrievably lost. There are now a great number of sick and many die . . .[14]

A Portuguese sailor in Recalde's flagship, *San Juan*, who was captured later, told his interrogator that although this was one of the best provided ships, 'there died four or five every day of hunger and thirst.'[15] And one of several Scottish fishermen taken aboard Recalde's ship as pilots confirmed that the ships were not only without victuals, but 'in great extremity for want of knowledge.'[16]

To gain some idea of the misery aboard it is only necessary to look at the English ships, which had not been so long continuously at sea, nor so damaged, and which had safe havens and supplies sent out to them, yet the men were dying by the day. They had arrived back off Harwich on the 17th – sufficient proof of the continuous south or southwesterly winds which had driven the Armada northwards in those first days after Howard had left them, for it had taken him five days to make good a distance of 200 miles. Hawkins had taken his squadron into Harwich; Howard and Drake had continued down to the North Foreland to anchor off Margate. On the 20th Howard wrote to Burghley:

Sickness and mortality begins wonderfully to grow amongst us; and it is a most pitiful sight to see, here at Margate, how the men, having no place to receive them into here, die in the streets. I am driven myself, of force, to come a-land, to see them bestowed in some lodging; and the best I can get is barns and such out-houses; and the relief is small that I can provide for them here. It would grieve any man's heart to see them that have served so valiantly to die so miserably.[17]

One of the worst affected ships was the *Elizabeth Jonas*; before the Armada arrived in the English Channel she had lost over 200 of her 500 crew to disease. Despite all attempts to purify her by replacing her ballast and thoroughly smoking her hold and orlopes with fires of wet broom the infection, whatever it was, had remained in her; she was now so short-handed that Howard sent her into the dockyard at Chatham. He and everyone else judged the infection was seated in the pitch used to caulk her. Probably it was in the drinking water or

The Spanish Armada consisting of 130 Shipps whereof 72 were Galleasses and Galeons in wch were 19290 Souldiers, 8350 Marriners, 2080 Gally slaves & 2630 great Ordinance. y Navy was 3 whole yeares sparing

The Fleete of Portugall consisting of 12 Vessells, in wch were 3330 Souldiers, 1233 Marriners, 400 Canons

some item of her provisions or galley equipment, or was passed from survivors of the original epidemic. Howard was no less worried about the other ships: the men had been in them so long, some for the whole eight months since the start of the emergency, they had few clothes left and no money to buy new. He urged Burghley to send down a thousand pounds worth of 'hose, doublets, shirts, shoes and such like', and money so that he could pay off the sick and discharge them.

It is evident from a letter Hawkins wrote to Burghley on September 5th, that sickness and death continued, for he reminded Burghley that the wages of those who died had to be paid to their friends, and 'in place of those which are discharged sick and insufficient, which indeed are many, there are fresh men taken,' which in fact cost the Exchequer more.[18]

The English fleet was being kept in commission even at this date, practically a month after the battle off Gravelines, and while the separated demoralised groups of the Armada were being driven hither and thither by storms in the North Atlantic, because there was still no certain news either of them or of Parma. In fact, Parma had long given up, if indeed he had ever had any hopes of invasion. Philip's Ambassador in Paris was receiving reports 'from all parts that the Duke of Parma is very sad and downhearted'.[19] Parma's own intelligence reports indicated that Medina Sidonia could not return; he knew that pinnaces from Seymour's squadron in the Downs were watching his ports, as were Justin of Nassau's flyboats and cromsters; he knew of the fate of the two Armada galleons which had drifted down to the Nieuport shoals. There was no possibility of his army getting out, let alone crossing the Channel. On August 29th he had written to Philip to inform him of this, and tell him he was dividing his troops into three bodies; one he was sending down the Rhine to Bonn, another he was taking to Brabant on the inland flank of the Zealanders, the third he was leaving to garrison Flanders.

Elizabeth, her council and commanders at sea remained anxious; conflicting rumours were rife, and when Hawkins and Drake discharged several of the merchant ships in their squadrons – which had been more a hindrance than help in any case – Howard was annoyed. It was not until towards the end of the first week in September that tensions eased. Howard divided the smaller Royal ships into two squadrons for the autumn and winter so that one could be on the Flemish coast while the other waited in the Downs; the Queen began to think about sending Drake after the treasure fleet returning from the Indies, a sure sign of returning normality.

Much has been made of Elizabeth's miserly neglect in paying the seamen who had beaten off the Spanish threat, and allowing them to rot on the streets of the port towns; this impression comes chiefly from the letter Howard wrote soon after returning from the pursuit, the opening paragraph of which has been quoted here, and another written on September 8th when he was paying off many of his merchantmen, and was consequently short of money:

I am driven to make Sir John Hawkyns to relieve them with money as he can. It were too pitiful to have men starve after such a service. I know her Majesty would not, for any good. Therefore I had rather open the Queen's Majesty's purse something to relieve them than they should be in that extremity; for we are to look to have more of these services; and if men should not be cared for better than to let them starve and die miserably, we should very hardly get men to serve . . .[20]

A thorough reading of Howard's, Burghley's and especially Hawkins' correspondence and accounts leaves an impression, not of uncaring neglect, but

The English Fleet whereof the L.ᵈ Charles Howaᵈ was L.ᵈ Admirall. & S.ʳ Fran: Drake vice Admirall.

Don Alphonſo Duke of Medina, Cheife Comander of y Spaniſh Fleele. & Iohn Martin Recalde, a great Seaman.

of individuals struggling manfully and it seems honestly to overcome administrative bottlenecks caused by the sheer, unprecedented scale of the effort England had put forth. Howard paid men from his own purse, protesting 'before God, I had rather have never penny in the world than they should lack',[21] apparently selling his own plate to do it and taking money from Drake's Spanish prize. How much of this went to his own adherents to ensure their loyalty, how much to the sick and the common sailors, how much was exaggeration to press his case with Burghley can never be known, but his letters have the ring of genuine indignation; thus when he took the gold from the *Rosario*:

. . . for, by Jesus, I had not 3£. (£3.00) besides in the world, and had not anything could get money in London; and I do assure you my plate was gone before. But I will repay it within 10 days after my coming home. I pray you let Her Majesty know so. And by the Lord God of Heaven, I had not one Crown more; and had it not been mere necessity, I would not have touched one; but if I had not some to have bestowed upon some poor and miserable men, I should have wished myself out of the world . . .[22]

Some 15,398 men served in the English fleets – considerably more than Philip had thought possible – and during the whole year, 1588, John Hawkins disbursed over £92,000 on naval stores and wages[23] – against an ordinary annual expenditure of some £6,000. If some money and victuals and ammunition did not arrive at the right place at the right time, it is not surprising. Much of the sickness and death in the fleet was due to an infectious or contagious disease rather than weakness or scurvy caused by want of provisions, and probably the most serious charge against the administration is that the fleet ran out of powder and shot at the crucial stage of the battle off Gravelines and in any case would not have been able to maintain that action without the ammunition taken from the Spanish prizes. It is true everyone had underestimated the likely 'hugeness' of the Spanish fleet and ships, and the amount of shot which would be required to disperse it, but a very great proportion of the shot fired in the actions up-Channel was wasted, and still they had sufficient after four actions to fight the decisive battle of Gravelines. As Medina Sidonia wrote on August 21st off the Shetlands:

This Armada was so completely crippled and scattered that my first duty to Your Majesty seemed to save it, even at the risk we are running in undertaking this voyage, which is so long and in such high latitudes. Ammunition and the best of our vessels are lacking, and experience had shown how little we could depend upon the ships that remained, the Queen's fleet being so superior to ours in this sort of fighting, in consequence of the strength of their artillery, and the fast sailing of their ships.[24]

The Armada's close order while being harassed up-Channel had been a triumph of seamanship; by the end of the first week in September, after rounding Scotland, then being driven northwards again in the Atlantic it was still largely together, which appears an even greater triumph. Individual ships and small groups had lost contact in the storms and fogs but somehow most had rejoined; the fact that Calderon in the vice flagship of the hulks was one of these indicates that Medina Sidonia had been holding back as he had in the skirmishes up-Channel, conforming to the movements of his slowest and worst sailers.

It was by now, September 8th, eight full weeks since the first squadrons had been towed out from Corunna to await a favourable wind; since then they had been continuously at sea. A small quantity of fresh provisions had been purchased in Calais, perhaps a few mules had been slaughtered for meat off Scotland, a small quantity of fresh fish had been purchased from fishing boats south of the Shetlands, and Calderon had distributed small quantities of a private stock of delicacies to the sick and wounded aboard various flagships, but all these

The Spaniards dispatching Messingers to the Prince of Parma requiring him forthwith to joyn him-selfe with them.

The Army of 1000 horse, and 22000 Foot, which ye Earle of Leicester comanded when hee Pitched his Tents att Tilbury

things could have reached no more than a fraction of the thousands in the fleet. What everyone needed was Vitamin C – something that was not discovered for centuries; all they knew they needed was good, fresh food, particularly vegetables and citrus fruit; as Drake had put it a month before, 'I doubt it not but ere it be long . . . the Duke of Sidonia . . . shall wish himself at St Mary Port among his orange trees.'[25]

Gaunt from hunger, cold in far northern seas they were unaccustomed to, often drenched by squalls, wet from leaking seams in the planking, breathing foul gas from the ballast and the nauseating stink of the stale, thin excrement and vomit of the sick and wounded who relieved themselves where they lay, close-packed in the orlope, all must also have been exhibiting the apathy which is one of the first signs of scurvy. It could begin to afflict crews after four or five weeks; after six weeks on salt tack it was inevitable: by eight weeks listlessness, swelling and bleeding gums and blotched skin would have begun to tell their tale. No one recorded it, but there can be no doubt it had fastened on the men. It makes the feat of keeping together even more remarkable. The sailors who hauled on braces, bowlines and sheets, the soldiers who manned shifts at the pumps and formed human chains passing buckets up on deck, carpenters' gangs who clambered amongst the clutter of the hold with lanterns to try and discover fresh leaks, or patched and shored all too visible leaks from seams working apart and losing their caulking, all were apathetic and weak, not simply through cold and hunger and the bitter taste of defeat and fatalistic feelings induced by the loss, day after day, of a few more of their shipmates, but because they were suffering from scurvy, the seaman's disease that claimed more lives and more ships than all naval battles together in the age of sail, and was to claim their lives by the thousand, and many of their ships.

The main body of the fleet with Medina Sidonia was somewhere to the north and west of Ireland by this time, there was no way of knowing exactly where, for they were not on a regular trade route and there was consequently little knowledge of the coastline or depths; charts were inaccurate. All they could do was attempt to make good the southwesterly course decreed by the French pilot. That they had been able to work a good way to the south since being blown northwards from off the Hebrides is suggested by an account from the vice flagship of the Castilian squadron, the *San Juan Bautista*, commanded by Marcos de Aramburu. He had become separated from the rest of the fleet on August 27th in 59 degrees north, but by September 8th had worked down to 55 degrees – abreast the north of Ireland. Probably Medina Sidonia with the worse sailers to look after was somewhat higher and the group of a dozen or so in company with Recalde higher still since they had sagged further north after passing the Shetlands. That the wind was again unfavourable is made clear by an account from another separated vessel, the *Gran Grifon*, flagship of the hulks. Her hull seams had opened so much that she could do nothing but run before whatever wind was blowing, and on September 8th and 9th she was heading north. On the 10th the wind went round to the north-east; she turned again and drove back before it. This was, of course, exactly what was needed, and both the main fleet with Medina Sidonia and Recalde's smaller group undoubtedly made good progress southwestwards for the next three days, passing down clear to the west of Ireland – only just clear it seems.

On the 11th the wind went round again to sou-sou-west, heading them; the *Gran Grifon* went round with it and ran back, nor-nor-easterly on her purposeless chase; Aramburu in the *San Juan Bautista*, evidently not confident that he had cleared the southern capes of Ireland, tacked north-westerly. Almost

This salamander pendant, in gold and rubies, was recovered from the wreck of the galleass *Girona*, which ran aground at Lacada Point, just east of the Giant's Causeway in Ulster. Out of 1300 men on board, only 9 were saved.

certainly Medina Sidonia did the same, and Recalde. On the 12th the wind backed into the south and that night blew up into a gale; the ships with their depleted crews could do nothing but run before the high, driving crests of the seas, and by next morning they had become scattered over scores of miles. Medina Sidonia, counting sails, saw only about 60 of the 95 he had had with him at the beginning of the month; with Recalde's *San Juan* only one patache could be seen in a waste of rolling water. The old Admiral himself was in his bunk as he had been since Gravelines, critically ill.

This was the final blow that broke the Armada. Although the wind veered into the north-west on the next day, the 13th, allowing the main body with Medina Sidonia to steer sou-sou-west and clear the southern tip of Ireland next day, others must have run east or south-east, as Aramburu did in the *San Juan Bautista*. Why they did so is not apparent from the accounts; for some it was perhaps that the state of the men and sails and rigging did not permit much else; others were so leaky after the latest battering that the emaciated hands at pumps and buckets could not compete with rising water in the holds and they had to make for the nearest land; still others had probably lost all hope of making Spain and were seeking any land where they might obtain fresh water and food and a rest to build their strength and make repairs; many captains, probably, were simply confused now they found themselves alone and leaderless. For whatever reasons they seem to have either sailed easterly, or made so much leeway while steering south or south-easterly that they found themselves jammed hard up against the Irish coast, and as the wind backed into the west, they were unable to weather the projecting capes.

For the English in Ireland it was a nervous time. Sightings of Spanish ships were reported from north to south along the Atlantic coastline, many duplicated so that it seemed as if the whole Armada was descending or, as Sir Richard Bingham speculated from Galway, 'new forces (were) come from Spain directly'. The garrisons were small isolated companies, some made up of English regulars, some of Irish mercenaries, all together not many more than 2,000 men. If the Spaniards were to succeed in joining together they would far outmatch any force that could be put into the field against them, even without the support they would receive from the local people; that was the fear, and at a time of such acute perceived danger the possibilities of the enemy being so wasted by starvation and depleted by scurvy as to be virtually harmless, even if they occurred to anyone, could not form a basis for action. The order went out from the new Lord Deputy in Dublin, Sir William Fytzwilliam, to 'apprehend and execute all Spaniards found of what quality soever'. Given the helpless state of the 'invaders' and the anxiety of the English, fed with propaganda about the Spaniards' cruel designs, and long experience of the rebellious Irish, the scene was set for a massacre.

Ireland was a wild country. Large areas had been colonised by the English from the 12th century onwards, but while these Earldoms and Baronies remained, the families had lost their colonial aspect over the centuries and become by intermarriage and identity with the country as Irish as the people themselves; these were the 'Anglo-Irish'. Some, like the Geraldines who held the great Norman Earldom of Desmond in the south-western province of Munster, remained powerful; they pretended allegiance to the Crown as represented by the Lord Deputy in Dublin, but conspired against the English for their own ambitions – as indeed they conspired and fought against each other.

Besides the Anglo-Irish Earls and lesser Lords, there were indigenous Irish clan chiefs, who held sway particularly in the less accessible, marshy or

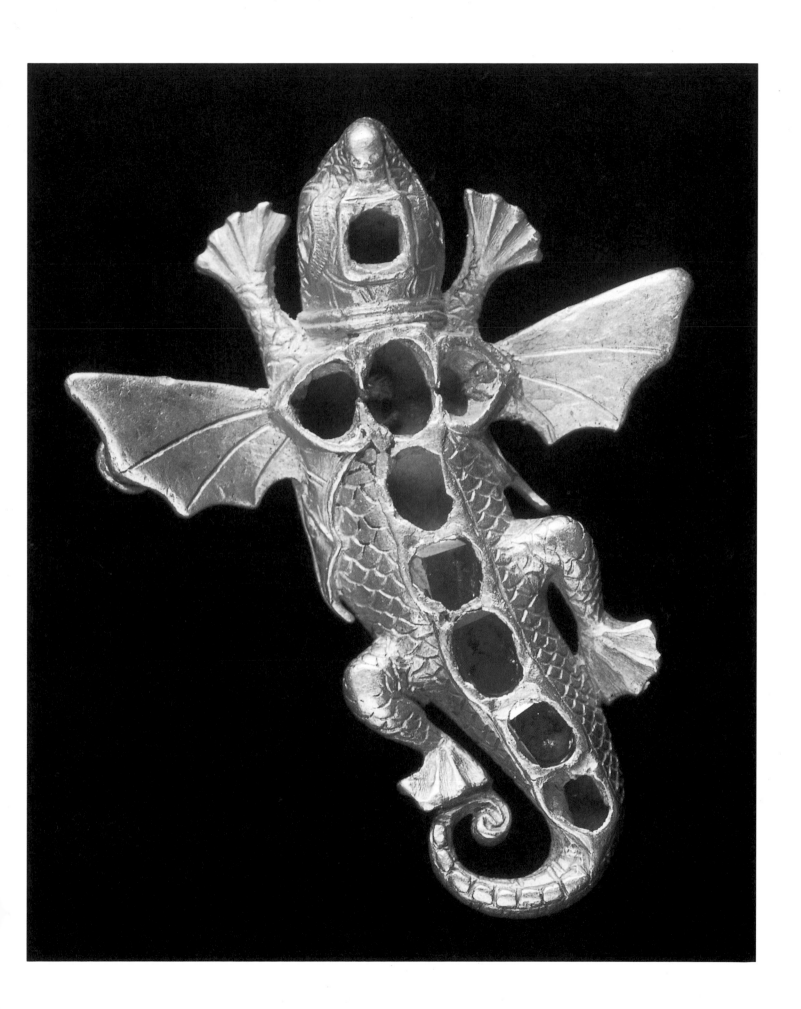

mountainous regions of the west and north-west. English Lord Deputies never had sufficient money or troops to keep the peace among all these factions and in practice Elizabeth's writ did not extend much beyond the five counties of the 'Pale', a small English enclave in the east around Dublin, and a number of chartered seaport towns in the south and south-west. Here, where some trading and seafaring wealth made possible a more decorous, urban life, the English language, dress, manners and the reformed Protestant religion retained a precarious hold, outposts of civilisation amid the surrounding barbarism – so it was perceived. The native inhabitants were regarded as savages, as indeed they were by the Spaniards who landed from the Armada. Captain de Cuellar, who had narrowly escaped summary execution for allowing his galleon to sail ahead of the fleet flagship the previous month, was one of the few who observed them for a long period and survived; he wrote:

The nature of these savages is to live like beasts among the mountains, some of which are very rugged in the parts of the island where we were cast away. They live in huts made of straw. The men have big bodies, their features and limbs are well made, and they are agile as deer. They eat but one meal a day, and that at night, and their ordinary food is oaten bread and butter . . . On holidays they eat meat, half cooked without bread or salt. They dress in tight breeches and goatskin jackets cut short but very big, and over all a blanket, and wear their hair down to their eyes. They are good walkers and have great endurance. They are always at war with the English, who garrison the country there, and both defend themselves from them and prevent them coming into their territory, which is all flooded and covered with marshy ponds . . . Their great bent is to be robbers and to steal from one another, so that not a day passes without a call to arms among them. For when the men of one hamlet learn that there are cattle or anything else in another, they go at once, armed, by night, and shouting war whoops kill one another, and then when the English learn which village has gathered in and stolen most cattle they swoop down on it and take it all away; and these have no other help than to fly to the mountains with their wives and flocks, for they possess no other property, neither household stuff nor clothes. They sleep on the ground, upon rushes freshly cut and full of water or else frozen stiff. Most of the women are very pretty but ill-dressed. They wear nothing but a shift and a blanket over it, and a linen cloth much folded on their heads and tied in front . . .[26]

Similar descriptions of the lawlessness and feuding between the clans were penned by an English Lord Deputy, Sir Henry Sidney, who toured the whole country in 1575 – escorted by 400 foot and 200 cavalry. In Galway he held a court:

Wherein I found plenty of murder, rape, burning and sacrilege, and besides such spoil of goods and cattle as in number might be counted infinite . . . and indeed the whole country not able to answer a quarter of that which was affirmed to be lost amongst them . . .[27]

While plunder and fighting seemed as natural to the Celtic character as bards and poetry, the English presence undoubtedly aggravated the trouble. During Elizabeth's reign great efforts had been made to pacify the country and create more 'plantations' of settlers; in pursuing these aims English administrations had been as crass as any conquerors in a minority whose superior material culture gave them delusions of higher worth. A 19th-century authority on the English conquest, J. S. Brewer, could not find in any of the 'numerous projects for keeping Ireland in order any indications of a nobler aim or a loftier purpose than that of retaining Ireland for the benefit of England at the smallest possible cost and trouble . . .';[28] And in despair at the Irish refusal either to govern themselves or be governed the English authorities attempted to obliterate all traces of

Irishness, banning long hair, moustachios and mantles, bards and rhymers; to listen to an Irish minstrel was an offence, to do so more than once was to court the loss of both ears. Meanwhile English and Scots settlers – like most settlers in a strange and hostile environment – being in the front line, behaved on the whole worse than their governors; J. S. Brewer again:

They learned to regard the Irish as fit subjects for plunder, to commit all sorts of atrocities under the degraded name of patriotism, to fill the whole country with discontent, immorality and disorder . . . While on the part of the native Irish the feeling they were beyond the pale and protection of English law tended to increase their lawlessness and violence. Hunted down like wild beasts, they turned like wild beasts on their pursuers. As the Englishman learned to associate the name of Irish with all that was vile, savage and degrading, the Irishman was naturally taught to connect all forms of oppression, cruelty and wrong with the name of Englishman; to hate what his conqueror loved, and to love what he hated . . .[29]

The Irish were quite as oppressed by their own chiefs and anarchic clan system, but the foreign invader attempting to cut out their soul, their Irishness, was a more obvious focus for discontent; resistance became bound up with religion, the Roman Catholic faith to which their ancestors had been converted. Although this had fallen into such disrepair by the 1570s that Sir Henry Sidney could report many parts of the country 'profane and heathenish', a new wave of missionaries arrived from the continent in the 1580s, as they had in England, burning with counter-reformationary zeal, and these found naturally fertile soil. Brewer wrote, 'In no country on earth has the priesthood been so completely identified with the sacred cause of nationality as in Ireland.'[30]

Religion also provided hope for external succour; Irish and Anglo-Irish leaders continually urged the Pope and Philip of Spain to wage their crusade against the heretic English in their country where they would receive the support of all the Irish people. In 1579 one of these, Sir James Fitzmaurice – earlier described by Sir Henry Sidney as 'subtle, malicious and hardy, a papist in extremity'[31] – succeeded in gaining some practical help and with a few Italian, Spanish, Portuguese, Fleming, French and Irish mercenaries raised rebellion in Munster. The following summer more Spanish and Italian mercenaries were brought to the province by a small squadron commanded by Recalde; they occupied the fort of Smerwick, where they landed, but were besieged by the then Lord Deputy, Lord Grey de Wilton, and soon surrendered to terms. The terms were not honoured. All were massacred as pirates, except for a few men of quality who were put up for ransom in the usual way. Afterwards the English forces were turned loose on the local rebels and their leaders, the Geraldines of the ancient Earldom of Desmond, with such ferocity that over the following months more than 30,000 were killed or starved to death. A contemporary described the results:

Out of every corner of the woods and glens they came creeping forth upon their hands, for their legs could not bear them; they looked like anatomies of death; they spake like ghosts crying out of their graves; they did eat the dead carrions, happy where they could find them; yea and one another soon after . . .[32]

Such was the land, tortured by hatreds and bad faith, fear, bigotry and atrocity, on which the Armada ships began to fall and anchor or beach and tear themselves on spurs of the rock-bound coast. And those Spaniards who were not drowned probably emerged like those inhabitants of Munster in 1580 and 1581 with their legs scarcely able to carry them, their sunken faces like anatomies of death.

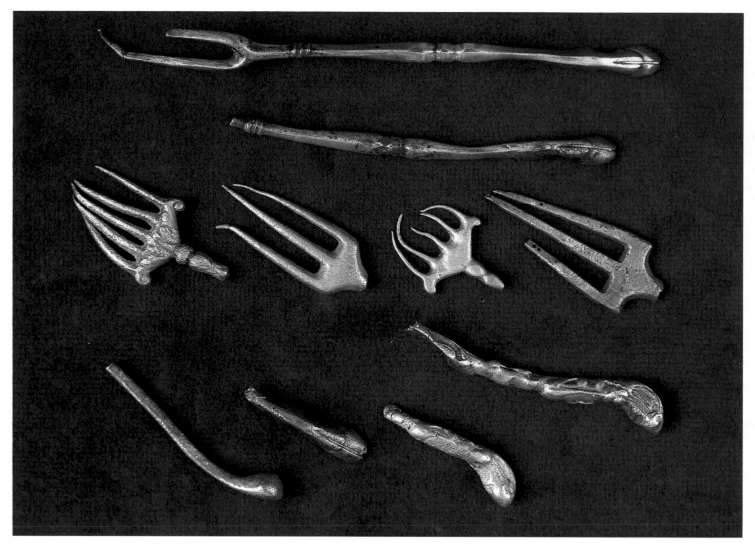

Silver forks and candlesticks
recovered from the wreck of the
Girona.

Gold and silver coins, and a gold ring
on which is mounted the figure of a
salamander, recovered from the wreck
of the *Girona*.

A stillness of apprehension had fallen over the country, English and Irish alike, ever since the first reports of the Armada in the Channel. In August an English official, Sir George Carew, had described how the people 'stood agaze until the game be played, not daring to discover (reveal) their real intentions. They are so possessed of fear that I have never seen a greater appearance of quiet.'[33] Tension mounted with the news of ships on the coast.

One of the first to come in was the huge Levanter, *Trinidad Valencera*. She had sprung a leak forward during the great storm of September 12th and, with water gaining on the pumps, had steered eastwards to seek land; running past Malin Head, the northern cape of Donegal in the extreme north-west of the island, she headed into a sandy bay just short of the entrance to Lough Foyle, and jarred up on a shallow spur of rock which held her fast. From the evidence of her remains, Colin Martin has deduced she was drawing about 25 feet when she struck, and must have been close to sinking.

Her commander, Don Alonso de Luzon, taking 'five more of the best of his company' ashore in their damaged boat was met by 'four or five savage people – as he termeth them – who bade them welcome.' These were of the local O'Doherty clan. After a while some 20 more local men joined them and the initial friendliness gave way to demands;[34] de Luzon later told his interrogater that he was relieved of a bag containing 1,000 reals, and a 'cloak of blue rash, richly laid with gold lace'. He managed to hire a boat to get his men ashore, but had to pay the hugely inflated sum of 200 ducats for it and the only food he could buy for his starving company were some ponies which they slaughtered and cooked, and a small quantity of butter. Nevertheless, during the next two days he succeeded in getting his men ashore with their arms, all except about 40 who drowned when the ship broke up on the 16th. He then started leading them towards a castle where, he was told, there was an Irish Bishop named Cornelius. This was either the O'Doherty castle at Illagh (now Calliagh), near Derry, some 30 miles heavy walking around the western shore of Lough Foyle, or another close by.

After four days he arrived within sight of the castle, but a local force of Irish mercenaries in English pay, commanded by two cousins of the neighbouring Earl of Tyrone, Richard and Henry Hovenden, and a major Kelly, were waiting for them. Numerically de Luzon's force was the stronger; he seems to have had over 500 men, including those rescued from the sinking *Barca de Amburg*, while the garrison troop was no more than 150 horse and foot.[35] But of course the Spaniards were in no condition to fight; many were critically ill and the rest had had no time to recover strength after their ordeal; they were, moreover, in a strange country without any knowledge of their compatriots, whom they must have supposed had sailed on towards Spain, and they were told by Kelly and the Hovendens that unless they surrendered 3,000 English soldiers would appear shortly to cut their throats. Despite all this and the fact they had no provisions or means of obtaining any de Luzon decided to resist, probably guessing the likely fate of his men if he were to surrender. There were a few skirmishes that evening.

Next day Kelly and the Hovendens promised that if the Spaniards laid down their arms they would conduct them all to the Lord Deputy in Dublin only 30 miles away – in fact it was five times that distance – and de Luzon submitted. Whether he believed the Irish officers would keep their word will, of course, never be known, but at least he could expect to save the lives of those worth ransom, and the alternative was to see his force reduced gradually until starved into submission.

They laid down their arms, which were collected and removed, then the

Dunluce Castle, near the Giant's Causeway, seat of the Irish chieftain Sorleyboy M'Donnell, who assisted in the escape of some of the Spanish sailors from Ireland.

mercenaries fell on them, robbing them of everything they had, even the clothes of the ordinary soldiers, leaving them naked for the night. Next morning they separated out Don Alonso, the officers and gentlemen volunteers, five servants and some friars, and ordering the rest into an open field between a line of arquebusiers and another of mounted lancers proceeded to slaughter them, according to one survivor 'killing over 300 with lance and bullet.'[36] Some 150 of those fortunate enough not to be hit by the first volley and charges, and fit enough to hobble or run from the horses into a nearby marsh escaped the massacre and managed to make their way to the castle they had been heading for originally; there they found shelter and care from Bishop Cornelius. Don Alonso and the 40 or so gentlemen judged worth ransom were taken on a long march towards Drogheda on the east coast.

By this time many more ships had come to anchor or gone aground along the length of the western coastline. Among the first after the *Valencera* were Recalde's *San Juan* and Aramburu's *San Juan Bautista*. At dawn on the 15th these two had found themselves together close in to the spur of the Kerry coast ending in the Blasket islands, unable to beat off against a westerly wind. Perhaps because of the danger, Recalde had risen from his sick bed; he ordered the helm up and, guided either by one of the Scottish fishermen he had taken or by knowledge he had acquired himself in 1580 when bringing the Spanish and Italian mercenaries to the aid of Fitzmaurice, ran in through a narrow and perilous channel between the islands and surrounding rocks. Aramburu, supposing he must know what he was doing, put his own helm up and followed through the milling, frothing breakers on either hand, and both dropped anchor safely in the lee of Great Blasket Island. The patache which was the only vessel to have kept company with Recalde through the storm of the 12th, followed them in and also anchored.

Recalde sent one of his Scottish fishermen and seven other sailors in a boat to prospect for fresh water and provisions, but they were seized by an English detachment and brought to the port of Dingle for interrogation. They painted a grim picture of conditions in the flagship with only 25 pipes of wine left 'and very little bread; and no water but what they brought out of Spain, which stinketh marvellously; and their flesh meat they cannot eat, their drouth (thirst) is so great.' By another account the (salt) beef was 'corrupt'; 200 of the company had died; the Admiral was 'very sick', as were the Master, one of the pilots and

Eleven out of a presumed set of twelve cameos of Roman emperors were recovered from the wreck of the *Girona*. This is the best preserved; almost in its original condition, it still bears at the sides its original complement of four pearls, held on a fine gold wire.

The cross of the Order of St John belonged to Fabricio Spinola, captain of the *Girona*.

numerous soldiers and mariners; the rest of the men were 'all very weak.'[37] No doubt after their interrogation these men were hanged; nothing more was heard of them. Meanwhile a force of some 200 arquebusiers and a few cavalry watched the Spanish ships from the cliffs overlooking Blasket Sound to prevent a landing.

On the same day Recalde and Aramburu had come in, the rudderless galleass, *Zuniga*, was also caught on a lee shore some 50 miles to the north, off county Clare; she managed to run in to shelter up a creek and anchor. And next day, still further north, off the coast of Sligo near Streedagh Point, three large ships from Recalde's scattered group dropped anchor a mile or so off-shore; one was a Castilian galleon, yet another *San Juan*, commanded by Don Diego Enriquez, another was the *Lavia* of the Levant squadron with Captain Cuellar aboard, and the third another Levanter. It is a sign of the miserable condition of the crews that having anchored they did nothing, according to de Cuellar not even able to make repairs, waiting perhaps for a change of wind. News of their presence was carried to the English garrison. The next day a vessel came to anchor or ran aground in the Bay of Tralee; 25 of her company gave themselves up. After interrogation they were all executed, it is assumed on the orders of Lady Denny, wife of the English commander in the area, Sir Edward Denny, who was in Dublin.

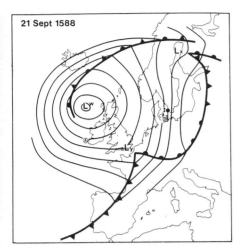

21 Sept 1588

The study by the Climatic Research Unit at the University of East Anglia suggests that the great gale of 21 September 1588 which finally broke the Armada originated as an Atlantic tropical cyclone, 'this being near the peak date for such systems entering higher latitudes on recurring tracks which carry them far to the north-east. By 21 September, Low 'W' had probably been rejuvenated and deepened by drawing in Arctic cold air in its rear.' This was the low whose effects the Duke of Medina Sidonia encountered earlier on 18 September as a severe storm in southern Biscay.

A large number of other vessels chiefly from Recalde's group which had not been able to work far enough south to clear Ireland, were still beating off the coast against the onshore wind; on the morning of the 21st the wind rose until it was blowing a westerly gale, the most ferocious yet: 'a most extreme and cruel storm the like whereof hath not been heard a long time', the Clerk to the Council of Connaught reported, and added that it gave the English authorities 'very good hope that many of the ships should be beaten up and cast away upon the rocks.'[38] The hope was fulfilled. The wearied, sickly Spanish crews could do nothing but resign themselves to the next world as they were driven helplessly before gigantic seas hurled up from the vastness of the Atlantic, unable in some cases to take in their canvas which split like rags. A few by chance found their way into sheltered anchorages, many drove up on rocks and foundered or were pounded to pieces by the seas. Thousands of the men were drowned, more than a thousand slaughtered on the shore as they were washed up more dead than alive, offering as much resistance to the waiting troops and irregular bands of plunderers as baby seals. Such was their pitiful state that one Scottish mercenary named McLaughlan MacCabe could boast of killing 80 with his own axe from a ship wrecked off Tralee.

The crews of the ships anchored off Streedagh Strand experienced a similar fate. Exposed to the full fury of the blast and the great seas rearing and tumbling as they surged into the shallows, these three vessels all dragged their anchors and, as Cuellar recorded, 'were driven on a sandy beach surrounded on every side by great rocks, a most terrible spectacle'.

Commending himself to God and Our Lady, Cuellar climbed to the poop:

. . . and from thence I looked about on the great spectacle of woe. Many men were sinking in the ships; others throwing themselves into the water, went down and never came up; some were on rafts and water-casks; captains threw their gold chains and their money into the sea, and some gentlemen I saw clinging to spars; others left on the ships cried aloud calling upon God; and some were swept off by waves which took them right out of the ships. And as I was staring at this horror, I knew not what to do, for I cannot swim and the waves and the storm were very great; and on the other hand the land and the beach were full of enemies who were going about skipping and dancing for joy at our misfortune. Whenever any of our men reached land, two hundred savages and other enemies rushed upon them and stripped them of everything they wore, leaving them stark naked, and without any pity beat them and ill used them. All this could be plainly seen from the wrecked ships . . .[39]

Cuellar and the Judge Advocate who had spared his life a month before were two of the last remaining aboard the *Lavia*, which was being pounded to pieces, quite literally, beneath them; according to Cuellar's account all three ships were dashed in pieces within one hour, and 'not three hundred men escaped. More than a thousand were drowned.' Finally he and the Judge Advocate launched themselves into the waves on a board the size of 'a good-sized table'. Almost immediately the Judge was swept off by a giant comber and drowned:

As he went down he shrieked aloud, calling upon God. I could not help him, because when the board was left with the weight on only one side, it began to twirl around with me, and at that moment a log of wood almost broke my legs.

He clung on and was washed ashore, battered and bleeding and unable to stand; as he crawled out from the water's edge his clothes were so covered with blood that 'the enemy and savages who were on the beach stripping all those who had succeeded in swimming ashore' left him alone. He made his way painfully into the dune grass where he was joined by another survivor, a youth, naked, shivering and so petrified he could not even tell him his name. When night came down over the savagery Cuellar fell into a fitful sleep, waking to the sound of a fresh band of English and Irish arriving to join in the pillage of the wrecks. In the morning he found the shivering youth was dead.

There he lay on the field with more than 600 other bodies which the sea had cast up. The crows and the wolves fed upon them and there was nobody to bury any of them . . .

Cuellar hobbled off painfully in search of sanctuary in a monastery he must have learned of, perhaps from a 'savage' who took pity on him, but when he came to it he found it had been burned down and desecrated and the monks had fled into the hills, no doubt fearing they would meet the same fate as his compatriots. In the chapel he found 12 Spaniards hanging.

Similar scenes of cowardly, pack brutality, greed and gratuitous lynching were played out along other stretches of coastline over the next few days as ships and their broken crews continued to be tossed ashore, probably more than 30 vessels all told from first to last. There were acts of mercy as indeed were to save Cuellar, and often Spanish survivors were cared for by Irish communities at risk to their own lives were they to be caught by the English or those chiefs who were presently supporting the English cause; but in general the miserable creatures washed ashore saw only the most depraved face of English and Irish alike; that there were special circumstances in a cruelly divided and mistrustful land, that terror was a weapon employed deliberately by a minority ruling over a potentially rebellious people, that Spaniards in the Indies and Portuguese in the spice islands treated the natives as their compatriots were treated in Ireland cannot disguise the terrifying depths to which human nature sank in the aftermath of this equinoctial gale, nor fail to throw a shadow over the English naval triumph which had forced this disaster on the Spaniards.

But this is a modern reaction. If, at the time, the responsible men felt any remorse or shame it does not show in their correspondence, only a sense of great relief and gratitude to the Lord who had delivered them from their mortal enemy. Thus Sir George Carew, Master of the Ordnance in Dublin Castle, writing to Walsyngham on September 28th with a rough estimate of the Spanish losses:

. . . The miseries they sustain upon these coasts are to be pitied in any but Spaniards for there have been wrecked between Lough Foyle in Ulster and the Dingle in Kerry 16 sails, many of them great ships. Of those that came to the land by swimming, or were enforced thereto by famine, very near 3,000 were slain; so that it is supposed that there have perished of them in this land by sword and sea about 5,000 or 6,000 . . . Her Majesty has great cause to praise God that hath so miraculously delivered her most malicious enemies into her hands without loss of her subjects, and broken the bond between them and this people so that their hope from Spain is now gone . . . There is no rebellion in the whole realm, so much terror prevails.[40]

A few days later Sir Richard Bingham, Governor of Connaught, wrote in the same vein to the Lord Deputy, Sir William Fytzwilliam: 'this may appear the great handiwork of God, who hath drowned the remain of that mighty army, for the most part on the coasts of this province.' By his estimate 15 or 16 ships had been wrecked on his coast and 6,000 or 7,000 Spaniards had perished, 'of which there hath been put to the sword, first and last, by my brother George, and in Mayo, Thomond (Clare) and Galway, and executed one way and another, about 7 or 800, or upwards.' He later revised this to '1,100 or upwards'.[41] These figures did not include those who perished from wrecks in Ulster and Munster.

Some weeks later the Lord Deputy himself toured the coast and saw the mass of wreckage and the bodies still being washed up from the sea, over 1,100 bloated and blackened corpses along one five-mile stretch where Cuellar's ship had been wrecked, and he wrote to Walsyngham 'since it hath pleased God, by his hand, upon the rocks to drown the greater and better sort of them, I will, with his favour, be his soldier for the despatching of those rags which yet remain.'[42] The 'rags' were the fugitives being sheltered by the Irish clans, and in particular some 300 sick left behind in Ulster from a force collected by Don Alonso de Leyva.

Don Alonso had found shelter from the gale of September 21st in Blacksod Bay on the projecting elbow of Connaught just below Streedagh. His *Rata Encoronada* had run in in company with the *Duquesa Santa Ana*, a large converted hulk serving in the Andalusian squadron, and both had anchored. The *Rata* subsequently dragged and drove aground; the *Duquesa* rode out the storm in a more sheltered arm of the bay, and de Leyva, having got his men ashore, marched them round to her. They made repairs and put to sea with both ships' companies, intending to make for Scotland; they had not cleared the coast of Donegal, however, when another storm blew up and forced them to run into a rocky inlet now called Loughros More Bay; there the *Duquesa*'s cables parted and the hulk was wrecked, de Leyva himself suffering serious injury to one of his legs.

He now proved he had as much steel as dash and charm in his character, for hearing from one of the local Irish – perhaps a priest as he spoke Latin – that there were three Spanish ships at anchor in Killybegs Bay on the northern coast of Donegal Bay some 20 miles due south, he marched his combined force across the heights between, having himself carried in a chair. He found two of the three ships were wrecked beyond repair and only one remained serviceable, the galleass, *Girona*. There were far too many men for her alone, so it was necessary to weed out the most seriously ill and wounded, who were in any case reluctant to hazard themselves to another passage. Then with some 1300 packed into the galleass, he set sail on a favourable wind, again making for Scotland. He cleared the northern capes of Ulster and was well on the way to his goal when the wind went into the north and blew up, forcing him to turn and run, smashing the rudder which had been repaired in Killybegs, and driving him out of control down to the north-eastern coast of Ulster, where he ran on a spur of rock running out from Lacada Point just east of the Giant's Causeway. The galleass was pounded to pieces in short time and all but nine of the men aboard were drowned, among them de Leyva and a host of young gallants who had followed him.

It was a cruel irony that de Leyva should have met his end here since the local chief, Sorleyboy M'Donnell, whose seat, Dunluce Castle was hard by, was involved in the escape of other Spaniards from Ireland. The survivors of Kelly's massacre at Illagh, having been looked after by Bishop Cornelius, then passed from one group of Catholic sympathisers to another, found their way to Sorleyboy and so by boat to Scotland. Other fugitives followed the same escape route, as did Cuellar, who arrived there the following year after a series of desperate and scarcely credible adventures.

His summary of the attitude of the Irish he had come across in Ulster is an indication of why Sir William Fytzwilliam, the Binghams, Captain and Lady Denny and other English realists in power had felt it necessary to take the measures they had.

These savages liked us very much, for they knew we were great enemies to the heretics, and had come against them, and had it not been for them, not one of us would now be alive. We were very grateful to them for this, although they were the first to rob and plunder those of us who reached the land alive. These savages got a great quantity of jewels and money from us and from those 13 ships of our fleet, for there were many people of great possessions on board who were all drowned . . .[43]

Of the men of property who neither drowned nor died from exhaustion subsequently, as did several of Alonso de Luzon's column from the *Valencera* while being marched eastwards, the Lord Deputy held almost 100 in Dublin and Drogheda. These were sent to England for ransom negotiations; they had evidently been able to build up their strength in captivity, for one group of about 30 while being conveyed in the pinnace, *Swallow*, managed to overpower the crew and sail the vessel safely to Corunna; there, it seems the unfortunate Irish sailors paid the ultimate penalty so many of the Spaniards had paid in their country.[44]

There were other escapes from Ireland; both the galleass *Zuniga* and Aramburu's *San Juan Bautista* got away from their anchorages on an easterly wind on September 23rd, and made sufficient offing to sail southwards clear of the coast. Five days later the *Zuniga* was caught in a westerly gale and driven into the English Channel and up as high as Havre de Grâce on the Normandy coast opposite Portsmouth before she found shelter. Aramburu weathered the storm, and got home to Spain, as did Recalde, who sailed from Blasket Sound on September 28th. There were others who left no record, who are only indicated in English summaries. Of the records that do exist, the *Gran Grifon*'s is one of the more remarkable: after driving back and forth aimlessly at the mercy of the wind direction for the best part of three weeks, her company had given up hope when on the afternoon of September 27th Fair Isle between the Orkney and Shetland Isles was sighted directly ahead. They managed to drop anchor in a sheltered spot that evening, and the next day, apparently while moving to a safer haven, went aground in a rocky inlet. The company of 300 scrambled to the cliff-top via the ship's yards and subsisted on the island with the few crofting families until November when a boat was found to take them to Scotland – all but some 50, who had died. There they and survivors from Ireland and, it was said, from Norway, were looked after by Scottish Catholics and finally provided with ships paid for by Parma which took them to Flanders; some fell victim to the Sea Beggars, but others, including Captain Cuellar arrived safely and eventually made their way home. They were a minute fraction of those thousands who perished off the coasts and on the beaches of Ireland or whose ships foundered in the Atlantic – precisely how many thousands from how many ships will never be known.

A large proportion of the main body of the fleet remained with Medina Sidonia. They could not have passed down far from the Irish coast; Calderon sighted an island on or before September 10th, and tacked away north-westerly to keep clear; 'it is believed,' he wrote, 'that the rest of the Armada will have done the same.'[45] By the 14th his hulk, *San Salvador*, had managed to work down to 51 degrees, just below Cape Clear at the south-western tip of Munster, but far enough off not to see it. He set course sou-sou-westerly 'for Corunna'.

Now there was only the open Atlantic and Biscay between the main body with the fleet flagship and the coast of Spain, and the chief enemies became scurvy and disease, hunger and lack of drinking water; it was a matter of whether the winds would allow them to reach port while there were still men left to work the yards and man the pumps. Medina Sidonia himself had succumbed to 'fever and flux', dysentery probably, and had been in his bunk for much of the past two weeks, while his personal retainers fell away until there were scarcely any to attend him. Ships and men became hollow shells of suffering beneath the images of the cross on stretched, salt-dry and patched sails; and each day more emaciated corpses were committed to the sea and sank slowly from the gaze of those who expected to follow them.

The same westerlies which drove most of Recalde's group and other stragglers on to the Irish coast allowed Medina Sidonia to steer southwards, although sagging well to leeward of the supposed course to Finisterre. Some 60 vessels were in company as they crossed Biscay, but a storm on the 18th scattered them so that approaching the latitude of the north coast of Spain only 11 remained with the *San Martin*. This storm was caused in all probability by the same cyclonic system which, curving northeastwards, caused the great gale of September 21st on the Irish coast.[46]

Land was sighted on the 21st, reported to Medina Sidonia as an island some 20 miles from Corunna; in fact they were 250 miles further to the east, well into Biscay and near the port of Santander. Pataches towed the flagship to an anchorage off the port, and Medina Sidonia was taken ashore before a violent south-westerly blew up, forcing the ship to weigh and run for Laredo. As the wind died over the next few days the ships which had been accompanying him straggled in by ones and twos to various ports, all damaged, several missing masts, the surviving men listless despite the sweet smells from the land, and the sight of trees; several vessels had practically no one fit to back the yards and drop the anchors, and simply went aground.

Calderon's hulk entered Santander on the 23rd; he went ashore and found Medina Sidonia in bed 'very ill'. The same day the Duke managed to get off a letter to Philip:

The troubles and miseries we have suffered cannot be described to Your Majesty. They have been greater than have ever been seen in any voyage before, and on board some of the ships that have come in there was not one drop of water to drink for a fortnight.

On the flagship 180 men died of sickness, three out of the four pilots on board having succumbed, and all the rest of the people on the ship are ill, many of typhus and other contagious maladies. All the men of my household, to the number of 60, have either died or fallen sick, and only two have remained able to serve me. God be praised for all He has ordained.

Great as have been these miseries and afflictions we are now more pressed than ever, for the men are all ill, and the little biscuit and wine we have left will be exhausted in a week. We are therefore in a wretched state, and I implore your Majesty to have some money provided speedily for the relief of necessaries . . .[47]

He also sent Don Francisco de Bovadillo to Philip with a note saying that he would be able to testify to his (the Duke's) inability to continue in command, for he had returned almost at his last gasp. Up to this time Philip had been receiving optimistic and often completely fictitious reports of English losses; he was in no doubt that the enterprise had failed though, and had already started planning another. Exactly what Bovadillo told him will never be known; it was probably not to the credit of the naval management of the expedition since the Chief of Staff, Diego Flores, was later imprisoned; on the other hand he may simply have been one of the chosen scapegoats; Parma was another, while in the fleet itself talk was of the slackness of some of the ships in the fighting[48] – exactly which is not apparent. No one yet knew the full extent of the losses, and whatever Bovadillo said did not affect Philip's decision to prepare another expedition; meanwhile he sent an administrator, Garcia de Villejo, to take charge of affairs in Santander.

The scene that greeted him on his arrival was overwhelming; only a fraction of the returned ships had come in here, yet:

There are over a thousand sick, and if the men be all disembarked at once, the hospital
would be so overcrowded that, although there has been nothing contagious yet, I greatly
fear that something of the sort will appear. It is impossible to attend to so many sick, and
the men are bound to fall ill if they sleep in the ships full of stench and wretchedness . . .

I believe that, with sailors and soldiers together, we have 7,000 mouths to feed – 2,000
seamen and 5,000 men-at-arms – and it is pitiable to see them. No one can believe that the
arrival of this letter will cause matters to be remedied; but I write it, even if it is to be put
to the fire . . .[49]

Medina Sidonia had already left on a horse litter to be borne the length of Spain to
his home. What his feelings were may be imagined; he still blamed himself and
his inexperience, still insisted that Philip had been wrong to entrust him with the
command; and no doubt the ghastly confusion he had left behind and the sick
and dying continued to cause him anguish when his mind returned to them, as it
must have done between bouts of fever. His sense of responsibility did not
extend to foregoing any part of the salary or expenses owing to him. He had been
hugely out of pocket before sailing from Lisbon and had recently contributed to
hospital expenditure in Santander; he had implored Philip to send relief for the
men, yet before leaving Santander he told de Villejo he wanted '33,000 ducats,
20,000 being a special grant given to him by His Majesty, 7,000 due to him as
salary, and 6,000 he lent here for the Hospital expenditure.'[50]

Men continued to go down sick and die over the next weeks as more ships
straggled in; 65 vessels of all types had returned to Spanish ports by the end of
October, 64 were reported as missing, excluding a galley that took no part. A
few of these appeared later, and it is possible that a few more, especially it is
suggested the hulks from the Hansa ports, found havens in Norway or inside the
Baltic; yet it is significant that an Ambassador from Denmark who travelled to
Hamburg on September 4th, and from thence to Holland, reported having heard
'no news of the arrival of any ships of the Armada on the Norwegian, Danish or
Hamburg coasts.'[51] Any vessels which found shelter in the Baltic must surely
have strayed from the fleet during the passage up the North Sea after August
12th, when Howard left them, certainly before 20th/21st when Medina Sidonia
passed the Shetlands heading west with the wind astern, thus over two weeks
and probably three weeks before the Ambassador left Copenhagen. And at that
time when the Armada was the topic of the hour and rumours and false reports
were on every sailor's lips, it would be strange if ships from the beaten fleet did
pass into the Baltic without anyone at Copenhagen or Hamburg hearing of it.
The probability is that the dreadful example made of Don Christobal de Avila
served to concentrate the captains' minds and keep them with the fleet as it sailed
westerly around the north of Scotland, and that the three hulks in the missing list
whose fate is not known were wrecked or foundered in the Atlantic.

Ten of the squadron of 22 hulks that sailed from Corunna were lost; the Levant
squadron suffered an even higher proportion of losses, eight out of 10, most with
known wreck sites on the Irish coast; only Martin de Bertendona's flagship,
Regazona, and the *Trinidad de Scala* arrived home. Of the other squadrons, apart
from the pataches, only the Castilian and galleass squadrons suffered serious loss
on the return voyage; the Indian guard galleon *San Juan* of Don Diego Enriquez
was wrecked on Streedagh Strand, one converted merchantman in Blasket
Sound near Recalde and another failed to return; of the galleasses, the *Girona* was
wrecked in Northern Ulster and the *Zuniga*, forced into Havre, sailed some
weeks later but was forced back by the weather and remained there for months.

Only one Portuguese galleon, the Marquis de Penafiel's *San Marcos*, failed to complete the voyage home, and from the Guipuzcoan, Biscay and Andalusian squadrons only four sizeable ships were lost, making a total of 27 important vessels which went missing on the northabout passage.

Besides these, two large ships had been lost to the English after the first day's fighting in the Channel, the galleass flagship had became a total loss off Calais harbour, two first line Portuguese galleons and one or perhaps two other large vessels were lost after the battle of Gravelines, and two others including Oquendo's flagship were lost after returning home, thus eight or nine to add to the 27 lost on passage, giving a total of 35 ships lost besides smaller craft, one of which is known to have been lost off Dunkirk. The official 'missing' list includes 20 pataches, so fleet losses as a whole may have been as high as 55.[52] Looked at another way, 26 wreck sites have been found on the Irish coast, others at Tobermory off the west coast of Scotland, Fair Isle and Devon, thus 29 wrecks are known; to these can be added the *Zuniga* at Havre, the hulks *San Pedro Menor*, which ended her days at Morvien in Brittany and *Barca de Amburg* known to have foundered at sea, the two prizes lost to the English in the Channel, the four or five lost at Calais and Gravelines plus one patache at Dunkirk and the two ships lost after returning home, and the total of known losses comes to 41. It is clear, therefore, that between 41 and some 55 vessels of all types were lost during the campaign, with the probability that it was nearer to the higher figure. If ships which were so damaged as to be little further use are added, it seems that Philip lost almost half his fleet. While the damage inflicted by the English guns caused a number of these losses, directly or indirectly, the high proportion of Levanters and hulks in the total makes it certain that light construction and poor performance to windward played an even larger part; simple lack of fresh food, especially citrus fruit, must also have played a significant role.

That most of the ship losses were due to the ordinary hazards of the sea, and most of the ships saved were those which remained with the fleet flagship for most of the time suggests that Medina Sidonia had no cause to blame himself; indeed his circumnavigation of the British Isles with the largest fleet of sailing ships ever assembled to that time and against repeated enemy assaults, with no safe haven to re-provision or refit was a heroic feat of endurance. And during his passage up-Channel, burdened as he was with supply hulks and heterogeneous, mainly slow and clumsy converted merchantmen which were no match for Elizabeth's warships, and with instructions which obliged him to join Parma off Flanders, there is no single point at which – so far as the accounts reveal – he could have created the conditions for success.

Nevertheless, it is probable that he was the wrong man to lead such an enterprise; inexperienced, un-confident and introspective leaders inclined to maximise difficulties do not win difficult campaigns; in that age especially, the contrary qualities were needed, as Machiavelli listed them, audacity, impetuousness, imperiousness. He knew his own limitations too well. He did his best; in his own field of energetic administration and conciliation he was superb; he cannot be faulted for competence or personal courage or, in the final test, endurance almost to death. Further than that, it is not permissible to go. Santa Cruz, had he lived, Alonso de Leyva, had Medina Sidonia been killed in the fighting, would perhaps have managed to push different decisions through the Councils of War, but neither could have overcome the geographical and naval disadvantages. Against the English and Sea Beggars' fleets a sustained invasion of England was, as Parma had recognised, not possible. It is easier to imagine a greater disaster under another more audacious and imperious leader than any

Prayer of Queen Elizabeth, in her own hand. A transcript reads as follows:

Most powreful and Largist Giving God whos eares hit hathe pleased so beningly to Grace the petitions of us thy devoted sarvant not with even measure to our disiars, but with far amplar favor hathe not only protected Our Army from foes pray, and from Seas danger but hast detained malesicius desonors even having fors to resist us from having power to attempt us or assaile them. Let humble acknowledgement and most reverend thankes sacrifice supply Our want of Skil to Comprehand suche endles Goodnis and unspeakable Liberalitie Even Suche Good Lord as Our Simple tounges may not Include such wordes as merites suche Laudes, but this vowe Except most deare God in Lieu of bettar merite that Our brethes we hope to ther Last Gaspes shal never Cease the memoriall of Suche flowing Grace as thy bounty fills us with but with suche thogths shal end the world and lene to the.

Al this with thy good Grace we trust performe we shal.

successful outcome – whatever Philip's real intentions may have been.

As for the men who died, it is impossible to estimate their number; they ran into many thousands, and probably more wasted away from starvation and disease than drowned or were slaughtered in Ireland; the *San Martin* lost 180 of her complement of 469 before she reached Spain; it is not difficult to imagine at least another 50 of her sickly crew expiring in the chaotic conditions after arrival, bringing the total to 50 per cent dead. If all the ships returning lost the same proportion and the 35 large vessels listed above and say 10 smaller lost their entire complements, then the death toll could have reached over 18,000; it may have been higher. That is speculation; no one will ever know.

The English lost no ships, and suffered little damage, none that could not be made good within weeks, and while it is impossible to know how many men they lost in the fighting and before and afterwards to disease, it could not have amounted to much more than 2,000 over the whole period of mobilisation; yet that is more speculative even than the Spanish figure; all that is certain is that their loss was minor by comparison.

What is not and never was in doubt is that in political, strategic, tactical, material and human terms Philip II had suffered a shattering defeat in a campaign which can be compared with Salamis, Lepanto, Trafalgar, Tsushima as one of the epics of naval history.

The architect of defeat was Philip II himself, yet it was the English commanders, who knew their advantage and held to it, who 'coursed' Medina Sidonia up-Channel without allowing him any respite, who chased him north 'with a brag countenance' and largely empty guns, who ensured that Philip's mistakes could not be retrieved. Elizabeth entrusted the fate of the kingdom to Lord Howard, and the event proved her choice wise; he listened to the experienced sea rovers and their advice was sound; if any one of them should be raised from comparative obscurity as the unsung hero of the campaign, it should perhaps be John Hawkins, Sir John, who fashioned the fleet and ensured that it was ready when the time came to meet the challenge. It is appropriate that he commanded a ship whose name was to become the proudest in the naval tradition of his country, *Victory*.

Most powerfull and largest Giving God whos
oari hit hath plcasid therbeinigly to
Grace the pittios of thy demots not within
miasure our pleas but Whampear fauor hath
not oly protecteb our strong froour
pray and thy Seat compt but hast retoind
malicious seboures wen hae ferb
to resist vs froo hae g powir to
attempt vs or assault thir Let
humbli acknowligcnt and most rewirin
thakis sacrifici supply the our want
of skil to copreheb enahi unhis Goodnes
and vinspitable Liberaliti Ewen Suche
good Lord as our Sempli toumed may
not Includi enahi Words as mirite
enahi Lawd Whast this VoWi exsept
as it were God in Lein of better
mirite that our brithio Wi hope
to thir Last Gospib what minir
Cease to thir mimoriall of enahi
Flowng Grace as thy Bounty
froo vs ut but it enahi Hog to
shad in the World Leur to thir
At this W thy good Grace
Wi trust efformi
Wi shall

Postscript

Naval battles are seldom, if ever, 'decisive' for more than a season. Oceans cannot be occupied, nor held from fortified strongpoints. Naval supremacy, like freedom, cannot be taken for granted, it has to be looked to constantly. It is more useful to regard the results of naval battles as defining existing economic, technological and geographical boundaries. The Armada campaign did just that. It changed nothing in the situation that made it necessary in the first place. Spanish-American treasure remained the dynamo of Philip's empire, and the focus of envy for all trading and piratical states of the Atlantic coastal fringe. The years 1579 to 1592 have been termed by historians 'the Royal silver cycle'; 1588 is simply a date in the middle. If anything, the result of the campaign set the existing situation in stone; it weakened Elizabeth financially, forcing her to extraordinary levies and borrowings and encouraging her to further expensive, piratical exploits, which only served – if that were necessary – to make Philip more determined to bring her down.

The loser, Philip, learned from defeat; he built a Royal navy with warships capable of taking on the English at their own game, attempted to expand his gun foundries, noted his fatal mistakes of divided command and the unaddressed problem of the shoal waters off the Flemish coast, took steps to improve the fortifications of the key points in the defensive system of the Caribbean and had special fast, heavily-armed frigates called 'galizabras' built to carry the treasure home independently of the slow annual *flotas*.

The winner, Elizabeth, gained extraordinary fame, but nothing else. She learned nothing; perhaps there was nothing much to be learned except that Philip represented an even graver danger than she or her advisors had supposed; she could never be free of fear of another Armada; she needed to continue subsidising the Dutch and French Protestants to prevent Philip gaining access to a deep-water port from which he might launch a successful invasion; she had to keep down the Irish in case he should land there; and to provide the subsidies and the land armies she sent to the continent, she had to cut naval expenditure and rely, as before, on London merchants and courtiers to take shares in the joint-stock piratical ventures that she sent out in the hope they would pay for the increasing expenses of the war. These suffered from the old disadvantage that short-term profit and long-term national aims were usually incompatible; prizes proved harder to come by, and the treasure which sustained Philip's credit was never captured. 1588 was in most respects – although with one exception, seen presently – the high-water mark of the great Elizabethan adventure and of most of the great names associated with it. Their subsequent history makes sad reading.

Drake was sent out with a veritable Armada of his own in 1589: 150 vessels, mostly English and Dutch merchantmen, headed by seven of the Queen's warships, a land force of some 10,000 under Sir John Norreys, and the

Portuguese Pretender, Dom Antonio; the aim was first to destroy the vessels surviving from the Armada in their harbours, next attack Lisbon, raise rebellion in the local populace and reinstate Dom Antonio on the Portuguese throne, and finally take an island in the Azores and hold it for the rest of the war. Not one of these goals was even remotely attained; the most memorable moment of the whole disastrous voyage was provided by Elizabeth's handsome young favourite, the Earl of Essex – her 'Wild Horse' – who came out to join the expedition in Spain and challenged the Commander of the garrison in Lisbon to single combat – it was not accepted. Elizabeth was so displeased with Drake after the costly failure she did not employ him for another five years; he had to content himself with representing Plymouth in Parliament.

Hawkins and Frobisher were sent out to the Spanish coast and the Azores the following year, but too late; the treasure fleet had arrived home. Returning empty-handed, Hawkins wrote to Burghley to tell him of his disappointment, ending that since it was God's pleasure, he was content. Elizabeth had not lost her sharp tongue. 'God's death!' she exclaimed. 'This fool went out a soldier and is come home a divine!'[1]

Next year, 1591, it was Lord Thomas Howard's turn to cruise off the Azores for the returning treasure fleet. He was surprised by a superior force sent out by Philip to escort the *flota* through the danger area, and his vice Admiral, Sir Richard Grenville, commanding Drake's favourite *Revenge*, was either too late in embarking men who had been put ashore sick or deliberately chose not to run from the enemy but to sail through them. He was forced into a fight against overwhelming odds which he sustained for 15 hours; then with most of the crew dead or wounded, the colours were struck against his wishes. He himself was mortally wounded and died later in the Spanish flagship, while the *Revenge* was so shattered she sank in a gale before she could be got back to Spain. It is a tribute to the remarkable sturdiness of Elizabeth's ships, to Hawkins' careful maintenance and to the seamanship of the English officers that the *Revenge* was the only Royal ship lost during the entire course of the unofficial and official war with Spain, a truly remarkable record. The last fight of the *Revenge* became a legend immortalised in the 19th century by Alfred Lord Tennyson; Grenville's contemporary, Monson, remarked that she was 'taken by the Spaniards by the unadvised negligence and wilful obstinacy of the Captain, Sir Richard Greynville.'[2]

The following year a force commanded by Sir John Burrough succeeded in capturing one of the richest single prizes of these twilight years, the *Madre de Dios*, an enormous Portuguese carrack, laden with peppers, cloves, maces, nutmegs, cinnamon, green ginger, frankincense, galingale, mirabolans, aloes, zocatrina, camphire, silks, damasks, taffetas, sarcenets, pearls, musk, civet, amber-griece, carpets, elephants' teeth, porcelain, ebony and many other strange, exotic wares and drugs, all together estimated at some £800,000. An orgy of looting by the sailors greatly reduced the return for the expedition's backers, one of whom was Elizabeth; nevertheless she netted something over £60,000 for an original outlay of £3,000.[3] The appetite for eastern trade had been whetted in the autumn of 1588 by the return of Henry Cavendish from a voyage of circumnavigation; it was said that when his ship was brought up the Thames to lie before the Queen's House at Greenwich 'every sailor had a gold chain round his neck, and the sails of the ship were of blue damask, the standard of cloth of gold and blue silk. It was as if Cleopatra had been resuscitated . . .'[4] Now the *Madre de Dios* fired a number of other merchants and adventurers to mount expeditions to the East.

Meanwhile Elizabeth's attention was drawn to the Continent; she was supporting the Huguenot Henri of Navarre – who had ascended the throne as Henri IV of France – against the French Catholics of the Holy League. Philip, supporting the League, was manoeuvring to gain access to French ports from which he might mount an invasion of England, and in the winter of 1593–4 his commander in Brittany moved troops into the Camaret peninsula below the great natural harbour of Brest and began constructing a fort to command the sleeve of water leading up to Brest. The prospect of Spaniards controlling harbours in Brittany seemed to Elizabeth as dangerous as Spaniards in Ireland, and in the summer of 1594 Frobisher was sent with 8 warships and a force of some 3000 men under Sir John Norreys to reduce the fort. They did so after a short siege, putting all survivors to the sword. This was Frobisher's last service for his Queen; he was wounded and died soon after bringing the squadron back to Plymouth.

Hawkins and Drake were not long in following him. Both were at an age when they might have retired full of honour and reputation, leaving adventurers of the rising generation, of whom there were plenty, to continue their exploits against the Spaniards. But both remained obsessed with the idea of cutting off Spanish treasure at source and so crippling Philip; and once again, and for the last time Elizabeth gave them their heads, contributing six Royal ships to their joint-stock venture, for which she was to receive one third of the returns. The original idea was to capture Panama, and a force of some 1500 troops was embarked in a fleet of altogether 27 vessels. At the last moment Spanish galley raids on towns on the coast of Cornwall and reports of another invasion Armada being prepared by Philip caused Elizabeth to prohibit their sailing. It was only after news of a treasure ship said to have taken refuge in Puerto Rico that she allowed them to go in August 1595.

The expedition was plagued from the start by disagreements between the joint leaders. Drake's inspirational temperament clashed with Hawkins' insistence on thorough organisation, both traits no doubt exaggerated by the age of the two and 'there passed many unkind speeches, and such as John Hawkins never put off till death . . .'[5] There was an unfortunate diversion to the Canary Islands on the way, warning the Spaniards of their goal, then Hawkins became ill and took to his bunk, 'so discouraged, and . . . his heart even broken' by mistakes he considered had been made 'through the perverse and cross dealings of some . . . who preferred their own fancy before his skill.'[6] He died off Puerto Rico in the afternoon of November 12th as the fleet was preparing for the assault; his body was committed to the sea.

The attack on Puerto Rico failed and Drake, reverting to his youthful character, sailed for the Spanish Main and attacked, looted and burned Rio de la Hacha, Santa Marta and Nombre de Dios, without however gaining substantial plunder. Finally the troops were landed for an assault on the isthmus, but the Spanish were ready and forced them back to the ships. One of the many who succumbed to the fevers of the region was Drake himself; he died at sea off Porto Bello on January 28, 1596.

Thus both men who had done more than any other individuals to shape the Elizabethan legend, the one forcing through and administering a revolutionary change in warship design, the other a seaman of intuitive genius who had come to represent all that was most daring and successful in plundering the King of Spain, found their final resting place appropriately enough in the waters of that alluring triangle of the Spanish Main which had occupied so many Elizabethan dreams, and not least their own.

Philip, meanwhile, was still gathering ships and stores for the second great Armada, which he had had in mind since he learned of the defeat of the first. As news of the preparations continued to come in Howard managed to persuade Elizabeth of the wisdom of the pre-emptive strategy which Drake and Hawkins had always advised. Veteran troops, English and Dutch, were withdrawn from the Netherlands in secret and a great fleet of 17 Royal ships, 18 Dutch men-of-war and 47 merchantmen was concentrated in Plymouth to carry them and other levies to Spain. Howard in the *Ark Royal* and Essex in a post-Armada galleon *Repulse* were joint leaders, with a glittering array of subordinate commanders, Lord Thomas Howard in the *Merhonour*, Sir Walter Raleigh in the *Warspite*, Sir Robert Southwell in the *Lion*, Sir Francis Vere, commander of the English Netherlands army, in the *Rainbow* and a host of other veterans and gallants. The story was put about that they were going out to the Azores to meet the homecoming West Indies fleet and they arrived off Finisterre in early June with the Spanish quite unaware of their presence. The three best sailers with the fleet were sent out ahead to capture enemy scouts which might raise the alarm; when these picked up intelligence that the outward-bound Indies *flota* was gathering in Cadiz, the fleet sailed there directly, achieving complete surprise when they arrived in the early morning of June 20th.

Time was wasted in arguments about where to land the troops until it was decided to make a naval assault instead. This was attempted next day against four galleons of the Indian guard formed up at the mouth of the harbour; there was an artillery battle until about four in the afternoon, then the galleons got under sail, either to put about and return with the other broadside or to retreat higher up the harbour; instead they went aground. Immediately the lighter draft vessels were sent in and boarded and took two while the other two were set alight by their own crews. With the harbour now in English hands, Essex landed troops and, such was the effect of the surprise, carried the town with little loss; finally the castle surrendered.

Next day was given over to looting the town and ships while Essex and Howard negotiated a sum for ransom with the leading citizens; 120,000 ducats was eventually agreed. The *flota* collected in the harbour and said to be worth some six or seven millions had to be left out of the calculation since the ships were destroyed by the Spanish rather than allowed to fall into enemy hands.

It is pleasant to record that the victors at Cadiz behaved with restraint and magnanimity: as Monson – there as captain of the *Ark Royal* – recorded, 'the noble treating of the prisoners has gained everlasting honour to our nation, and the generals in particular.'[7] And when after a fortnight the town was put to the torch, the churches were expressly spared; some were damaged but only because the flames spread from nearby buildings; about a fifth of the town's stock of houses was gutted.

Medina Sidonia, as commander of the defences of Andalusia, had collected some 5,000 men and was waiting to see where the next blow would fall, sending off anxious messages to Philip reminiscent of his letters from the Armada: he lacked money, provisions and munitions. It was no doubt true: one Spanish commentator at the time stated that if the English had marched to take Seville there would have been no obstacles in their way. Howard opened negotiations with his old antagonist, offering to exchange prisoners for Englishmen serving in Spanish galleys, and was successful in obtaining the return of 51 of these poor men.

Undoubtedly in its initial stages the best planned and most brilliantly executed grand enterprise of the reign, the expedition disintegrated almost as soon as it left

Cadiz. State interest which required the destruction of Philip's Armada ships was abandoned either for the hope of quick plunder or the desire to get home as rapidly as possible with the considerable plunder already acquired. Essex emerged with rather more credit than Howard. He was eager at first to waylay the returning Indies *flota* at the Azores; Howard and others ruled this out on the usual grounds of provisions. Then, after they had failed to find the Armada ships at Corunna or Ferrol, Essex wanted to sail into Biscay to look for them at Santander or Los Pasages – where a great many would have been found; the rest were in Lisbon. He was overruled again. The only exploit after Cadiz was the looting and burning of two small towns near Cape St Vincent; from one of these Essex took the extensive library of Jerome Ossorio, Bishop of the Algarve, and after his return presented it to the new library at Oxford, the Bodleian.

The sack of Cadiz, and the loss of the Indies *flota*, was the greatest humiliation Philip suffered at Elizabeth's hands and he was stung into hastening his Armada preparations for immediate retaliation. The plan this time was to send the force to Ireland, where his emissaries were in constant communication with the Geraldines of Munster, the Earl of Tyrone in Ulster and various Irish Bishops, including Cornelius. Tyrone and his fellow conspirators in the north, O'Donnell, O'Dogherty, Cormack, Maguire, the Magees, O'Rourke, Macwilliam Burke, Macarty, O'Cahan, Maginnis and others – as listed in a document from that summer – were promising to put 6,000 foot and 1,000 horse into the field against the English garrisons totalling only some 4,000 men, if Philip would send them arms and equipment.[8]

By the end of September some 100 ships, only 20 of them warships, and a force of over 16,000 men had been gathered in Lisbón under the command of the *Adelantado* – or Governor of Castile – Don Martin de Padilla Conde de St Gadea. Philip urged him to sail as he had urged Santa Cruz to sail with the first Armada long after the campaigning season was past. Padilla's Vice Admiral, Diego Brochero de Anaya, and other sea-officers joined in a written protest – to no avail. Philip commanded them to go. Padilla managed to get to sea on the 18th October; 10 days later, about the latitude of Finisterre, he was struck by a south-westerly gale and his force scattered; about a third of the ships were lost, and sailors deserted by the score from those that eventually limped back to port. The Venetian Ambassador commented, 'if His Majesty intends to use his fleet next year, he will have to reconstitute it.'[9]

Since the sack of Cadiz money had been a serious problem for Philip; it had, of course, been his most serious problem before that, but now with their eyes opened to the apparent ease with which the English could enter his supposedly secure main fleet base, European bankers were reluctant to advance further loans unless at even more exorbitant rates than before. In November, for the third time in his reign, he declared himself bankrupt, repudiating his debts and leaving himself free to use the mortgaged revenues from the Indies. Next year, 1597, he came to a settlement with his creditors, whereby they forfeited part of both their capital and interest. It is said that men were ruined in all the commercial centres of Europe.

Meanwhile he had the Armada reconstituted; once again it was not ready to put out before late summer – and not properly ready then – and it was September before Padilla took it to sea. The plan now was to put the troops ashore at Falmouth where there was a good deep-water harbour just to the east of the Lizard, and there to establish an advanced base at the entrance to the English Channel and to windward of the English fleet bases. It was a much more realistic scheme than Medina Sidonia had been burdened with, and if successful threatened real danger for Elizabeth. Once again the Atlantic weather took a hand; the ships were scattered by a gale in Biscay and forced back to Spanish ports. The legend attributing the defeat of the first Armada to God blowing with his winds, and the song Elizabeth composed to the same effect, which was sung during the victory celebrations in 1588, were more appropriate to these later attempts:

He . . . hathe done wonders in my daies
He made the winds and waters rise
To scatter all myne enemyes.[10]

It was Philip's last throw against the heretic woman. His health broke the following spring, and by the end of July he was lying immobile on his bed in the Escorial, his body suppurating with ulcers giving off a nauseating odour, waiting for death to release him from torment. He drifted off at last on September 13th, firm in his faith, grasping his parents' crucifix; the last sounds he heard were probably the singing of Mass in the chapel nearby.

His death did not signify the end of the war. That did not come until Elizabeth had died after a similarly protracted and malodorous final decay in March, 1603; all her favourites had gone long since, Leicester, her enduring love in the midst of the victory celebrations for the Armada, her 'Wild Horse' Essex more recently after ruining his reputation by failing in Ireland when the Earl of Tyrone, despairing of Spanish aid, had raised rebellion; afterwards Essex had justified her name for him by staging a mad, ill-prepared rebellion in London, and had paid the price with his head. Burghley had died before him in the summer that Philip died, but not before ensuring the succession as first minister to the Crown for his son, Robert Cecil, an equally shrewd head known for his devilish cunning as 'Robert le Diable'. Howard remained; he was as upright and fastidious a dresser as ever, but since Hawkins' death abuses had been creeping back into the naval administration, and he was not vigorous enough in his age to combat them; in any case, he had always been too steady and cautious a man to catch Elizabeth's heart.

She sat in one spot for days on end, staring silently or sighing and breaking into fits of crying, refusing to go to bed lest she should not get out again. Dying was far harder for her, with her sharp and unconventional intelligence, than it had been for Philip.

When I was fair and young, and favour graced me,
Of many was I sought, their mistress for to be;
But I did scorn them all, and answered them therefore,
Go, go, go seek some otherwhere,
Importune me no more![11]

At last on March 21st, she allowed herself to be persuaded into bed and death came to her two days later as she slept. Sir Robert Carey, one of the gallants who had joined Howard's fleet while it was following the Armada up-Channel, and 'had a glorious day of them' at Gravelines, was ready with horse to carry the news to Edinburgh where James VI of Scotland was now James I of England.

The brilliance of Elizabeth's Court, her wit and the legend she created in her own lifetime, the fame of her seaman-explorers and would-be colonisers, the daring of the adventurers who singed the beard of the most powerful monarch in Christendom, and the simultaneous flowering of English poetry and drama have generally obscured the sober and workaday, but historically more significant rise of the Dutch rebels during the same period. Behind the fireworks shot off by

Elizabeth's flamboyants, the simple sailors and not so simple merchants of the northern provinces of the Netherlands, in particular Holland, were quietly engrossing the trade of the western world.

The process had started before the rebellion against Philip's rule; indeed rebellion was its natural consequence. The blocking of the Scheldt by the Sea Beggars had shifted the focus from Antwerp – by then financial/industrial capital of Philip's empire – north to Amsterdam; when Parma recaptured Antwerp his policy of tolerance extended to allowing Protestants to emigrate with their money; many European cities benefited, Amsterdam most of all. While grand English expeditions to Spain and the West Indies, and subsidies and the maintenance of English troops in the Netherlands and France bled Elizabeth's treasury – and English and Zealand privateers gradually made the seas so unsafe for Spanish ships without escort in the great *flotas*, that the captains, deprived of legitimate prey, turned to piracy – finance and trade, the hidden springs of history, burgeoned around the shores of the Zuider Zee.

It was not so much the defeat of the first Armada that allowed the northern rebels to consolidate into a merchant Republic, the 'United Provinces', but the dispersion of Parma's efforts caused by the Armada. Later he was drawn westward into the French civil war. He died in 1592 without being allowed to prove what he might have done to reconquer and unify the Netherlands for Spain.

Meanwhile the United Provinces – known later as the Dutch Republic – developed into a merchant and naval power of the first rank and within some 10 years of Elizabeth's death had become as pre-eminent on the world oceans as Venice had once been in the Mediterranean.

The beginnings can be traced from before Philip's first Armada: already in 1585 weekly commodity price-lists were being printed in Amsterdam; already the market there was capable of buying up the cargoes of whole fleets and providing return freights; the Dutch 'fluyt', a cheap, mass-produced vessel with simple rigging, requiring about a half or even a third the crew of a comparable English merchantman, was fully developed and undercutting all competitors in the staple bulk trades of the Baltic and western Europe. By 1598 wind-powered sawmills were operating in Amsterdam to produce the standardised timbers for mass-shipbuilding. The same year, at a time when the English were still sending out adventurers to explore trading routes to the east, five competing Dutch companies fitted out 22 ships for the spice islands. Three years later 65 ships sailed for the east in 14 fleets, and the following year, 1602, while Elizabeth still reigned, the competing companies were amalgamated into the United Netherlands East India Company. Since this and the later West Indies Company were breaking into the jealously-guarded preserves of Portugal and Spain, they were invested with rights to make war, conquer, settle and administer overseas possessions as sovereign powers within the larger sovereignty of the United Provinces.[12]

It was these two great mercantile groupings which broke the Spanish and Portuguese monopolies and practically drove their ships from the seas; and it was the Dutch Admiral Pieter Heyn who in 1628 succeeded in the age-old dream of capturing a Spanish treasure fleet. It was the Dutch Admiral Maarten Tromp who destroyed the last Spanish Armada sent north in 1639, not against England, but to relieve the Spanish Netherlands from Dutch assault. The Spanish commander, Don Antonio de Oquendo, son of Medina Sidonia's squadron commander, sought shelter in the Downs after being harassed up-Channel by the Dutch. So low had English power sunk by this time that Tromp attacked them there, in English waters, in the presence of an English squadron which tried vainly to intervene. Oquendo lost four-fifths of his fleet, driven ashore, sunk or taken as prizes, and although he managed to get his shattered flagship and a few others home was a broken man and died shortly afterwards, as his father and Recalde had died shortly after their return from the first Armada.

Under the shelter of the Dutch assault on Spain the English were able to colonise the north American seaboard and increase their trade and merchant fleet, but the great monopolies were in the hands of the Dutch; Amsterdam was the commercial, financial and industrial capital of the world, and when the French decided to build up their Royal navy, it was to Dutch shipbuilders and Dutch patterns they turned, not English.

English historians' natural concern to highlight the Elizabethans has misrepresented their importance; undoubtedly they formed a colourful pattern in the tapestry, undoubtedly Hawkins was largely responsible for the most efficient ocean-going navy in the Atlantic system of the time but England remained an essentially agricultural country with a predatory fringe of sea rovers and a national policy of highway robbery. Elizabeth had no money for much else. It was only later, after revolution, that the English, re-creating a great navy with new traditions of state service foreign to the Elizabethans, started their rise to world power by cutting the Dutch sea routes to the oceans, as they could so easily by virtue of their position and deep-water harbours, and causing the grass to grow in the streets of Amsterdam.

The moving finger wrote then – as, of course, it writes today – in the ledgers of merchants and bankers; neither Drake nor Elizabeth nor Philip, nor his great Armada, nor the Protestant nor the Catholic faith, nor the sufferings of the thousands of soldiers and sailors, nor the tears of the families from whom they were ripped could cancel half a line.

> That moving finger writes;
> and having writ,
> Moves on . . .

Notes

Abbreviations used in the references:

Arm. I or II
J. K. Laughton, Ed., *State Papers Relating to the Defeat of the Spanish Armada*, Navy Records Society, (2 vols), 1894. (Dates of letters are usually old style, ie minus 10 days).

Calderon
Pedro Calderon's Account in *Sp.* (see below).

Car.
J. S. Brewer, W. Buller, Eds., *Calendar of Carew Manuscripts, 1575–1588*, London, 1868.

Dom.
R. Lemon, Ed., *Calendar of State Papers, Domestic, 1581–1590*, London, 1865.

IJNA
International Journal of Nautical Archaeology and Underwater Exploration.

Ir.
N. Hamilton, Ed., *Calendar of State Papers Relating to Ireland*, London, 1885.

MM
Mariner's Mirror, Journal of Society for Nautical Research.

Med. Sid. Diary
Medina Sidonia (diary) to Philip, August 1588, printed in *Arm.* II, pp. 354ff. and *Sp.* pp. 293ff. (References following all from *Sp.*).

Relation
'A Relation of Proceedings' (Engl.), in *Arm.* I.

Sp.
M. A. S. Hume, Ed., *Calendar of Letters & State Papers Relating to English Affairs preserved in . . . Simancas, Vol. IV, Elizabeth, 1587–1603*, London, 1899.

1. The Prudent King

1. Braudel, II, p.1236.
2. Kamen, *Spain*, p.89.
3. Elliott, *Imp. Sp.*, p.208.
4. Charles to Juana, 25 May 1588, cited Kamen, *Sp. Inq.*, p.79.
5. to de Espinosa, early 1569, cited Parker, *Philip*, p.94.
6. F. Alvarez, *Politica Mundial de Carlos V y Felipe II*, Madrid, 7th ed. 1963, pp.205–10, cited Pierson, *Philip*, p.43.
7. Braudel, *op. cit.*
8. See Pierson, *Philip*, p.50.
9. Alvarez, *op. cit.*
10. Thompson, *War & Govt.*, p.288.
11. Philip to Parma, 4 Sept 1587, *Sp.*, p.137.
12. Philip to Card. Archduke, 14 Sept 1587, Lloyd/Naish, p. 8.

2. The Virgin Queen

1. T. Glasgow Jr, 'The Navy in the First Elizabethan undeclared War, 1559–1560', *MM*, Vol.54, No.1, Feb 1968, p.26.
2. *ibid*, p.33.
3. Rowse, *Engl. of Eliz.*, p.302.
4. Bindoff, *Tudor Engl.*, p.176.
5. Neale, p.65.
6. Cerovski, p.42.
7. *ibid*, p.75.

8. C. Hatton, cited Neale, p.213.
9. Rowse, *op. cit.*, p.312.
10. See Wilson, pp.129ff.
11. See Williamson, *Hawkins*, p.102 and Andrews, p.20.
12. Dom., p.357, cited R. Pollitt, 'Bureaucracy and the Armada: the Administrator's Battle', *MM*, Vol. 60, No. 2, May 1974, p.120.
13. See Rowse, *Engl. of Eliz.*, p.373ff.
14. See Thompson, *War & Govt.*, pp.73ff.
15. Neale, p.277.
16. *ibid*, p.81.
17. Mattingley, pp.92–93.
18. 2 April 1587, cited Mattingley, p.92.

3. The Sea Rovers

1. J. Sugden, 'Edmund Drake of Tavistock', *MM*, Vol.59, No.4, Nov 1973, p.436.
2. Williamson, *Hawkins*, p.145.
3. *ibid*.
4. See J. Sugden, 'Sir Francis Drake; A Note on his Portraiture', *MM*, Vol.70, No.3, Aug 1984, p.303 and Andrews, p.61.
5. cited Waters, p.536.
6. ibid.
7. cited Andrews, p.61.
8. cited Waters, p.535.
9. John Stow and Edmund Howes, *Annales . . .*, p.808, cited Richard Boulind, 'Drake's Navigational Skills', *MM*, Vol.54, No.4, Nov 1968, p.355.
10. Drake to Q.E., 13 April 1588, *Arm.*I, p.148.
11. cited *Arm.* I, p.148.
12. Kenny, p.77, and see Williamson, *Drake*, p.302.
13. cited Waters, p.179.
14. *Arm.* II, p.103.

4. The Reluctant Commander

1. See Thompson, *War & Gov.*, p.205.
2. See *ibid*, p.73.
3. cited I. A. A. Thompson, 'The Appointment of the Duke of Medina Sidonia to the command of the Armada', *Hist. Journ.* XII, 2 (1969) p.209.
4. *ibid*, pp.200–1.
5. Parma to Philip, 31 Jan 1588, *Sp.*, p.201.
6. See for inst. Mendoza to Philip, 16 Jan, *ibid*, p.194.
7. Medina Sidonia to Idiaquez, 16 Feb 1588, *Sp.*, pp.207–8.
8. Thompson, *Hist Journ.*, *op. cit.*, pp.212–14.
9. Fr. Juan de Victoria, *Noticias . . .*, Madrid, 1842, cited P. O. M. Pierson, 'A Commander for the Armada', *MM*, Vol.55, No.4, Nov 1969, pp.396–7.
10. Philip to Med. Sid., 20 Feb 1588, Lloyd/Naish, pp.12–13.
11. Parma to Philip, 20 March 1588, *Sp.*, p.237.
12. cited Thompson, *Hist Journ.*, *op. cit.*, p.199.
13. cited Pierson, *MM*, *op. cit.*, pp.383ff.
14. See R. J. Lander, 'An Assessment of the numbers, sizes and types of English and Spanish ships mobilised for the Armada Campaign', *MM*, Vol.63, No.4, Nov 1977, pp.359ff. and C. Martin, 'Spanish Armada tonnages', *ibid*, pp.365–67.
15. See Martin, *Full Fathom*, pp.132–33.
16. cited Mattingley, pp.191–2.

17. 1 April, Lloyd/Naish, p.14. See also *Sp.*, p.246.
18. Med. Sid. General Orders, May? 1588, *Sp.*, p.290.
19. Note of certain plunder, *Arm.* II, pp.209–10.
20. See 'Full Statement of the Armada sailing from Lisbon', 9 May 1588, Med. Sid. to Philip, *Sp.*, pp.280ff. Summary, p.285 lists 130 galleons, hulks, despatch vessels, zabras, galleasses, galleys, *plus* 10 caravels, 10 falucas (fellucas).
21. Med. Sid. to Philip, 14 May, *Sp.*, p. 296.
22. Med. Sid. to Parma, 10 June, *Sp.*, p.309.
23. Med. Sid to Philip, 21 June, *Sp.*, p.314.
24. Med. Sid. to Philip, 24 June, *ibid*, pp.317–8.
25. Philip to Med. Sid., 1 July, Lloyd/Naish, p. 25.
26. Philip to Med. Sid., 5 July, *Sp.*, pp.326–28.

5. The Lord High Admiral

1. See 'Full Statement of Armada sailing from Lisbon', 9 May 1588, Med. Sid. to Philip, *Sp.*, pp.280ff.
2. Kenny, p.6.
3. Cerovski, p.68.
4. Kenny, p.75.
5. See R. Pollitt, 'Bureaucracy and the Armada: the Administrator's Battle', *MM*, Vol.60, No.2, May 1974, p.121.
6. *ibid*, p.126.
7. Ld. Howard's Commission, 21 Dec 1587, *Arm.* I, pp.19–21.
8. Howard to Burghley, 21 Feb 1588, *Arm.* I, p.79.
9. Howard to Burghley, 29 Feb 1588, *ibid*, p.85.
10. *ibid*, pp.85–6.
11. Wynter to the Principal Officers, 28 Feb, *Arm.* I, p.81.
12. Drake to Q.E., 13 April, *Arm.* I, pp.148–49.
13. Howard to Burghley, 8 April, *ibid*, p.138.
14. Howard to Walsyngham, 14 June, *ibid*, p.202.
15. *ibid*, p.200.
16. Howard to Burghley, 13 June, *ibid*, p.198.
17. Howard to Walsyngham, 15 June, *ibid*, p.204.
18. Howard to Walsyngham, 13 July, *ibid*, p.258.
19. Howard to Walsyngham, 6 July, *ibid*, p.247.
20. Howard to Walsyngham, 13 July, *ibid*, p.258.
21. Howard to Walsyngham, 17 July, *ibid*, p.273.
22. See C. Martin 'Spanish Armada tonnages', *MM*, Vol.63, No.4, Nov 1977, pp.355–67.
23. See I. A. A. Thompson, 'Spanish Armada Guns', *MM*, Vol.61, No.4, Nov 1975, pp.355–371.
24. See M. Lewis, cited *ibid*.
25. 11.65 to 10.85 lbs per gun advantage to the English – see I. A. A. Thompson, *ibid*, Table 10, p.368.
26. These details are not included in *Sp.*, but are printed in Martin, *Full Fathom*, pp.266ff.
27. T. Glasgow Jr, 'Gorga's Seafight', *MM*, Vol.59, No.2, May 1973, pp.180–1.

6. The Craft and Mystery of the Sea

1. G. Waymouth, *The Jewell of Artes*, m/s, 1604, cited Waters, p.295.
2. W. J. Carpenter Turner, 'The building of the *Gracedieu . . .*' in *MM*, Vol.40, 1954, pp.55–72.
3. See W. A. Baker, 'The Arrangement & Construction of early 17th Century Ships,' *American Neptune*, Vol.XV, No.4, 1955, p.20. For shipbuilding and ship design I have used

the above article and W. A. Baker, 'Early Seventeenth Century Ship Design', *American Neptune*, Vol.XIV, No.4, 1954 and the same author's '*Mayflower II Scale Plans & Rigging Specifications*', Hingham, Mass., together with Eds. W. Walisbury, R. C. Anderson, 'A Treatise on Shipbuilding and a Treatise on Rigging written about 1620–1625', *Soc. for Nautical Research*, 1958, and several specialised articles in *MM*.

4. See Oppenheim, *Admin.*, p.125 (*Madre de Dios* 100ft keel, 165ft overall, 46ft 10in beam).

5. *ibid.*, p.124.

6. Baker, 'Early 17th Century Ship Design', *op. cit.* p.11 gives 0.36 of keel length.

7. See R. W. Unger, '4 Dordrecht Ships' in *MM*, Vol.61, No.2, May 1975, p.111.

8. See Oppenheim, *Admin.*, p.129.

9. Derauve, Durosquel, p.56.

10. Howard to Burghley, 8 April 1588, *Arm.* I, p.138.

11. See Vischer's Armada engravings, National Maritime Museum, and G. S. Laird Clowes, *Sailing Ships, their History and Development*, Part I, HMSO for the Science Museum, 1959, p.55.

12. See Waters, p.576.

13. P. Padfield, *The Sea is a Magic Carpet*, Peter Davies, 1959, p.72.

14. See Waters, p.576.

15. *ibid*, and G. V. Scammell, 'European Seamanship in the Great Age of Discovery', *MM*, Vol.68, No.4, Nov 1982, p.360.

16. cited Scammell, *ibid.*, p.359.

17. See *ibid*, p.364.

18. R. Holinshed & others, *Chronicles*, cited Waters, p.168.

19. Howard to Walsyngham, 6 July 1588, *Arm*, I, pp.247–48.

20. See Waters, pp.30–38.

7. The Guns, the Gunner and the Crew

1. C. Martin, 'El Gran Grifon: An Armada Wreck on Fair Isle'. *IJNA*, 1972, I, pp.63–64.

2. cited Oppenheim, *Admin.*, p.155.

3. Oppenheim, *Monson*, IV, p.33.

4. Binning, p.109.

5. See detailed discussion of this in Padfield, *Guns*, pp.59ff.

6. J. Montgomery, *Censuria Literaria* v. 139, cited J. Corbett, *Drake and the Tudor Navy*, Longmans, 1899, p.289.

7. cited Padfield, *Guns*, p.62.

8. Major J. G. D. Elvin to author, 9 Nov 1982.

9. See Padfield, *Guns*, p.63.

10. Wynter to Walsyngham, 11 Aug 1588, *Arm.* II, p.11.

11. See Martin, *Full Fathom*, pp.214ff.

12. See Inventory of *Rosario*, *Arm*, I, p.190.

13. For technical details of construction see F. Howard, 'Early Ship Guns, Part I: Built-up Breech-loaders' in *MM*, Vol.72, No. 4, Nov 1986, pp.439ff. and Part II – 'Swivels' in *MM*, Vol.73, No.1, Feb 1987, pp.49ff: also official Catalogue of the Museum of Artillery in the Rotunda, Woolwich, 1934.

14. cited Oppenheim, *Admin.*, p.334.

15. For detailed analysis, Spanish gun weights, see I. A. A. Thompson 'Spanish Armada Guns', in *MM*, Vol.61, No.4, Nov 1975, pp.355ff., esp. Tables p.361.

16. J. F. Guilmartin Jnr, 'The Cannon of the Batavia . . .', *IJNA*, 1982, II, pp.133–44, esp. pp.140–41.

17. Above argument refuted by R. Barker, 'Bronze Cannon Founders . . .' in *ibid*, 1983, 12.1. pp.67–74, and by the Elizabethan officer, Monson: see Oppenheim, *Monson IV*, p.43.

18. See Table in Oppenheim, *Admin*, p.318; Padfield, *Guns*, pp.37–8, 54; *Royal Armouries Catalogue*, Tower of London, pp.394–95; Oppenheim, *Monson IV*, pp.36–41.

19. See Padfield, *Guns*, p.38.

20. C. R. D. Bethune, Ed., *The Observations of Sir Richard Hawkins*, Hakluyt, 1847, p.190.

21. *ibid*, p.214.

22. Thompson, 'Spanish Armada Guns' *op. cit.*, p.368, gives the Spanish 441 culverin, demi culverin, saker, against 324 cannon type.

23. See for instance, *Dom.*, p.244, and Oppenheim, *Admin.*, pp.159–60.

24. See N. A. M. Rodger 'Elizabethan Naval Gunnery', note in *MM*, Vol.61, No.4, Nov 1975, pp.353–54.

25. Corbett, *Fighting*, (citing W. Raleigh's 1617 Instructions), p.42.

26. W. Raleigh, *History of the World*, Part I, Book V, Chap.1, Sect.6, cited Hodges, p.26.

27. Corbett, *Spanish War*, pp.55–56.

28. *Colloquies of Tartaglia*, cited Hodges, p.12.

29. R. Hawkins, *Observations*, cited *ibid*, p.22.

30. Med. Sid. General Orders to the Armada in Lisbon, May? *Sp.*, p.293.

31. James Humfrey, *The Book of the Lawe of Olerone . . .*, 1568, Pepys Library, Cambridge, p.173, citing Ipswich Commissioners.

32. See Oppenheim, *Admin*, p.79.

33. Lloyd, *British Seaman*, p.33.

34. Howard to Walsyngham, 26 Aug., *Arm*. II, p.160.

35. cited Oppenheim, *Monson* II, p.248.

36. *ibid*, p.237.

37. Med. Sid. Instructions to the Shipmasters on the Armada at Lisbon, 21 April 1588, *Sp.*, pp.269–71 and see list of provisions in Armada, *ibid*, p.276.

38. See *Mary Rose* Museum, Portsmouth, and Souvenir Guide to the *Mary Rose*, and Derauve, Durosquel, p.40, and finds in the Ulster Museum, Belfast.

39. C. Martin to author, 14 April 1987, 'two distinct sizes of eating utensils – "individual portion" types and containers suitable for six or eight rations – were noted on the *Trinidad Valencera*.' See also Derauve, Durosquel, p.40.

40. Dr Margaret Rule (Research Director '*Mary Rose* Trust') to author, 8 May 1987. 'We certainly found mess kids and a very large number of plates and bowls. Most of these were found in a stowage area on the Orlop deck immediately above the galley.' And 'Souvenir Guide' to the *Mary Rose*.

41. For insights into the origin of the Spanish pottery found in Armada wrecks see Muckleroy, pp.97ff.

42. Derauve, Durosquel, p.66.

43. See Oppenheim, *Admin.*, p.139.

44. Rawlinson's Ballads, Bodleian Library, No.157 cited C. Bridge, *Sea Songs and Ballads*, Oxford, 1906, pp.10–12.

45. See *Mary Rose* Museum, Portsmouth; Ulster Museum, Belfast.

8. The Fighting Up-Channel

1. Howard to Walsyngham, 'A Brief Abstract of Accidents', *Arm*. II, p.55; Med. Sid. to Philip, 30 July 1588, *Sp.*, pp.356–57; and for rendezvous position Armada, May General Orders, *ibid*, pp.291–92; 'to windward of the Scilly Isles'.

2. Howarth, p.119.

3. Drake to Q.E., 13 April 1588, *Arm*. I, p.148.

4. 'A Brief Abstract . . .' *op. cit.*, p.55.

5. Harl. MSS 132 & 4685, cited Smith, pp.xvii–xviii.

6. Advices from England, 5 Nov 1588, from Genoese spy, Marco Antonio Micea, *Sp.*, p.480.

7. Philip's Instructions to Med. Sid., 1 April 1588, *Sp.*, p.248.

8. Howarth, p.116.

9. Med. Sid. to Philip, 30 July 1588, *Sp.*, pp.357–358.

10. *Relation*, p.7.

11. Pedro de Estrada, probably aboard *San Marcos*, cited Oppenheim, *Monson II*, p.301.

12. Alonso de Chaves, cited Corbett, *Fighting*, pp.4–5.

13. *ibid*, p.8.

14. W. Camden, cited Smith, p.xvii.

15. *Relation*, p.7.

16. Henry Whyte to Walsyngham, 8 Aug 1588, *Arm*. II, p.63.

17. Examinations of Emanuel Fremoso, in *San Juan*, *ibid*, p.219.

18. Jorge Manrique to Philip, 11 Aug 1588, *Sp.*, p.373.

19. *Calderon*, p.440.

20. Pedro de Estrada, cited Oppenheim, *Monson II*, p.302.

21. Med. Sid. Diary, p.396.

22. Howard to Walsyngham, 21 July 1588, *Arm*. I, p.288.

23. Report of deserters, Holland, 3 Aug 1588, *Arm*. II, p.79; *Calderon*, p.441.

24. Howard to Sussex, 22 July 1588, *Arm*. I, p.299.

25. *Relation*, p.8.

26. Petition of Capt., Master, Lt., *Margaret & John*, *Arm*. II, pp.106–7.

27. Don Pedro de Valdes to Philip, 21 Aug, *Arm*. II, p.135.

28. *Relation*, p.9.

29. Med. Sid. Diary, p.396.

30. Med. Sid. to Parma, 1 Aug, *Sp.*, p.358.

31. 'A Brief Abstract of Accidents', Howard to Walsyngham, 7 Aug, *Arm*. II, p.56.

32. *Calderon*, p.441.

33. *Relation*, p.10.

34. Med. Sid. Diary, p.397.

35. *Relation*, p.10.

36. See Williamson, *Drake*, p.334.

37. *Relation*, p.11.

38. Med. Sid. Diary, p.398.

39. *Calderon*, p.442.

40. Jorge Manrique to Philip, 11 Aug, *Sp.*, p.374.

41. Med. Sid. Diary, p.398.

42. *Relation*, p.11.

43. *ibid*, p.12.

44. Wm. Thomas to Burghley, 30 Sept, *Arm*. II, p.259.

45. See R. Pitt, Mayor of Weymouth, 24 July, *Arm*. I, p.303.

46. Med. Sid. Diary, pp.397–98.

47. Med. Sid. to Moncada, 2 Aug., *Sp.*, p.359.

48. Med. Sid. Diary, p.398.

49. *ibid*, p.399.

50. *Calderon*, p.443.

51. Sir Geo. Cary to Sussex, 25 July, *Arm*. I, p.234.

52. Med. Sid. to Parma, 4 Aug, *Sp.*, p.360.

53. Med. Sid. Diary, pp.399–400.

54. Seymour to Q.E., 11 Aug, *Arm*. II, p.1, Seymour to Walsyngham, 7 Aug, *ibid*, p.3; see also Borough to Walsyngham, 7 Aug, *ibid*, I, p.336.

55. Estrada, cited Oppenheim, *Monson II*, p.306.

56. Med. Sid. to Parma, 6 Aug, *Sp.*, pp.362–63.

9. The Battle of Gravelines

1. Parma to Philip, 7 Aug, *Sp.*, p.365.

2. Manrique to Idiaquez, 11 Aug, *ibid*, p.375.

3. Advices of the fleets, 11 Aug, *ibid*, p.377.

204   4. Mendoza to Philip, 27 Dec, *ibid*, p.183.

5. Philip to Archduke (to pass on to Santa Cruz), Jan 1588, *ibid*, pp.187–8.

6. Parma to Philip, 31 Jan, *ibid*, p.199.

7. Parma to Philip, 22 Feb, *ibid*, p.211.

8. Parma to Philip, 20 March, *ibid*, p.236.

9. Med. Sid. to Philip, 14 May, *ibid*, p.296.

10. Parma to Mendoza, 22 March, *ibid*, p.241.

11. Philip to Parma, cited Howarth, p.153.

12. Fernando Duro, *La Armada Invencible*, Madrid, 1884, II, p.10, cited Thompson 'The Appointment of Med. Sid. . . .', *op. cit.*, p.205.

13. Philip to Med. Sid., Supplementary Secret Instructions, 1 April, *Sp.*, p.250.

14. cited Thompson, 'The Appointment of Med. Sid . . .' *op. cit.*, p.201.

15. Thompson, *ibid*, p.200, note 21.

16. Philip to Archduke, 14 Sept 1587, attached to Philip to Med. Sid., 1 April 1588, in Lloyd/Naish, p.9.

17. Assumption from Med. Sid. to Philip stating this intention, 10 June, *Sp.*, pp.302–3.

18. Parma to Philip, 22 June, *ibid*, pp.315–16.

19. Recalde to Philip, 11 July, *ibid*, 334–35.

20. Philip to Med. Sid., 7 Aug, *ibid*, p.363.

21. Parma to Philip, 22 June, *ibid*, p.315 note.

22. See H. E. J. Stanley (Ed.), *The Three Voyages of Vasco da Gama*, Hakluyt, 1869, pp.366–67.

23. Seymour to Walsyngham, 12 July, *Arm.* I, pp.254–55, and see Seymour to Walsyngham, 20 July, *ibid*, p.286, 'The Duke intent only to employ them for Wakerland' (Walcheren).

24. Wynter to Walsyngham, 20 June, *ibid*, pp.213–14.

25. Dale to Leicester, 17 June and 21 June, *Sp.*, pp.312–13.

26. Parma to Philip, 8 Aug, *ibid*, p.366.

27. See Med. Sid. Diary, Sunday 7, re Tello's report, p.400.

28. Med. Sid. to Philip, 1 Aug, *Sp.*, p.358.

29. Med. Sid. Diary, p.399.

30. Dale to Leicester, 21 June, *Sp.*, p.313.

31. Med. Sid. to Parma, 6 Aug, *ibid*, pp.362–63.

32. Philip to Med. Sid., Instrs. 1 April, *ibid*, p.246.

33. Drake to Q.E., 13 April 1588, *Arm.* I, p.148.

34. Wynter to Walsyngham, 11 Aug, *ibid*, II, p.8.

35. Estrada, cited Oppenheim, *Monson* II, p.306.

36. *Memoirs of Robert Carey*, London, 1905, p.9.

37. Advices of the Fleets, 11 Aug, *Sp.*, p.376.

38. *Calderon*, p.443.

39. Manrique to Philip, 11 Aug, *Sp.*, p.373.

40. Med. Sid. Diary, p.401.

41. Richard Tomson to Walsyngham, 9 Aug, *Arm.* I, p.347.

42. Wynter to Walsyngham, 11 Aug, *Arm.* II, p.10.

43. Sir H. Palavacino's Relation, *ibid*, p.207.

44. H. Whyte to Walsyngham, 18 Aug, *ibid*, p.63.

45. Relation of galleass *Zuniga*, 4 Oct, *Sp.*, p.461.

46. Med. Sid. Diary, p.401.

47. Seymour to Q.E., 11 Aug, *Arm.* II, p.2 and Wynter to Walsyngham, 11 Aug, *ibid*, pp.9–10.

48. *Relation*, p.16.

49. Whyte to Walsyngham, 18 Aug, *Arm.* II, p.64.

50. Estrada, cited Oppenheim, *Monson* II, p.307.

51. Relation of galleass *Zuniga*, *Sp.*, p.461.

52. *Calderon*, p.444.

53. *ibid*.

54. Wynter to Walsyngham, 11 Aug, *Arm.* II, p.11.

55. *Calderon*, p.444.

56. Med. Sid. Diary, p.402.

57. Wynter to Walsyngham, 11 Aug, *Arm.* II, p.10.

58. Emanuel Fremoso's deposition, *ibid*, p.221.

59. Deposition of Sp. prisoners from Pimentel's ship, *ibid*, p.80.

60. *Calderon*, p.445.

61. Drake to Walsyngham, 8 Aug, *Arm.* I, p.341.

62. Fenner to Walsyngham, 14 Aug, *ibid* II, p.40.

63. Ubaldino's narrative, cited Lloyd/Naish, p.72.

64. Matthew Starke's deposition, 21 Aug, *Arm.* II, p.102.

65. Advices from London, 21 Aug, *Sp.*, p.392.

66. Brief Abstract of Accidents, 17 Aug, *Arm.* II, p.58.

67. Howard to Walsyngham, 8 Aug, *Arm.* I, p.341.

68. Drake to Walsyngham, 8 Aug, *ibid*, p.342.

69. Hawkins to Walsyngham, 10 Aug, *ibid*, p.360.

70. The Council to Seymour, 7 Aug, *ibid*, pp.335–36.

71. Memorial for Richard Drake, 10 Aug, *ibid*, pp.355–56.

72. cited Strickland, pp.267–68.

73. See Howarth, p.184.

74. Tomson to Walsyngham, 9 Aug, *Arm.* I, p.350.

75. Seymour to Q.E., 11 Aug, *Arm.* II, p.2, and Wynter to Walsyngham, 11 Aug, *ibid*, pp.11–12.

76. Gorges to Walsyngham, 10 Aug, *Arm.* I, p.357.

77. Med. Sid. Diary, p.403.

78. *Calderon*, pp.446–47.

79. Howard to Walsyngham, 17 Aug, *Arm.* II, p.54.

80. Hawkins to Walsyngham, 10 Aug, *Arm.* I, p.361.

81. Henry Whyte to Walsyngham, 18 Aug, *Arm.* II, p.64.

82. Tomson to Walsyngham, 9 Aug, *Arm.* I, p.350.

83. Drake to Walsyngham, 10 Aug, *ibid*, p.364.

84. Med. Sid. Diary, p.404.

85. Sedgwick, p.10.

86. *ibid*.

87. *ibid*, pp.7–8.

88. Resolution, Council of War, 11 Aug, *Arm.* II, p.6.

89. Fenner to Walsyngham, 14 Aug, *ibid*, p.40.

90. *ibid*, pp.41–42.

10. Wreck and Massacre

1. Carey to Walsyngham, 8 Sept, *Arm.* II, p.186.

2. cited *ibid*, p.240.

3. *Calderon*, p.447.

4. Relation of galleass *Zuniga*, 4 Oct, *Sp.*, p.461.

5. Med. Sid. Diary, p.404.

6. Oral legend investigated by the late Frank Lynder, with the help of Magne Flem; Kristina Behnke to author, 6 May 1987.

7. Bjørn Ringstad, Molde, to author, 10 Aug 1987; Bjørn Jonsen Dale, Oslo, to author, 10 July 1987.

8. E. van Meteran, *'The miraculous Victory . . .'*, cited in Blacker, p.417.

9. *Calderon*, p.448.

10. Carey to Hunsdon, 1 Sept, *Arm.* II, p.137.

11. *Calderon*, p.448.

12. Med. Sid. to Philip, 3 Sept, *Sp.*, p.411.

13. Drake to Walsyngham, 20 Aug, *Arm.* II, p.97.

14. Med. Sid. to Philip, 3 Sept, *Sp.*, p.412.

15. Emanuel Fremoso's deposition, *Arm.* II, p.221.

16. cited Martin, *Full Fathom*, p.36.

17. Howard to Burghley, 20 Aug, *Arm.* II, p.96.

18. Hawkins to Burghley, 5 Sept, *ibid*, p.163.

19. Mendoza to Idiaquez, 30 Aug, *Sp.*, p.409.

20. Howard to Walsyngham, 8 Sept, *Arm.* II, p.183.

21. *ibid*, p.184.

22. Howard to Walsyngham, 6 Sept, *ibid*, p.168.

23. See R. Pollitt, 'Bureaucracy and the Arm . . .', *MM*, *op. cit.* p.130.

24. Med. Sid. to Philip, 21 Aug, *Sp.*, p.393.

25. Drake to Walsyngham, 10 Aug, *Arm.* II, p.364.

26. Sedgwick, pp.69–72.

27. cited *Car.*, 1589–1600, p.lxxvi.

28. Intro. to *Car.*, pp.xxxi–ii.

29. *ibid*, p.xiii.

30. *ibid*, p.xvii.

31. *Car.*, 1589–1600, p.lxxv.

32. Spenser, cited Black, p.479.

33. Carew to Vice-Chamberlain, Dublin, 4 Aug, 1588, *Car.*, p.470.

34. Exam. of Sp. prisoners, 13 Oct, *Arm.* II, p.273.

35. See Fallon, p.135.

36. Juan de Nova's deposition, *Sp.*, p.508.

37. Emanuel Fremoso's deposition, *Arm.* II, pp.223–224; Pier Carr deposition, *ibid*, pp.226–228.

38. Ed. Whyte's Report, cited Douglas, Lamb, Loader, re 21 Sept.

39. Sedgwick, pp.20–22. The following quotations from Cuellar are pp.16–17, 24–25, 29.

40. Carew to Walsyngham, 18 Sept 1588, *Car.* p.471.

41. Bjngham to Fytzwilliam, 21 Sept, *Arm.* II, p.238 and Bingham to Q.E., 3 Dec, *ibid*, p.300.

42. Fytzwilliam to Walsyngham, 28 Oct, *ibid*, p.286.

43. Sedgwick, pp.73–4.

44. See David Quinn, 'Spanish Arm. prisoners' escape from Ireland', *MM*, Vol.170, No.2, May 1984, pp.117–18.

45. *Calderon*, p.449.

46. See Douglas, Lamb, Loader, 18 Sept.

47. Med. Sid. to Philip, 23 Sept, *Sp.*, p.432.

48. See de Villejo to de Prada, 10 Oct, *ibid*, p.467.

49. *ibid*.

50. *ibid*.

51. Mendoza to Philip, 24 Sept, *ibid*, p.434.

52. See Spanish Statement of vessels lost, *ibid*, p.343–44.

Postscript

1. cited Williamson, *Hawkins*, p.322.

2. Oppenheim, *Monson* II, p.263.

3. Black, p.413.

4. Letter from London, Mendoza, *Sp.*, p.491.

5. Captain J. Troughton, cited Williamson, *Hawkins*, p.388.

6. Hawkins to Q.E., via Captain Troughton, cited *ibid*, p.342.

7. Oppenheim, *Monson* I, p.354.

8. Relation from Ireland, June 1596, *Sp.*, p.626.

9. cited Oppenheim, *Monson* II, p.17.

10. cited Lloyd/Naish, p.84.

11. Verses attributed to Q.E. from *The Art of English Poesy*, 1589, cited *ibid*, p.83.

12. See, for instance: V. Barbour, *Capitalism in Amsterdam in the 17th Century*. Johns Hopkins, Baltimore, 1950, pp.17ff; C. R. Boxer, *The Dutch Seaborne Empire 1600–1800*, Hutchinson, 1965, pp.20ff; C. Wilson, *Profit and Power*, Longmans, 1957, pp.3ff; P. Padfield, *Tide of Empires. Decisive Naval Campaigns in the Rise of the West*, Routledge, Vols. 1 and 2, 1979–81.

Selected bibliography

K. R. ANDREWS: *Drake's Voyages*, Weidenfeld, 1967.

S. T. BINDOFF: *Tudor England*, Penguin, 1950.

T. BINNING: *A Light to the Art of Gunnery*, London, 1669.

J. R. BLACKER (ED.): *The Portable Hakluyt's Voyages*, Viking, NY, 1965.

J. B. BLACK: *The Reign of Elizabeth*, Oxford, 1959.

F. BRAUDEL: *The Mediterranean & the Mediterranean World in the Age of Philip II*, Collins, 1972.

W. CAMDEN, ED. W. T. MACCAFFREY: *The History of the Most Renowned and Victorious Princess Elizabeth . . .*, Chicago, 1970.

J. S. CEROVSKI (ED.): *Fragmenta Regalia . . .* Sir Robert Naunton, reprint Associated University Presses Inc, Washington, 1985.

C. M. CIPOLLA: *Guns and Sails*, Collins, 1966.

J. CORBETT (ED.): *The Spanish War 1585–87*, Navy Records Society, 1898.

— *Fighting Instructions 1530–1816*, Navy Records Society, 1904.

C. G. CRUIKSHANK: *Elizabeth's Army*, Oxford, 1966.

J. DERAUVE, J-M. DUROSQUEL (EDS.): *Tresors de l'Armada*, Crédit Communal, Brussels, 1985.

K. S. DOUGLAS, H. H. LAMB, C. LOADER: *A Meteorological Study of July to October 1588: The Spanish Armada Storms*, University of East Anglia, Norwich, 1978.

K. S. DOUGLAS, H. H. LAMB: *Weather Observations and a tentative Meteorological Analysis of the period May to July 1588*, University of East Anglia, Norwich, 1979.

J. H. ELLIOTT: *Imperial Spain 1469–1716*, Arnold, 1963.

C. ERIKSON: *The First Elizabeth*, Macmillan, 1983.

N. FALLON: *The Armada in Ireland*, Stanford Maritime, 1978.

H. W. HODGES, E. A. HUGHES (EDS.): *Select Naval Documents*, Cambridge, 1936.

D. HOWARTH: *The Voyage of the Armada, The Spanish Story*, Collins, 1981.

H. KAMEN: *Spain 1469–1714*, Longman, 1983.

— *The Spanish Inquisition*, Weidenfeld, 1965.

R. W. KENNY: *Elizabeth's Admiral*, Johns Hopkins, Baltimore, 1970.

M. LEWIS: *Armada Guns*, Allen & Unwin, 1961.

C. LLOYD: *The British Seaman 1200–1860*, Collins, 1968.

C. LLOYD (ED.): *The Health of Seamen:* Navy Records Society, 1965.

C. LLOYD, G. NAISH (EDS.): *The Naval Miscellany, Vol IV*, Navy Records Society, 1952.

C. MARTIN: *Full Fathom Five*, Chatto & Windus, 1975.

G. MATTINGLEY: *The Defeat of the Spanish Armada*, Cape, 1959.

K. MUCKELROY (ED.): *Archaeology Under Water*, McGraw Hill, 1980.

J. R. NEALE: *Queen Elizabeth*. Cape, 1934.

Z. NUTTALL (ED.): *New Light on Drake*, Hakluyt Soc. II, Series 34 (1914).

M. OPPENHEIM (ED.): *The Naval Tracts of Sir William Monson*, Navy Records Society, 1902.

M. OPPENHEIM: *A History of the Administration of the Royal Navy*, London, 1896.

A. D. ORTIZ: *The Golden Age of Spain 1516–1659*, Weidenfeld, 1971.

P. PADFIELD: *Guns at Sea*, Hugh Evelyn, 1973.

G. PARKER: *The Dutch Revolt*, Allen Lane, 1977.

— *Philip II*, Little Brown, 1978.

P. PIERSON: *Philip II of Spain*, Thames & Hudson, 1975.

A. L. ROWSE: *England of Elizabeth*, Reprint Society, Macmillan, 1950.

— *The Expansion of Elizabethan England*, Macmillan, 1955.

M. RULE: *The Mary Rose*, Conway Maritime, rd., 1983.

R. A. SABATINI: *Torquemada & the Spanish Inquisition*, London, 1913.

W. SALISBURY, R. C. ANDERSON (EDS.): *A Treatise on Shipbuilding & a Treatise on Rigging written about 1620–1625*, Society for Nautical Research, 1958.

W. SCOTT (ED.): *Memoirs of Robert Carey, Earl of Monmouth*, London, 1905.

H. D. SEDGWICK JR (TRANS.): *A Letter Written on Oct. 4, 1589, to King Philip II*, London & NY, 1896.

A. R. SMITH (ED.): *Spanish Armada List*, 1588, London, 1886.

C. STONE (ED.): *Sea Songs and Ballads*, Oxford, 1906.

A. STRICKLAND: *The Life of Queen Elizabeth*, Hutchinson, 1904.

I. A. A. THOMPSON: *War & Government in Hapsburg Spain 1560–1620*. Athlone Press, 1976.

D. W. WATERS: *The Art of Navigation in England in Elizabethan and Early Stuart Times*, Hollis & Carter, 1958.

J. A. WILLIAMSON: *The Age of Drake*, Black, 1946.

— *Hawkins of Plymouth*, Black, 1949.

C. WILSON: *Queen Elizabeth & the Revolt in the Netherlands*, Macmillan, 1970.

Some *Mariner's Mirror* articles not listed in the references:

K. R. ANDREWS: 'The Elizabethan Seaman', *MM*, Vol.68, No.3, Aug 1982, pp.245 ff.

L. A. CLAYTON: 'Ships and Empire: the Case of Spain', *MM*, Vol.62, No.3, Aug 1976, pp.235 ff.

P. CROFT: 'English Mariners trading to Spain and Portugal, 1558–1625', *MM*, Vol.69, No.3, Aug 1983, pp.251 ff.

T. GLASGOW JNR: 'List of Ships in the Royal Navy from 1539 to 1588 . . .', *MM*, Vol.56, No.3, Aug 1970, pp.299ff.

G. V. SCAMMELL: The English in the Atlantic Islands *c.*1450–1650, *MM*, Vol.72, No.3, Aug 1986, pp.295 ff.

— 'Manning the English Merchant Service in the Sixteenth Century', *MM*, Vol.56, No.2, May 1970, pp.131 ff.

Index

Storm

Gallan Head

Lewis I.

PENTLA

Faro Head

Row Stoir Assynt

L. Brenn

Kenna Flochmore

WESTERN

North I.

ISLANDS

South I.

Rum I.

Barra I.

Coll I.

Mull

Tire is I.

Jura I.

Storm

Ila I.

Cantire

Boot I.

Arran I.

Tory I.

Fair Head

Firth of Clyd

North I. of Arran

Wigtown

Coleraine

C. Telling

London Derry

The Mull of Galloway

Donagall

Down Patrick

Killala

Slego

Carlingford

MAN I.

Calfe of Man

Dundalk

Carlingford B.

Drogheda

Dundalk B.

The

I R E-

IRISH SEA

Galway

DUB-

LIN

Liffe R.

Holy Head

South Iles of Arran

Wicklow

ANGLESEY

LAND

Gallway B.

St.

Ennis

Brayehiquilt P.

Cardigan B.

Shannon Mouth

Limerick

GEORGE'S

Wexford

Carnsore P.

Cardigan

Dingle Is.

Hedley B.

Tralee

Waterford

Waterford

Milford Ha.

Castlemain or Dingle B.

Corke

CHANNEL

Bishops & his Clerks

Pembroke

Kilmare R.

Bantry

Kinsaile

Corke Hr.

BRISTOLL CHANNEL

Beer Hn. or Bantry Bay

Old Head

Lundy I.

Barnstap.

Cape Cleare

Haveland Pt.

Lands End

Exeter

Plymouth

The Ilands of SCILLY

Falm.

Truro

Dartmouth

Lizard Point

The BRITI

Morlaix

Pampol

The BRI

Ushant

H. Gravelot delin.   Published by John Pine Junr.